BEYOND IBM

BEYOND
◄IBM►

Lou Mobley and
Kate McKeown

McGRAW-HILL PUBLISHING COMPANY
New York   St. Louis   San Francisco

3/2/89

1 2 3 4 5 6 7 8 9 DOC DOC 8 9 2 1 0 9 8

ISBN 0-07-042625-2

LIBRARY OF CONGRESS CATALOGING-IN-PUBLICATION DATA

Mobley, Lou.
    Beyond IBM / Lou Mobley and Kate McKeown.
      p. cm.
    Bibliography: p.
    Includes index.
    ISBN 0-07-042625-2
    1. International Business Machines Corporation—Management.
2. Computer industry—United States—Management. 3. Electronic
Industries—United States—Management. I. McKeown, Kathleen R.
II. Title
HD9696.C64I4863   1989
338.7′61004′0973—dc19   88-13225
                                                            CIP

Book design by Kathryn Parise

To our families,
with our love
and our thanks

◄ CONTENTS ►

◄ PREFACE ►

Lou and I finished the first draft of this book on October 31, 1987. On November 12, Lou's heart stopped. I'm certain he felt no prolonged pain or fear, although I think there was a moment of surprise.

I'm telling you this first, because Lou was such a brilliant, wonderful soul that as you read this book, you might get the urge to call and ask him to have lunch with you to discuss the nature of the universe. He isn't available for lunches any more. I'd give everything I own to have a bowl of split pea soup with a slice of lemon floating in it—his favorite working lunch—with him just one more time in this life.

Businesspeople operating in the information age have to contend with two fundamental facts of this new era. First: every day, things change faster. Second: every day, people are more different from each other than they were the day before. The needs and wants of customers shift with confounding quickness, and the aspirations and abilities of workers mutate almost overnight. The two irreducible jobs of management—deciding things worth doing and getting things done—are more challenging now than they were in the relatively stable, relatively uniform industrial era. Our book is about how to do cutting-edge leadership, marketing, and finance.

But first, we look back at the industrial age. What management insights can we take with us from the age we're now departing? We look to the best of the receding era for the answer to that question: IBM was the industrial age superstar.

For thirty-two years, Lou helped engineer the meteoric growth of the company whose market value was the highest of any company in the world. As a young man, Lou wrote speeches and letters for Tom Watson, Sr., learning intimately that great executive's vision and values. Later, Watson Sr. asked Lou to build a business history of IBM. Lou ransacked IBM's records and scoured the memories of all IBM executives to find, as he put it, "the skeletons in the closet and the angels in the air." Lou personally gleaned the essence of IBM's entrepreneurial explosion under Watson Sr., but the story was never written down. Tom Watson, Jr., took over IBM and put the business history project on ice indefinitely, saying, "The story isn't over." In fact, it had only begun.

In 1950, Tom Watson, Jr., asked Lou to join the fifteen-man task force that launched the computer. In the glorious summer of the industrial age, Lou created the management development operation that forged IBM's leaders. He personally directed IBM's Executive School. All of IBM's CEOs after Watson Jr. and before John Akers took a crash course in leadership, marketing, and finance from Lou. Lou was an insider's insider, and he had the kind of mind that whizzed past details and identified the essentials. Now they are written down, in Chapters 1 and 2.

In Chapter 3, our book pivots from IBM to leadership, marketing, and finance beyond the industrial age—beyond IBM. It's an overview chapter. It distills four themes that provide a context for the systems, tools, and information outlined in the rest of the book.

The leadership and marketing sections of the book speak for themselves. I feel obliged to put in a good word for the finance section, however. The finance section provides systems for managing and planning a business. Because so few businesspeople really, deep down inside, understand finance, we start with a friendly crash course in what it all means. It's nuts-and-bolts. But once you've digested Chapters 10 and 11 you'll never be mystified about what your numbers mean or what to do about them. Then in Chapter 12, we present an overview of the larger economic environment in which we're all operating.

I have just a few comments about the mechanics of the book. Some of the anecdotes in the book are from Lou's past, some from mine, and some from our joint experience. We decided to identify our individual experiences by writing I (Lou) or I (Kate) at their beginnings. Everybody who read our early drafts found the construction distracting. We discussed putting all the anecdotes in the third person, and thought it boring. We considered pretending they were all joint experiences, but some of them took place before my parents met, so that was out. In the end, we decided to leave it, hoping to diffuse your potential discomfort by this little disclaimer up front.

Do you remember how your eighth-grade librarian taught you to scan books for main themes? Neither do I. So I've written chapter digests that appear at the end of each chapter of our book. They recap our main points. You can read them before the chapter, after the chapter, skip them altogether, or my favorite option, tear them out and mail them to your friends suggesting they buy the book.

Lou and I love charts and graphs. All expert opinion about how to sell lots of books suggests that charts and graphs make your book look like a textbook and people hate textbooks. Never, they say, should a potential book buyer, leafing through your book, be accosted by something nonverbal that requires figuring out. We compromised. Most of our beloved charts and graphs are in an appendix. If you hate having to go all the way to the back of the book to find one, write to me and I'll commiserate.

There's one more thing I want to tell you about Lou. He'd hate it if I left this out. In 1980, during open heart surgery, Lou had a near-death experience. He would always say that as a result of that profound moment, he had no fear of death at all. He would say that he had a conviction—more than a belief—that the individual consciousness survives death. I agree with him. I believe his story isn't over.

—Kate McKeown
Washington, D.C.

◄ ACKNOWLEDGMENTS ►

First, our thanks to Maya Porter, whose editorial and research talents were invaluable. She helped with every aspect of this project, and it is much richer because of her intelligence, insight, and energy.

Tom Quinn, our McGraw-Hill editor, has been unflagging in his support and his enthusiasm. His editorial suggestions have been incisive and very helpful. But in our heart of hearts, we feel most grateful for his unswerving presence. There was never a moment during this long process that we didn't feel he was right with us.

Lynn Bunis transcribed the fifty-five tapes we made in the course of writing this book. Her interest and commitment were heartening. Sometimes when she was transcribing a tape in which we were gnawing futilely on some issue, she'd type right into the transcription her assessment of our blind spot, as well as suggestions for clearing it up. We loved it.

Chris Mobley made thorough financial analyses of companies for us, often on short notice. He also kept all our hi-tech tools running, often on even shorter notice. His patience and graciousness never ran thin.

Bob Block, inventor and entrepreneur extraordinaire, freed us to give our full attention to our book by taking charge of the refining and marketing of our financial planning software. He has also been a good and true friend.

Arthur Lipper has been a staunch and shining ally throughout. We're pleased to have his Foreword—drawn from his unique vantage for studying entrepreneurs in the wild—to augment our observations about the nature of these overnight executives.

Our agent, Peter Livingston, was committed to this book before we ever put pen to paper. We're grateful for his instincts and his early efforts on our behalf.

We want to acknowledge our first great teachers, Dwayne Orton (for Lou) and W. Edwards Deming (for Kate). You never forget your first love, they say. Certainly, never your first mentor.

Walter Wingo, Don Wilson, and C. J. Houtchens attacked our manuscript with sharp knives. It's leaner and meaner—or is it leaner and friendlier?—for their careful honing.

Even if our manuscript were the most astounding work since *War and Peace*, if the McGraw-Hill marketing and production people didn't turn their skilled hands to it, you'd never see it. Our thanks to them, especially to Lucia Staniels, Lori Glazer, Tom Tressel, Bobbi Mark, Gilly Hailparn, and Margery Luhrs.

Myriad other people have contributed to our work and to our thinking over the years. We can't list them all, but these few, all of whom know how they've helped, just can't go unnamed: John Hevener, Herschell Doss, Bernard Hickey, Kate Marshall, Jeff Davidson, Bob Schwartz, Rick Martin, Deborah Fialka, Chuck Waters, Bernie Wandell, Leslie Evans, Lao Russell, Mary Wallace, G. Edward Busch, and the delightful people at both the Heindl Printing company and the Tenleytown Public Library in Washington, D.C.

◄ FOREWORD ►

A Special Message for Entrepreneurs

The first two chapters of this book are about the creation and development of the world's most consistently value-adding commercial enterprise. The book as a whole is one of the more instructive business management books I've read, as well as being fascinating, both as a history and as a philosophy text. The Mobley Matrix is described in detail in the finance section. It will become, I predict, one of the most widely used presentation formats benefitting entrepreneurs, managers, lenders, and investors.

But *Beyond IBM* does indeed go beyond the story of IBM. It is a superior business management book, covering leadership, marketing, and finance. There are so many well conceived thoughts, expressed in such highly quotable form, that few readers who speak publicly or write for publication will be able to restrain themselves from plagiarizing the clear, lucid text whose authors manifest an eloquent economy of language.

One of the reasons I found *Beyond IBM* such an important book is that I spend my life in the midst of entrepreneurial America. *Venture* has more than 450,000 subscribers, more than 70% of whom are either owners or partners in their businesses. Many of these subscribers also have an involvement in creating businesses other than their principal one. Each month in *Venture* we "cover" more than 100 companies, particularly the younger, innovative, entrepreneurially managed companies. Also, as chairman and founder of the Association of Venture Founders I am in continuing contact with hundreds of successful entrepreneurs. Both as a vocation and an avocation, I am deeply involved in a broad range of entrepreneurship education activities. I am therefore sensitive to the educational needs of our country's most economically productive group, those who are willing to assume the responsibility for the lives of others by becoming employers.

Beyond IBM addresses directly the psyche, interests, and needs of employers. It is a book for and about employers. It is a book about constant change and the need to welcome—rather than to be frightened by—the prospect and certainty of change.

What do entrepreneurs do best? Recognize market niches and, if successful, create products that will satisfy the demand and, if truly successful, defend the niche created.

What do entrepreneurs do worst? Predict future events, particularly those which they believe they have an ability to influence. Entrepreneurs almost always believe they can control their destiny, and the need to control their destiny is an important part of an individualistic drive that results in their becoming entrepreneurs.

Entrepreneurs who read and study *Beyond IBM* will gain an enhanced ability to understand their current situation and to better plan for their future circumstances. It is cash and not accounting concepts such as profit and loss that dictates how a company must be managed. It is a company's current and future cash level that determines appropriate and available strategies, therefore ultimate value. Using the Mobley Matrix will significantly increase an entrepreneur's understanding, true understanding, of his or her current and therefore likely future position. A better understood position is one which is easier to control.

Why can't IBM, perhaps one of the very greatest and best managed of companies, create an environment wherein entrepreneurs can flourish? Since IBM has all of the resources available to accomplish almost any task, why have they not been able internally to develop and retain successful entrepreneurs? Can it be that this most enlightened and well managed of enterprises does not want to be burdened with those who are overly individualistic? Can it be that the baggage accompanying entrepreneurs, almost by definition contemptuous of authority and impatient with bureaucracy, is more troublesome than acceptable from the perspective of an organization whose size requires discipline and orchestrated motivation more than it does the innovation of individual entrepreneurs? Would "an" IBM be advantaged by having the skills and insights of a substantial number of entrepreneurs, those willing to assume a personal risk in the pursuit of profit? Would that advantage be sufficient to compensate for the internal havoc such inspired individuals are capable of generating? Although IBM could benefit from entrepreneurs, it probably won't be able to make the necessary accommodations.

Many companies are currently asserting that they both want and have developed a strange new hybrid, which *Venture* has dubbed "corporateur." A corporateur is an individual having some, or perhaps many, of the characteristics of an entrepreneur save for the willingness to accept a full measure of personal risk and responsibility in return for the freedom, other benefits, and obligations, of being an employer.

In their chapter on managers and executives, Lou and Kate do an excellent job of describing the skills, knowledge, systems, and values that managers and executives must call on to perform effectively. They outline how a person grows from non-manager to manager to executive. Then they describe how entrepreneurs are overnight executives and have to grasp the essentials of business management quickly and on the job. Doing, rather than studying, is likely to be the normal entrepreneurship education curriculum.

Though many claim to crave the luxury of self-determination, only a few are really prepared for the responsibility and loneliness associated with being the captain of a vessel. The larger organizations, be they government or commercial bureaucracies, are just not suited to grow or house entrepreneurs. Those leaders gaining corporate promotion and power are not likely to be those persons having the characteristics of successful entrepreneurs. They are likely, however, to be better assessors of terrain and be better practitioners of the art of the possible. The winners within larger enterprises are those who tend to be more manipulative and less direct. They make fewer mistakes and fewer important wins. Also they may well be, or appear to be, "nicer" people or, at least, will have developed their people skills to a point where those more powerful than themselves "like" them. The successful entrepreneur is more likely to be intimidating to those having more power and to befriend those over whom he or she enjoys, and is burdened with, power.

Entrepreneurs are just very different people from those who succeed in the larger companies. This is not to say that they are better or worse. It is to say they are different. The characteristics and potential problems associated with gifted children are remarkably similar to those applicable to entrepreneurs. The following is selected from a listing of traits that appeared in the February 1988 issue of *Gifted Children Monthly*, a publication for the parents of children "having great promise," which I founded nine years ago.

high verbal ability

keen powers of observation

long attention span, persistence, intense concentration

creativeness, originality

ability to see relationships, make connections

sensitivity

high energy level

independence

a loner

Beyond IBM raises subliminally but effectively the issue of "winning," as do so many business books. It is unfortunate that winning is so frequently left undefined by many people embarking on a career path. Therefore, values other than the individual's are both imposed by others and self-imposed by the entrepreneurs. I believe that if there were an individualized, introspective determination of a personal definition of winning, there would be fewer disappointments resulting from the entrepreneurial process.

Entrepreneurs are parents of enterprise. They are similar in some respects to artists and architects who have visions and grand designs not always communicated effectively to others. In many cases, even the entrepreneur is not able fully to articulate the ultimate plan. Entrepreneurs proceed on the basis of "feel" and intuition. The entrepreneur must be able, however, to persuade those with needed resources of the ultimate success of the program since it is essential to gain access and control over the resources. Entrepreneurs do not usually lie. They do not even believe they are exaggerating or embellishing when they project future achievements and objectives—though the two can easily become interchangeable in presentations. Entrepreneurs are much more likely to become victims of fraud than they are to be perpetrators. Were entrepreneurs more cynical, they would suffer fewer disappointments and accomplish less. Entrepreneurs need to be in control. They truly believe that they can control future events and therefore do not have to lie to others for they can achieve the predicted results by force of willpower. The almost ever-present entrepreneurial need to control may well be insecurity-based. Nevertheless, to others the entrepreneur exudes confidence and gives every appearance of being in control at all times. The entrepreneur may be willing to seek advice but is seldom willing to place himself or herself in the position of being dominated by individuals or circumstance.

Achieving wealth is not one of the primary objectives of most entrepreneurs. They assume success and know that in our society commercial success and wealth are usually synonymous. However, it is the power accompanying wealth that is the sweeter fruit and more a driving force. The power to cause change, to create and develop, to make decisions and mistakes, is the entrepreneur's objective. The entrepreneur has a need to prove herself or himself. This need is frequently a result of having had a particularly strong relationship with a parent or, in the case of those in technology-based businesses, a group of prior colleagues or an employer. Entrepreneurs want to prove themselves right in the development of what they may well have been told wouldn't work or shouldn't be attempted. Entrepreneurs know that they can make something happen. Unfortunately, they sometimes knows that their company will achieve a specific result next year, even if the year has to have a few more months of revenue credit than the normal twelve. One of the problems facing investors in private companies is that the entrepreneur's definition of success may be related more to product and customer satisfaction than to immediate profit creation. Investors and entrepreneurs should frankly discuss specific objectives and goals before the investment is made.

Entrepreneurs starting businesses usually are self-financed or assisted by family and friends. Commercial funding and professional investment sources are usually not available to entrepreneurs. They typically accept sacrifice in income, and certainly—in the normal definition—in security, in starting their businesses. Having a focus on the future, entrepreneurs have difficulty focusing on the details of running a business. They are as impatient with administrative detail as they are with authority and bureaucracy.

There is a pervasive and destructive myth circulating that entrepreneurs enjoy risk. Quite the contrary is true. The entrepreneur is by nature risk-averse. The entrepreneur fears the randomness of events over which he or she has no control. Entrepreneurs are not generally found in casinos. Rather they are seen on ski slopes, sailing, mountain climbing, or in some activity that is challenging and may be frightening to observers but where the participant can be in control. Those who choose to become entrepreneurs or employers (if they indeed really do have a choice) do so as opposition to accepting the position of being employed and therefore having less control over their lives. If observers—particularly those who are the gatekeepers to other people's money—understood the entrepreneur's natural risk aversion, entrepreneurs would find financing easier to obtain. This would be a positive development, as entrepreneurs are our country's most productive resource.

Entrepreneurs are optimistic and certain of their ability to control their future, but they are natural worriers. Perhaps it would be better were they less certain of ultimate victory, as then they might invest some energy in covering their flanks and rear and even in locating possible reinforcements should the need arise. One of the aspects of *Beyond IBM* which I find most interesting is the enhanced ability the user of the Mobley Matrix has in distilling currents of change and displaying the results of forces driving businesses.

Impressing on entrepreneurs, particularly younger entrepreneurs, the need for alternative or contingency planning would be performing an invaluable educational service. Investors considering participating in an entrepreneur's dream should explore with the entrepreneur the question, "What if *it* (whatever the "it" is for that enterprise) does not occur as predicted? What will you do then?" Typically, the entrepreneur will not have a good answer. This reluctance to articulate the unthinkable, or the genuine lack of prior consideration to the possibility of a desired event not occurring, should not disqualify the project as an investment. Instead, they should give rise to a further questioning of projected events and perhaps, just perhaps, managerial maturity or, at least, objectivity.

Entrepreneurs, however, as well as their financiers and mentors, must remember that "first must come the dream and then the reality, as without the dream there will be no launching of the missile." The application of cold logic did not build this nation. Men and women with dreams created that which most of us enjoy. In many cases, they did "it" because no one they chose to believe told them they couldn't do "it."

I believe it would be wholly constructive were entrepreneurs given a focus and perspective that would permit them to:

1. Measure their successes in such a way as to understand that winning a lot is usually a result of lots of little wins and that these shorter term and perhaps, therefore, lesser gains should be understood as being important

2. Understand that not every situation is destined to work out as desired, and that most human endeavors fail to achieve the results orginally predicted by the original conceivers and initiators

3. Understand that truly important successes are usually only measured and measurable long after the event has occurred

4. Understand that survival, staying in the game, is vital for ultimate success

5. Understand that winning, in retrospect, may well be understood to have been a matter of having had the judgment and courage to withdraw at some point, while there were still resources available, for future recovery and counterattack

6. Finally, understand that losing money and currently perceived opportunity is a part of the process—not the end of the world.

I frequently think that a phoenix would be a better entrepreneurial symbol than the more traditional eagle. The overly macho entrepreneur is, of course, all too often chiefly fearful of either thinking of himself or of having others think of him as "chicken."

There are about 17 million incorporated businesses in the United States. The business discontinuance statistics are not as readily available and require much more study and qualification than those for new incorporations. It must be understood than perhaps more than half of all corporations are not really "in business" in terms of having employees, since they are used as entities for holding assets. When new entrepreneurs start new businesses, there is usually a good deal of activity engendered. People are employed, goods and services purchased, skills learned and transferred, products and services sold, premises leased or acquired, and taxes paid. Ultimately, a significant percentage of new businesses are terminated. This is very different from the destructive and erroneous cliché of a large percentage of new businesses failing. The President's Report on Small Business states that:

> "Ninety percent of the approximately 400,000 business that dissolve each year do so for voluntary reasons, such as retirement of the owner or desire to enter a more profitable field. Ninety-nine percent of "failed" businesses have fewer than 100 employees and over 80% are under 10 years old. Only 10% of businesses that annually cease operations do so for involuntary reasons. They may file for bankruptcy or be considered a failure if the organization ceases to operate and leaves outstanding debt."

Actually, bankruptcies are running about 60,000 a year, versus more than 600,000 new incorporations.

Another reason for the discontinuances is the inability of the new enterprise to obtain credit. It is therefore without creditors (who deny credit because they believe most new businesses fail in the first five years) to pay. There isn't a "failure" in the traditional sense but rather a discontinuance.

The key to making a new business succeed is cash flow. I believe that what entrepreneurs need more than anything else is a full and realistic understanding of cash-flow projections and profit margin analysis. The single best element of advice for entrepreneurs is not to run out of cash. And if an entrepreneur seeks credit, the best way of obtaining it is to demonstrate to the prospective lender when and how repayment will be accomplished.

It's cash availability, not profit, that is important to entrepreneurs. Profit is an accounting concept and the basis for taxation. Cash is what pays rent, salaries, and suppliers. Without sufficient cash, nothing works and the entrepreneur is at risk of becoming a consultant or lecturer to future entrepreneurs, on the need for cash. The primary purpose for laboring through the creation of a business plan is to understand the permutations of the projected development cycle in order to assess the amount and timing of needed cash. Every entrepreneur ought to read Chapters 10 and 11 of *Beyond IBM* very carefully. Others who also need to understand the essence of finance and cash flow should similarly study these pages.

The future can be frightening to those who have most to benefit from a maintenance of the status quo. The future is coming no matter how strong a defense is posted. Inevitably the future will be a composite of change. Entrepreneurs seek the challenge of constructive change and make things happen.

Beyond IBM is a book which will help readers achieve more than they would, had they not been exposed to this truly important book. It should be seen as a text for students of business and those too impatient to remain students. One of the quotes from the book which I have already used in talks is "Learning occurs when there is a felt need or clear relevance." For anyone involved in commerce, the relevance of *Beyond IBM* will be inescapable.

—Arthur Lipper III

◄ P A R T I ►

IBM AND BEYOND

◄ CHAPTER 1 ►

Tom Watson, Sr.— The Entrepreneurial Struggle

IBM was in chaos. It was 1914, and IBM's financial strains were so severe that company policy was to pay no bills that weren't at least six months overdue. The offspring of the first horizontal merger in history, IBM was an arranged marriage of three small, unprofitable, disorganized, rabidly independent companies. Its directors went looking for someone who might make an enterprise out of the flailing entities—somebody who could take three sow's ears and make one silk purse.

They found Thomas Watson. He agreed to become general manager provided he could share the profits as well as the risks of IBM—it was his chance to be an entrepreneur without capital. He was almost forty years old. Out of a job for six months, he'd been fired by National Cash Register, and had been tried and sentenced to jail for sabotaging competitors' sales efforts. An appeals court granted a new trial and Watson considered himself vindicated. The issue was ultimately settled by a consent decree. Watson's successful struggle to harness and exploit the meager resources of his brawling business sheds light on the way to build a business even today.

Watson Sr. took a close look at his businesses. At a time when executives defined their jobs, not by saying "I run a company" or "I'm an engineer" but rather by saying "I'm in steel" or "I'm in automobiles," Watson Sr. found himself charged with running a mutation in the business world—a conglomerate. IBM's name in those years was "The Computing- Tabulating- Recording Company." It sold computing scales, tabulating machines, and time recorders. It was on the tabulating machines that Watson bet the future of the company.

In 1954, Watson Sr. was eighty years old. Two years earlier, he'd made the weighty decision to make Tom Watson, Jr., the president of IBM. Watson Sr. had reached the point where he could no longer make personal visits and speeches to factories and sales offices. It was in the thousands of these meetings with IBM employees that he personally had planted and nurtured the values and beliefs and dreams— the culture, although he would never have called it that—of IBM. He wanted the ideals of IBM to be carried on, and he wanted people, particularly IBM employees to whom he could no longer explain what IBM was all about, to have a written account of what made IBM great.

Constructing business histories was a new discipline in 1954. Most IBM'ers didn't know the story of those early years of IBM. Everybody was having too much fun hammering out the future to look backwards. From the time I (Lou) joined IBM in 1938, until Watson Sr. gave me a special assignment in 1954, I took IBM's success for granted. And then Watson Sr. asked me to compile a history of IBM.

I had been with IBM sixteen years when Watson Sr. gave me the job. I had learned a lot about business, observing Watson as I came up through the ranks of IBM in engineering and in education. But only when I went to work on the business history of IBM did I fully understand the dimensions of what Watson Sr. had done.

I interviewed all IBM executives, active and retired. I was able to talk with the people who had been with IBM since 1914, when Watson Sr. took over. I read the minutes of all board meetings since IBM's birth in 1911, and studied all of IBM's annual reports. I spent days in a dusty old warehouse in Brooklyn where we stashed away our records, looking for the history of IBM not covered by our legends.

In the end, it was not the records that explained the secret of IBM's success under Watson Sr. Documents showed me clearly what the secret was not. It was not specific deals that saved the day; it was not clever maneuvers that slam-dunked competition; it was not fierce internal power plays that only the strong survived. Businesses have these, and IBM was no exception, but if anything, they hide rather than highlight the essence of greatness.

From my interviews with insiders who had witnessed the early days of IBM, I gradually pieced together the real story of IBM and Watson. My own memories and experiences fell into a larger context.

Watson led IBM to prominence. He built the foundation of the most valuable company in the world. The story of leadership, marketing, and finance in Watson Sr.'s era is better than fiction. From the early entrepreneurial struggle, to the strokes of pure luck, to the foundation of one man's determined command, to the growth of its people and its cash flow, IBM under Watson Sr. holds insights still relevant today.

Like all successful entrepreneurs, first and foremost, Watson Sr. had a vision. That vision spoke loud and clear to a need in the American business environment. Watson Sr. saw that clerks and accountants—record keepers—were proliferating much faster than the rest of American business was growing. The cost of pencil-pushing was exploding.

Watson found this record keeping to be a back-bending job of entering a fact, a number, reclassifying that fact and writing it again, grouping it with different facts and writing it again, perhaps dozens of times.

Ahead of his time, Watson had a conviction that information, just like cash registers and rifles and cotton gins, could be made of interchangeable parts. He believed that a human choice to record a number could be made once, and that number, encoded on a card, could be available, reclassifiable, and printable by a machine, forever—or at least as long as the card was not bent, folded, or mutilated. I heard him say a hundred times, "You can punch a hole in a card and that's a five...and you'll never have to write it down again. Machines can do the routine work. People shouldn't have to do that kind of work."

IBM's tabulating machines had been designed by Herman Hollerith to keep statistics for the Census Bureau. Watson saw that if he added printers to IBM's tabulators, he could automate record keeping and revolutionize the way business processed information. Watson bore down to make real what he believed in. He sold his vision to his customers, to his own directors and employees, and to his creditors. IBM's other divisions were gradually sold off, or died on the vine.

Note that Watson did not invent the technology that made his company a giant. He was listening to his business environment. He recognized that Hollerith's brainchild could speak to an urgent need. He added a crucial twist—the printers—to the product. And he sold and he sold and he sold. We've found that this is often the story of entrepreneurship. The creator of an idea and the innovator who brings it to market are two different people with different value systems. The creator brings something new into the world because of a compulsion to create. The innovator recognizes a human need for the product or service and takes steps to bring customer and product together; the innovator's compulsion is to make money by satisfying a need.

These two value systems can clash. Watson had a terrible time with Hollerith, who wanted nothing to do with turning his lofty statistics generator into office equipment. The best a creator and an innovator can do is recognize the difference between them and capitalize on the strengths of each and the synergy arising from their contrasting perspectives.

Watson Sr. first had to get money to engineer the machine he envisioned. In 1916, he convinced the Guaranty Trust Company to give him a $25,000 loan. He used the money to set up an R&D lab where the new record-keeping machine would be created. He said often that this was one of the two greatest sales jobs of his life, the other being when he convinced his wife Jeannette to marry him. Watson, like most entrepreneurs today, found that one round of financing was not enough. He had to get his credit extended twice before his dream took off. Monumentally optimistic, he christened a shabby little plant in Endicott, N.Y., surrounded by cornfields as far as he could see, "corporate headquarters." Then he mused, "There's just one thing that bothers me about this whole situation here. We just don't have enough room to expand."

In 1919, Watson Sr. introduced his new "printer-lister" machine to an enthusiastic sales force. In 1924, he became CEO of the company, and renamed it "International Business Machines." He was 50 years old, and he was poised to build, as his company's new name implied, a great multinational corporation.

The risks Watson took during his entrepreneurial era are not widely remembered. We think of him as an eagle-eyed autocrat, presiding over a monolithic IBM. It's easy to forget that his success actually came in the last third of his life. He risked everything he had to build a company.

Watson Sr., Autocratic Leader

Entrepreneurs are autocrats. They are inspired by consuming visions or purposes, and they surround themselves with others who buy into their dreams. Being the source of the vision or purpose, they feel that only they can order the group's efforts. Entrepreneurs see the people with whom they work as extensions of themselves in the world, and they ultimately make their decisions alone.

When an entrepreneur's dreams start to come true and the business begins to grow, it is natural for that individual to cling to the leadership style that worked so well in the creation of the company. This is precisely what Watson Sr. did.

Watson Sr. had another compelling reason to remain an autocratic leader as his business blossomed: that was the kind of leadership that his employees desperately wanted.

The Great Depression conditioned a generation of Americans as had nothing else in history, except perhaps the Civil War. It wrenched people's souls. A famished Scarlett O'Hara digs a turnip from the dirt with her fingers in *Gone with the Wind* and vows never to go hungry again. It was this sort of profound emotional commitment never to be hungry again that created a value set for the entire generation of people who lived through the Depression.

Men resolved that they would never again be without a job. This national resolve was institutionalized in the Employment Act of 1946. It committed the federal government to a goal of preventing unemployment from rising above the normal level of frictional unemployment. This national will still plays itself out when the federal government bails out large banks and corporations that are going under.

The American man in the 1930s, 40s, and 50s felt he was fulfilling the requirements of his role by having a steady job and providing for his family. The American woman felt that her fundamental responsibility was to make sure that her family was adequately fed and housed and clothed. The roles of men and women were solidified in the collective vision of the sanctity of the nuclear family.

These were the conditions that made safety, security, and belonging the uppermost values of a society—the society in which Watson Sr. was building IBM.

Watson provided a company that promised his employees the safety and security of a lifelong career and the feeling of belonging to a family. As the head of the family, Watson expected commitment, loyalty, and obedience. Looking back on Watson through the lens of today's values, we label him an autocratic, paternalistic leader. He was. And he was precisely what his followers wanted.

This is the lesson: a good leader is timely. Timeliness requires understanding a cultural value set at a particular time. We can never understand leadership until we understand followership.

Because of his own value system, Watson was able to appeal to other deeply held values in his followers. An economic depression reorients people to spiritual values, a concern for higher things. People begin to ask, "What is really important in life?" When people are suffering, they tend to come together to help each other. Witness a neighborhood street after a big snowstorm, or a community after a flood or hurricane.

In every speech and in every conversation, Watson spoke to these higher values. He hammered away at the vision of the IBM family spirit, the golden rule, human relations, service to others. He commissioned an IBM theme song containing the words, "We can't fail for all can see/ That to serve humanity has been our aim!" I'd come to work at nine in the morning and hear that song rolling through the hills of Endicott. A new class of salesmen would be singing it, so loud the people over in the factory could hear it. I remember how inspiring I found it.

The values of family and service and doing right were yearnings that the population broadly was feeling, but rarely could find expressed in industrial organizations. And these were Watson's own values. They were the ground of his corporate culture, though no one called it that then.

Watson's timeliness is a secret of IBM that few outsiders have ever understood. You hear simplistic analyses of Watson: "He had everybody under his thumb," or "He created organization men who sat under 'Think' signs and didn't think." Outsiders concluded that if Watson had a personal preference for white shirts, he would command everybody to wear white shirts and they would grudgingly oblige. This misconception teaches us nothing. Analyses of Watson that simply call him charismatic are also useless. Followers did what Watson wanted because they were committed to the timely cultural pattern called "the IBM family."

And there is something else meaty to be learned here. Certainly Watson deliberately went about creating the IBM spirit. But at least as important as his conscious effort was the fact that he was being himself, and his spirit attracted the people who wanted what he wanted. There is an implacable urge in all of the best executives to remain their own unique selves in the face of all of society's efforts to make them conform. The story of executives is a story of uniqueness, not a story of acculturation. You heard it here first. We'll cover that story fully in the chapter on managers and executives. Watson Sr. is one of the best illustrations there is.

While other executives were honing their skills at scientific management—designing ways to make jobs simple, repetitive, brainless functions—Watson was working on job enlargement—finding ways to expand people's responsibility and sense of accomplishment. When other companies were delighted to leave education to the schools and universities, Watson was borrowing money to fund in-house education programs. While other companies were calling people "labor," a commodity to be hired and fired at will, Watson called his employees "the IBM family" and insisted on a full employment policy. This policy nearly bankrupted IBM in the early thirties when Watson kept everybody working during the Depression. He filled warehouse after warehouse with unsold machines. Only the Social Security Act of 1936, which created a huge and instant market for punch card accounting machines, bailed him out.

Watson's "man proposition"—that if you want to build a company, you must first build men—was his obsession. It colored every decision he made about IBM. He built men through his "human relations" policies. These innovative policies made him distinctive among industrialists.

The only way to build a great company is to be distinctive. Imitate other companies and be prepared for mediocrity. Watson Sr.'s approach to human relations was only one of the ways he made IBM distinctive. His approaches to both marketing and finance were also different, even peculiar in his time.

It is easier to be timely than distinctive. To be timely, you have to look at what the culture is saying to you. To be distinctive, you have to ask what values are shifting, and in what direction they are likely to go. You work hard to find creative responses to emerging needs and wants. Watson Sr. did all this beautifully. It was an element of his charisma, an underpinning of his success.

While the driving values of Americans in Watson Sr.'s time were safety, security, and belonging, another value was emerging in the American culture—the value of achievement. Watson's IBM offered opportunity. People who joined the IBM family could better themselves. Just because you came aboard as a salesman didn't mean you couldn't hope to be a vice president someday. Watson hoped you would.

Watson comprehended the desire for achievement in many women in his time. Sharp, capable women were graduating from college to face bleak career horizons. Watson opened a path for them into IBM professional ranks by creating the entry-level job of "systems service girl." Women were hired to work in the field, guiding customers through the complex systems work that IBM machines required. Watson was criticized for "taking women out of the home." But, as usual, Watson did what he felt was right.

Watson's intuitive approach to people happened to be an integrated system that allowed IBM to overcome many of the difficulties inherent in bringing disparate people together to achieve economic goals. In other words, Watson, being himself and acting out his own convictions, happened upon a splendid management system for his day.

The people who became Watson's managers were driven by what Abraham Maslow called achievement needs. They were able to inspire their subordinates who had security and belonging needs. Watson himself was becoming self-actualized. Having experienced achievement sufficiently, savoring his own distinctiveness, Watson was free to strive for something more. He was drawn to people like the great artist and mystic Walter Russell, another individual whose thinking was far ahead of his time; Watson loved to visit Russell, with whom he explored metaphysical interests. Because he had moved beyond achievement himself, Watson could inspire achievement-oriented managers. In terms of maturity, a leader needs to be one notch above those he or she leads.

The two irreducible requirements of a management system are:

somebody decides what is worth doing, and somebody gets it done. Watson personally decided for IBM what things were worth doing. He built, in his human relations policies, a timely and distinctive way to get things done.

In essence, Watson's human relations policies saw to it that people were selected carefully, educated extensively throughout their careers, guaranteed employment, rewarded generously, and promoted as often as possible. Their individual needs and wants were respected through a policy that placed responsibility for each employee's satisfaction and advancements squarely on the shoulders of that employee and his or her manager—what Watson called the "man-manager relation." And IBM employees had an appeals system, the "open door policy," which allowed them to go over the boss's head when an issue couldn't be resolved between them.

IBM hired people on character first, skill second. People were given a sense of the IBM culture before they were hired. IBM spent ten times as much money training new people as the average company did. Even today IBM is, in terms of annual budget and student hours, the largest university in the world.

It was IBM's educational effort that allowed for promotion from within. When you were promoted, you were given appropriate education for your new job. It was the educational effort that permitted job enlargement—IBM didn't dump new responsibility on an unprepared employee but educated the individual to rise to the requirements of a larger job.

Since people were promised lifetime employment, nobody was afraid to make suggestions about how to improve productivity or to cut costs. While in most companies a labor-saving suggestion could cost your buddy a job, at IBM a good idea hurt nobody, and could bring a cash reward. And since people were expected to stay for life, the large investment in education paid off.

Every social system should have an appeals system, to protect the weak from the strong. At IBM, the "open-door" policy, in which a disgruntled employee could go all the way to Watson, was a vital, respected appeals system. It had teeth because management took every open-door action seriously and spent hundreds of management hours investigating and solving problems.

The labor union arose to fill the crying need for an appeals system in other industrial companies. A labor union tends to be inefficient because it substitutes one cast of managers (the union's) for another cast of managers (the company's). The results of union-company negotiations must be applicable everywhere, so an individual's unique problem can only be given broadbrush consideration. A union's focus basically boils down to wages and working conditions—only in these areas can uniform, verifiable policies be established. As institutions, unions can't help one person solve one problem in one novel way.

Unions didn't gain a foothold in IBM because they were not needed. Wages and working conditions were exceptional, and IBM's open-door policy settled grievances effectively.

While the hiring, education, full employment, and appeal policies we've discussed were bedrock at IBM, they were not considered a substitute for the one-on-one, face-to-face solving of problems or the seeking of opportunities that can go on between an employee and a manager. This is subtle, and very important.

Watson saw that policies that applied across the board could not possibly satisfy the needs of every unique human being at IBM. He institutionalized respect for the dignity of the individual in his man-manager relation. An employee's job satisfaction and career growth were the direct responsibility of the individual and his or her boss on the job. They were not the responsibility of a remote personnel department, an executive several levels removed, or a vice president in charge of anointing fair-haired boys. All policies were only guidelines for managers. The manager's job was to work with individuals to fit policies to needs. I heard Watson say in speech after speech to his managers, "Understand your man well enough that you can give him exactly what he needs, and don't be afraid of violating company policies if you know in your heart you're doing the right thing."

It is the uniqueness of the individual that gives him or her dignity. Watson knew this innately. Since individuals are unique, they must be different from each other, and these differences have to be respected. Watson knew that no rules, policies, or principles could be applied uniformly to all employees—or to all vendors or customers, for that matter.

I recall times when Watson was like a lion, tearing apart an employee, and five minutes later, with the next person in his office, he was as tender as a lamb. He knew intuitively that two different people, in two different situations, required two different leadership styles, and he was pragmatic enough to do what was necessary in each case.

You might ask how it is that an autocrat can be so adept at respecting differences. Watson drew upon the autocratic leadership style most often because it was what followers wanted. He was careful to listen to people. When he sensed the wants and needs of employees, customers, vendors, or whoever else was involved, he would make a decision that reflected their purposes, as well as his personal purpose and the purpose of IBM. Since his decisions respected the position and values of the people who would be affected, people generally agreed with him. Because IBM people so seldom objected to Watson's decisions, outsiders thought that Watson was calling all the shots. Not true. All successful autocrats must appeal to the wants of followers. Otherwise they'd get rebellion. They'd get labor unions. This is a subtlety of autocratic leadership that is seldom recognized: to a great extent, an autocrat will decree what his or her followers, deep down, desire.

Watson's vision for IBM came in part from inside himself, in part from the needs of his followers, and also in part from the needs of his customers and others in the larger business environment.

The leadership job of an executive today is fundamentally the same job that Watson did—to determine the purpose of his or her company. The best purposes include the values of employees, the wants of customers and other relevant outsiders, and the executive's own individual passions and dreams.

Watson's sensitivity to what people wanted, his respect for people's differences, and his drive to give people what they needed inspired his human relations effort. These urges propelled his sales effort, too.

Sales Under Watson Sr.

IBM's product was a big-ticket item with a relatively small market— executives. Watson recognized that his salesmen would have to do a different job of selling from that of most other salesmen in the world. Selling an IBM machine was not like putting a cash register in every store. The unique needs of the customer required more tailoring. Customers got one machine and later, again and again, they would see the need for "extensions" to do more jobs. An IBM sale was not a one-time event. Watson recognized that his factory people had to build quality, not quantity, and his field people had to manage relationships with customers.

Once the sales job was defined as managing a relationship with the customer, the salesman had all of IBM's resources at his fingertips to keep the customer happy. Every IBM sales class listened to talks by the manufacturing manager, the R&D director, the marketing manager, the service manager, even the editor of *Think* magazine. All would tell the class, "If you have any problems with a customer, pick up the phone and call me."

Watson loved salesmen. He loved to sell and to hire salesmen and to train salesmen and to reward salesmen. He dearly loved to promote salesmen and was often accused of favoritism, but in IBM's case, that bias paid off. IBM was just plain lucky in that the nature of its product guaranteed its salespeople on-the-job training to become executives.

People who made decisions to buy IBM machines were typically CEOs. To do a good job writing a sales proposal to a CEO customer, the IBM salesman had to understand thoroughly the customer's business. IBM salesmen saw many times and in many different situations the problems and considerations a CEO faces in the overall running of a business. The IBM salesmen didn't learn by discussing cases. Each proposal they wrote to sell a machine was a mini-case, but it was not merely an academic exercise in a business administration class; it was a concrete proposal on which the salesman's success and reputation depended. The finest kind of executive development a person can get is the development that takes place on the job. The fact that so many IBM executives lived through the process of selling to executives contributed incalculably to IBM's success.

Because IBM salesmen became IBM executives, the company's dedication to the primacy of the customer was self-perpetuating. Those who rose through the ranks serving the customer insisted that all of their employees be similarly dedicated. Even the financial breakthroughs of IBM grew out of Watson's dedication to serving the customer.

Finance Under Watson, Sr.

The financial story of IBM's first thirteen years was a constant cash crisis. They borrowed from Peter to pay Paul. Every board meeting contained discussion of "where will we get the money to pay..."

The financial story of the next thirty years was the rental policy. The rental policy allowed IBM to generate cash internally and to plan growth.

Watson Sr. scrutinized his business environment. He saw that many potential customers did not have enough cash to buy his expensive machines. He saw that a vast, stable market was waiting to be supplied with machines based on current technology. In these circumstances, Watson made an unusual and, it turned out, ingenious decision. He decided to rent his equipment. This meant that he continued to own all IBM machines.

Watson capitalized the equipment, putting it on the balance sheet as an asset. Capitalizing products took a lot of cash up front, and IBM made huge cash outlays as it paid employees and paid for materials. But since IBM owned all the equipment it made, it was able to depreciate all that equipment. It was a smart move, tax-wise. Moreover, depreciation turns into cash when revenue is collected. Once IBM financed its initial large investment, and the rental policy began to roll, IBM's cash flow from operations became predictable. In essence, the rental policy made IBM confident that it could consistently generate cash internally. Never again was IBM utterly dependent on lenders or stockholders for capital.

IBM's early foreign operations provided a home for all the rental equipment IBM owned when that equipment became antiquated in the United States. Customers in countries whose record-keeping methods were following the American systems by ten or fifteen years were delighted to get older IBM machines at a good price.

Watson Sr. loved doing business abroad. He believed that "When goods and services pass back and forth unrestricted across the boundaries of different countries, there will be no need to have soldiers marching back and forth along these boundaries."

There is a second reason that IBM was able to generate cash internally, again stemming from the nature of the product. Customers for IBM machines were executives. IBM wanted executives to own its stock so that they would be inclined to buy IBM equipment. Executives are not intimidated by a high stock price; they look at a company's price-to-earnings ratio and other indicators when they make investment decisions. They are not looking for cash dividends, but for ways to shelter the fruits of their investment from taxation. So IBM deliberately chose to keep its stock prices high and to retain earnings rather than pay cash dividends. Executives watched their investments in IBM appreciate, and IBM used the cash to grow. Much later, when IBM moved into the personal computer business, it announced stock splits so that the price of IBM stock fell into a range that non-executives—PC buyers—considered affordable.

Only successful companies reach the point where they can depend on cash flow from operations for new investments. Debt and equity were gravy for IBM once it was able to consistently generate cash internally.

IBM under Watson Sr. was able to stabilize its cash flow. It could then gear its rate of growth to its cash flow. This stability and predictability were crucial to IBM's future. The harnessing of cash flow and the confident control of growth rate were the secret of IBM's financial genius in Watson Sr.'s era.

Stable growth also meant that IBM's stock price appreciated. Sophisticated investors look for a future stream of earnings in evaluating stock price. They saw that IBM's income kept moving smoothly upward along a curve that was easy to extrapolate.

The rental policy imposed a discipline of good business on other areas of IBM. IBM had to be customer-oriented because a customer could ship back a machine at the end of any month. Watson's emphasis on service to the customer was underscored by the rental policy. Manufacturing policies that emphasized quality in production rather than quantity of production were appropriate for rental machines. Educated employees and job enlargement were important in a plant that emphasized quality rather than quantity. With stable growth and stable cash flow, a no-layoff policy was not difficult to maintain.

A steadily growing company is the easiest to manage. This is what Watson Sr. finally handed over to his son. In 1956, Watson Sr. made Tom Watson, Jr., already president for four years, the chief executive officer of IBM. Six weeks later Watson Sr. died.

The IBM business history Watson Sr. asked me to make was never completed. Watson Jr. postponed the project indefinitely, saying, "The story isn't over." He asked me to join a task force to take IBM into electronics.

Watson Sr.'s legacy was not lost. In the late 1950s, with the help of all his executives, Tom Watson, Jr., made a determined effort to decide what of his father's corporate culture should be preserved. We crystallized into IBM's "three beliefs" the essence of what we felt made IBM great.

The first belief was rooted in Watson Sr.'s human relations thrust, in which he drove home the importance of "the man proposition" and which he institutionalized by his continued emphasis on the "man-manager relationship." Watson Sr.'s solid respect for differences led Watson Jr. to IBM's first belief: respect for the dignity of the individual.

Everybody recognized that Watson Sr.'s love for sales, carried on by his sales managers who became top IBM executives, brought enormous success to IBM. Watson Jr. canonized the customer in IBM's second belief: service to the customer.

Watson Sr.'s emphasis on superior selection and continuous education for everyone, together with his emphasis on achievement and promotion, built a culture bursting with high expectations. Watson Jr. captured this in IBM's third belief: the ideal of excellence.

Those beliefs—respect for the dignity of the individual, service to the customer, and the ideal of excellence—capture part of the story of IBM's early triumphs, but not the whole story.

Looking back on Watson Sr. after my own IBM career and my work with dozens of other organizations, I see that Watson hammered out and happened upon a handful of insights that are as relevant in the information age as they were in the first half of the 20th century.

The first was his *vision*. Watson tirelessly took every opportunity to interact with outstanding people and institutions outside of IBM. He did a lot of walking around in his own company's factories and sales offices. For most of his career, he accurately perceived his business environment. He geared for changes looming on the horizon so that he and his company were already acting by the time other executives noticed a shift. And he poured passion and energy into his dreams.

The second was his *timeliness*. Watson continually asked the question: "What values in the political, social, and economic environment speak to the fundamental purpose and thrust of IBM?" Then he geared his company to the predominant and emerging values of his world.

The third was his *respect for differences*. Whether interacting with customers or employees, leaders of state or people on the street, Watson delighted in their uniqueness and respected their differences. He could thereby serve their interests, and allow them to serve his, in ways that best suited both.

The fourth was that Watson was *distinctive*. He was willing to be different from other executives and was willing to make IBM different from other companies.

The fifth was his mastery of *cash flow*. Watson confidently geared the growth of his company to the growth of his operating cash flow.

Watson Jr. embraced his father's insights. He inherited a company at a pinnacle of success. The punch card machine business had never been better. Watson Jr. could have settled in at IBM and presided over a large, prosperous punch card accounting machine company. But because he, too, was willing to be timely and to be different, he didn't.

Watson Jr. made a new vision for IBM. He and his management team took IBM beyond the edge of Watson Sr.'s horizon to become the most successful company in the world.

Chapter 1 Digest

Tom Watson Sr. built the foundation of the most valuable company in the world. The story of leadership, marketing, and finance in Watson Sr.'s era is better than fiction. From the early entrepreneurial struggle, to the strokes of pure luck, to the foundation of one man's determined command, to the growth of its people and its cash flow, IBM under Watson Sr. holds insights still relevant today.

IBM under Watson Sr. was an entrepreneurial superstar because:

1. *Watson made IBM timely.* The Depression conditioned a generation of Americans to grasp for safety, security, and belonging. Watson made IBM a safe "family." Through the lens of today's val-

ues, we label him an autocratic, paternalistic leader. He was. And he was precisely what his followers wanted.

2. *Watson made IBM distinctive.* While other executives were honing their skills at scientific management, Watson was working on job enlargement. While other companies left education to the schools and universities, Watson was borrowing money to fund in-house education programs. Imitate other companies and be prepared for mediocrity.

3. *Watson held to his vision.* He christened a ramshackle shed in Endicott, N.Y., surrounded by cornfields, "corporate headquarters." Then he mused, "There's just one thing that bothers me about this whole situation here. We just don't have enough room to expand." The executive today must do fundamentally the same job Watson did—determine the purpose of the company. Purpose includes the wants of customers and other relevant outsiders, the values of employees, and the executive's own passions and dreams.

4. *IBM served the customer.* Since an IBM sale was not a one-time event, Watson's factory people had to build quality, not quantity, and his field people had to manage relationships with customers. Watson loved salesmen: he loved to hire and train and reward and promote them. He was accused of favoritism, but his bias paid off. Because IBM salesmen became IBM executives, the dedication to the primacy of the customer was self-perpetuating at IBM.

5. *Watson's rental policy made cash flow stable and predictable.* The financial story of IBM during its first thirteen years was that they were short of cash; the financial story of the next thirty years was the success of Watson's rental policy. Watson saw that many customers did not have enough cash to buy his expensive machines so he decided to rent. It took a lot of cash up front, but once IBM financed the initial large investment, operating cash flow became predictable and IBM could gear its rate of growth to its cash flow. Stable growth also meant that IBM's stock price appreciated. Sophisticated investors saw that IBM's income kept moving smoothly upward along a curve that was easy to extrapolate.

◄ CHAPTER 2 ►

Tom Watson, Jr.—
The Making of a Monolith

The two decades of Watson Jr.'s tenure at the helm of IBM—the 1950s and 60s—were a quixotic marriage of forces: there was a visceral quest for stability coupled with explosive growth and two bet-your-company forays into new products.

During those years, Watson Jr.'s management team moved IBM from autocracy to bureaucracy. Our management development effort—which simultaneously buttressed and battled the dictates of bureaucracy—produced some radical insights into the nature of leadership. Systems thinking emerged as an eye-opening, powerful way to get our arms around rampant diversity and complexity.

The concept of marketing, under which sales was subsumed, was born during Watson Jr.'s era, and IBM was among its earliest midwives. We chanced upon the secret of industry leadership in the late 50s and exploited it in the 60s. We came to understand better how to use financial data from the past to inform decisions about the future.

When Watson Jr. became IBM president in 1952, he made a decision that changed the world. Against his father's intuition and advice, Watson Jr. made IBM an electronics company. (Watson Sr. felt that there was a small scientific market for computers, and no commercial market to speak of.) IBM applied its formidable industrial capability to building the machine that launched the information age.

I (Lou) served on the task force whose job was to move IBM into electronics. We didn't know, going in, what would be required. We knew that we had a huge job ahead of us. For example, when we started, IBM had a total of five electronics engineers. One of my jobs on the task force was to hire 3000 electronics engineers in two years. I had to place an open ad to lure experienced engineers from other companies—a first for IBM, since Watson Sr. had always believed that good people would find us on their own. Meanwhile, I hired students, and their professors, too, if I could get them.

We were playing catch-up with Remington-Rand (later Sperry-Rand), which had built the Univac computer based on J. Presper Eckert's and John Mauchly's patents. Eckert and Mauchly had invented the ENIAC, the first large-scale electronic digital computer, to do wartime ballistic calculations. Now they were working with Remington-Rand.

We had to develop our way around the Eckert and Mauchly patents, not knowing if we could design a data storage system that would do the job. We had to convince customers that they needed this machine, and that it really could do what we said it could—such things as calculating a day-long payroll job in five seconds. We had to gear up to manufacture the machine. We had to train customers in the intricate job of programming—in essence, creating the profession of computer programming. We had to teach our own field force to sell and service this complex new beast that was as different from a tabulator as a tabulator was from an abacus.

It was touch and go. Our CRT data storage design didn't work. We had the prototype machines sitting in our showrooms, and customers waiting in line to try them, but we couldn't keep them running. We had to start over, acquiring at great cost a non-exclusive license to use An Wang's patented design for magnetic core storage. We had a terrible time with the intermittent failure of the joints connecting the miles of wires to the electronic components in our machines. It took us months to diagnose and correct a cold soldering problem in our manufacturing process. Our sales force was trying to sell machines with 18-month lead times.

Our long-term debt almost doubled during those years. Creditors were willing to lend us $200 million over five years only because our operating cash flow remained solid.

Our strengths in finance, marketing, and leadership saw us through. Watson Jr. summarized why IBM was able to launch the large-scale electronic computer in five years: "First, we had enough cash to carry the costs of engineering, research, and production. Second, we had a sales force whose knowledge of the market enabled us to tailor our machines very closely to the needs. Finally, and most important, we had good company morale. Everyone realized that this was a challenge to our leadership. We had to respond with everything we had—and we did."

In the end, the move into electronics, along with several other key factors, required a total reorganization of IBM. The leadership story of IBM in Watson Jr.'s era is found in the move from autocracy to bureaucracy. We took the management system out of one man's mind and put it down in policies, rules, and regulations.

Of course, we never said to each other, "Hey, gang, let's build a bureaucracy!" Rather, we worked hard and fast to prevent ourselves from being overwhelmed by the exploding complexity of the company. We knew we had to move beyond Watson Sr.'s autocratic management system because it didn't work anymore.

The Building of the Bureaucracy

In an autocracy, the person at the top makes all important decisions. Had there been an organization chart in Watson Sr.'s day, it would have shown a huge tangle of lines leading to him. Watson Jr. inherited a company of 50,000 employees. Sales were growing by 20% to 30% a year. Watson Jr. couldn't make all the important decisions in a company of IBM's size and complexity. Decisions bogged down in the president's office.

Followers, too, demanded a different leadership style in the 1950s and early 60s. No longer were people so desperate for security. We'd won World War II and expected to settle into a world in which the forces of upheaval had been vanquished. The Employment Act of 1946 seemed to promise jobs to all but a few. We were ready for the Eisenhower years—prosperity, regularity, order.

People didn't need Daddy anymore to provide security and direction. Benefits replaced paternalism. We were suspicious of power concentrated in the hands of one individual. Bureaucracy, with its rules and policies designed to be uniformly applied, prevented leaders from being arbitrary. Fairness and predictability were what people wanted. Bureaucracy was evenhanded. It was timely.

IBM divisionalized in 1956 for the first time in IBM's history. Each division had its own president. For the first time, we made organization charts and paid attention to them. We developed position descriptions, and had formal appraisals. We had a wage and salary administration. These management tools laid the groundwork for a full-fledged bureaucracy to emerge.

The earliest practice of bureaucracy in western cultures was in the church and the military, both of which operated according to a strict hierarchy. Bureaucracy seemed to work when organizations became large and had to simplify administrative decision-making. As industrial age businesses like IBM grew large, bureaucracy looked like a natural way to organize.

Bureaucracy mandates fixed structures. Its logic tells you how to put something together. Bureaucratic organizations are expected to work like machines—start them up, and they do the same thing day after day, year after year. To keep everything "running smoothly" is a bureaucratic ideal. Just as machines are made of parts that do specific jobs, bureaucracies breed specialists, who do specific jobs. If several specialists do the same job, they must be clustered together.

A bureaucracy is primarily a closed system. Little input from outside is needed or wanted. The person above you on the organization chart reads the policies and the rules, tells you what to do, and you do it. Ka-chunk, ka-chunk. Authority is conferred by position. My box is higher than your box. And bureaucracy insists that information flow from the top downward. When it flows upward or laterally it is anathema, dubbed "the grapevine" or "out-of-channel communication."

Bureaucracy attempts to ward off chaos by preserving stability. Stability is guaranteed if you continue to do over and over what you did in the past. To make a decision, you look at precedents and policies. What to do tomorrow? Simple. Do what you did yesterday.

Bureaucracy lent itself to the economic environment of the industrial age. It was an era of mass production and mass consumption. You could spend two years engineering a widget, another year gearing up to manufacture it, and then expect to be able to make and sell thousands of widgets year after year. This type of production required plenty of property, plant, and equipment. To raise capital for heavy investment in fixed assets, you had to be big, and it seemed that to be big, you had to be bureaucratic.

Bureaucracy is oversimplification for the sake of efficiency. Complexities of real life confound bureaucratic operations. So even as we were hammering down the structural elements of our bureaucracy in IBM, we were improvising processes that allowed us to circumvent them.

For example, we knew that a bureaucratic organization would bury the development of the computer. No function, no specialist in our bureaucracy was equipped to handle dozens of essential elements of the project. For instance, no job description anywhere in the company covered creating a new profession, but we knew that for the computer to fly, we'd have to develop 10,000 career programmers in five years. Our engineering hierarchy was composed of electromechanical engineers—in essence, they designed doorbell circuits. We needed a tidal wave of electronics engineers, ten times more engineers than we'd ever had, in a couple of years; the engineering turf would never be the same.

To do an end run around the obstacles that we knew our baby bureaucracy would erect, we used a task force to launch the computer.

A task force is more like a network than a hierarchy. You park your job description at the door. A task force has a special goal, defined in time and scope. It is a change agent. It creates new ways of achieving new purposes. It pole vaults over all the status quo mechanisms of a bureaucracy to do something different. When the job is finished, the task force dissolves, having provided the bureaucracy something new to be stable about.

Management Development in IBM

A pivotal lever in the shift from autocracy to bureaucracy was IBM's management development program. I (Lou) headed up the task force that created the ongoing management development program for all IBM managers and executives. Our program was distinctive in that we approached leadership programmatically. We did not swallow bureaucracy as an ideology, as so many companies in that era did. Many still do.

For example, the logic of bureaucracy suggested that we train people. "Training" is taking something as is out of the head of the teacher and tucking it neatly into the head of the learner, molding that person to fit the needs of the corporation. We departed radically from much of the conventional wisdom about education of that era—starting with the idea of training.

Training people in the policies and procedures of IBM built our bureaucracy. To a degree, we did train first-line managers, and to a lesser degree, middle managers, in the policies and beliefs of IBM. Executives are not trainable.

Training is a process of acculturation: "Won't it be great when everybody acts the same way!" Development is a process of differentiation: "How can we create experiences in which each individual can learn what he or she needs to actualize his or her unique self?" In our management development program, we leaned toward offering people as much opportunity for development—rather than training—as they could handle.

We found that individuals at different levels of leadership maturity have profoundly different educational needs. We built a unique management development program based on that insight. Most other companies had constructed management development programs that were basically the same human resources and personal growth education offered to everybody, regardless of level of management maturity. In IBM, we built three different management schools—one for first-line managers, one for middle managers, and one for executives.

The time to offer people training or development is when they are first promoted into a job. Education is effective only at the time of felt need and clear relevance.

First-line managers need and want a lot of training. Newly promoted from non-manager ranks, they have to implement the policies, practices, and procedures of the company, so they need to know what these are. More importantly, new managers are embarking on totally new careers—they are now leaders. All previous formal education has been in followership. Schools teach people to be followers, not leaders: "I'm the teacher, you're the learner, now hear this..."

Leaders get things done with the efforts of other people. There are leadership skills and knowledge that can be taught, particularly in the areas of communication and motivation, the two most important elements of leadership. A leader can also learn problem-solving and decision-making techniques. This crucial knowledge, too, is rarely taught in schools.

Leadership skills, and of course policies and procedures, can be taught didactically, and first-line managers expect to learn this way. It's how they've learned all their lives.

We knew, however, that the best development is real-life work, and we encouraged managers to take advantage of opportunities everywhere to lead. Volunteer organizations, for example, are always delighted to find people willing to lead. You can make lots of mistakes and they are still thrilled to have you.

Middle managers performed a crucial role in companies when we first set up IBM's management development programs in the 1950s. Their key skills were in accumulating, analyzing, and disseminating large amounts of information. They were our original systems people. Middle managers also provided a link between executive policy-making and manager implementation of policies. One reason middle management is becoming obsolete today is that computers are doing much of the information processing that middle managers used to do.

As people grow and mature, they become more resistant to efforts to condition them through training, and they become more open to development experiences. They begin to want to develop their own uniqueness. In middle-management education, therefore, we introduced experiential learning—people did more role-playing and simulated project work. As new middle managers were spreading their wings and beginning to be proud of their own unique selves, we urged them to capitalize on their strengths rather than to focus on overcoming perceived weaknesses.

Good executives resist, and should resist, training. We used to say, "You can't hang the training bell around the neck of the executive cat." Executives are becoming self-fulfilled people. They know who they are, and what they want, and they have their own ideas of how to get there.

A mistake many companies make when setting up executive development programs is to put a manager in charge of designing and running it. Managers have no idea what people one or two levels of leadership maturity above them need, nor how to get it. Most schools don't know either. Executives know what they need, and it is likely that what any given executive wants is different from what all other executives want.

While managers get things done, executives decide what things are worth doing. Executives orient the business to the larger environment. To that end, they must escape from their own area of specialization and become generalists. They need to know enough about every field relevant to their business to ask discerning questions. If there are other people an executive must learn from—top-flight economists, for instance—the executive will seek them out. Executives who want to acquire knowledge tend to choose their own teachers.

Executive development is a process of differentiation, not a process of acculturation. Executives are minorities. They become executives precisely because they resist society's pressure to do what they are told. Executives remain their own unique selves.

I (Lou) personally directed IBM's Executive School. Development was experiential. For example, I would take a case study from a business school on valuation in a merger. I would not ask the executives to sit around and discuss it, with me telling them in the end the "right way" to think about the case. If I had done that, they would have learned to be consultants, not decision-makers. Instead, the executives would break into groups of three. In each group, two would be the CEOs of the two parties to the merger, and the third would be the investment banker whose job was to make the deal happen. Their task would be to work out a deal by the next morning. The executives often stayed up all night negotiating. They got an opportunity to try lots of different styles of negotiating, to see what behaviors led to agreements and what behaviors blocked agreement. When we discussed the exercise the next day, they could examine their experience and compare their conclusions with the other bleary-eyed executives who had gone through the same process. Everybody learned from the successes or failures encountered in each group.

I also brought in what we called "resource leaders." They were top people in fields such as finance, law, marketing, and governmental affairs. Their job was to encapsulate for our executives the essence of their expertise, and to answer the executives' questions.

In the 1950s, when we set up management development at IBM, we had about 100 executives per year going through our Executive School. IBM was growing fast, and needed executives fast, especially general managers for all the newly created divisions. IBM poured money and time into the growing of executives.

The story of entrepreneurial leadership today is a story of overnight executiveship for 950,000 people per year in America alone. That's the rate at which people are starting companies—and thereby carving out for themselves executive responsibility. What IBM executives took years and even decades to grow into, many people now catapult themselves into, on a smaller scale, in weeks and months. Entrepreneurs have to learn a manager's skills and knowledge and develop executive values and capabilities all at the same time. It's tough, and a lot of them fail. People in large companies trying to be "*intra*preneurs" face a similar challenge. In the leadership section of this book, we'll succinctly cover the skills, knowledge, systems, and values that will benefit leaders in the information age, some of which will be quite different from those valuable in the industrial age.

Like his father, Watson Jr. was a leader who created a vision for IBM that allowed the company to be enormously successful. Watson Jr.'s great personal contribution to IBM's vision was his lonely conviction, early on, that electronics was the way of the future. As IBM became bureaucratic, Watson Jr. delegated responsibility for formulating vision to his management team. This is the way the better bureaucracies handle the job of relating to their larger environment: each executive keeps track of a specific area of the business environment; acting together, the top management team integrates its observations and determines the direction of the company.

Like his father, again, Watson Jr. found a way to make IBM both timely and distinctive. His willingness to build a bureaucracy made us timely. His willingness to bust out of the bureaucracy when and where we could allowed IBM leadership to be distinctive. In addition to our commitment to our three "beliefs" and our management development programs, we relied on systems, particularly computer systems, to help us manage complexity more creatively than bureaucracy generally allowed.

Systems

The information age has been born out of systems thinking. The only way to capitalize on complexity is to order it with systems. Without systems, complexity dissolves into chaos. If there is one new insight that businesspeople today can learn from the Watson Jr. era, it is that you can apply systems to leadership, marketing, and finance. In brief, here is the story of systems thinking. Systems thinking evolved out of four pursuits—operations research, game theory, cybernetics, and finally, the most far-reaching, general systems theory.

Operations research was a World War II problem-solving methodology. It spoke to problems like: how do you search 1000 square miles of ocean in the least amount of time, using the least amount of fuel, with the maximum chance of finding victims of a ship sunk by a submarine? It applied complex math, designed to handle large numbers of variables in scientific theories, to real world problems. To solve for many variables, you have to solve many equations. Operations research was limited by the fact that calculations had to be done by mechanical calculators and slide rules. IBM's large-scale computers, with their ability to solve thousands of equations per second, took the lid off.

Game theory, developed mainly by mathematician John Von Neumann, deals with decision procedures involving conflicting interests, unknowable variables, and probability. The goal is to find the optimal action to take.

The game tree, for example, is a decision-making technique that game theory spawned and computers made practical. With the game tree, complicated problems are broken into sequential procedures like tree branches. You can start climbing at the trunk of the tree to see where an action will most likely lead. Or, from the upper branches, you can climb down the game tree toward the trunk to determine what actions taken at the lower levels enabled you to reach your ultimate goal. The computer picks optimal routes whenever it comes to a fork in the branches.

Game theory, which considers poker the quintessential game because it includes the element of bluff, has found numerous uses in exploring unknowns of science, economics, and business.

Cybernetics introduced the concept of feedback. It said: no communication is complete until feedback is received. Automatic control was possible once we understood the cybernetic cycle: plan, execute, evaluate (meaning, get feedback), then plan again, execute again, evaluate again, and so forth.

The thermostat controlling a furnace is a classic example of the cybernetic cycle. It reads the temperature in the room, compares it to the desired temperature, sends a signal to turn the furnace on or off, then starts all over. Feedback is fundamental to complex systems. A rocket, for instance, is on course only 2% of the time—the rest of the time it is correcting.

The cybernetic cycle defines an efficient closed system. When one group plans, executes, and evaluates a job, it is likely to be efficiently done. It is interesting to note that the U.S. government's three branches cover the three parts of the cybernetic cycle: the legislative branch plans, the executive branch executes, and the judicial branch evaluates. But the cycle was deliberately split by the framers of the constitution in the name of "least government is the best government." Since the planners are a different group from the doers, who are a different group from the evaluators, of course the U.S. government is inefficient, as so many people complain. It was designed to be.

There is a pivotal piece missing in the cybernetic cycle: how does the desired temperature get programmed into the thermostat? In other words, what larger purpose orders that lovely little cyclic system? General systems theory, which grew out of the life sciences, speaks to the meaning of systems. It says that the purpose that orders a system cannot be found within that system—purpose is what connects a subsystem to a larger system of which it is a part.

The notion of likening the functioning of a company to an organic system first flickered into our awareness with the breakthrough of general systems theory in the mid-1950s. We are still struggling to change our minds and our management systems to take advantage of this insight. The information age is pushing us along. Here's how:

Organic systems are open systems—they must exchange energy, material, and information with their larger environment, or they die. Industrial age companies, operating in a stable environment, could afford to operate much more like closed systems than can companies operating in our boisterous information age. Information age companies must stay tuned to their larger environment, or risk becoming irrelevant fast.

The principle of equifinality is a tenet of general systems theory that is especially interesting in a time when bureaucratic structures are being widely criticized for being unwieldy and stodgy, and for smothering innovation. Equifinality says that process upstages structure: if you want to achieve a certain result, it doesn't matter so much where you start; if the process you employ is consistent with your result, you'll get there eventually.

Suppose, for example, you have a structure like a glass full of dirty water and you'd like a glass of clean water to drink. You don't have to empty the glass. Just keep pouring in clean water, letting all the excess pour out over the rim of the glass. Pretty soon you'll have your glass full of clean water. If, on the other hand, you decide to restructure (you pour out the dirty water) and then you continue with no change in process (you pour in more dirty water), you'll never get something suitable to drink.

The bureaucratic imperative—when something goes really wrong, restructure!—needed a good dose of the process thinking that general systems theory offers.

The key to systems thinking is to ask: How is everything connected to everything else? What purposes relate the systems and subsystems you're concerned with? Jettison cause-and-effect thinking when you're dealing with complexity and when you experiment with ways to give meaning to many variables, as in the approach to financial strategy outlined in Chapter 8. Frederick Emery's book, *Systems Thinking*, is a non-technical book that fully explains the key tenets of systems theory.

The Birth of Marketing

Marketing is a beautiful systems story. It starts with a recognition that you don't have a customer until you have a product but you don't really have a product until you have a customer. Neither comes first. If you wait for one to cause the other, you may twiddle your thumbs for a long time. A systems approach to an opportunity suggests you work on all fronts simultaneously.

Marketing integrates information from designers, manufacturers, customers, salespeople, and finance people—everybody on a marketing team offers input and feedback about products and services.

Marketing wasn't invented until the 1950s. In Watson Sr.'s day, "sales" was the way a company related to customers. A product was designed, the factory geared up and produced it, and then the salespeople convinced customers to buy it. There was no easy channel for feedback to flow from customer to design engineer. The CEO of the company kept a finger on the pulse of the marketplace and told the designers what to do. Watson Sr., who dearly loved to visit sales offices and customers, was a master at this. In his own mind, he performed the environmental scanning function in addition to the integrative function that marketing undertook during Watson Jr.'s era.

Our thrust to launch the first large-scale computer was more a sales effort than a marketing effort: we designed a product that Watson Jr. thought the world needed, built the product, and then tried to convince people to buy it.

While full-fledged marketing teams were rare in IBM throughout Watson Jr.'s day—IBM still basically saw itself producing mass quantities of general purpose machines—by the time the 1960s rolled around, several of IBM's major projects, like the Apollo project with NASA and the Sabre project for computerizing reservations for American Airlines, were classic marketing efforts in which IBM and the customer worked closely together to create what the customer needed.

But in 1955, I (Lou) was heading up sales promotion for the first large-scale computer, and promote sales was precisely what I did. IBM spent enormous amounts of time and money introducing the finished product to our potential customers. The computer was such a radical innovation that many people, even our executive customers, were skeptical that it would work. Here we were, promising that we could do a day-long payroll job, for instance, in just about five seconds. To convince them, we'd fly them, at our expense, to Poughkeepsie, N.Y., where one of our two prototype computers was operating (the other was at World Headquarters in New York City). We'd give our potential customers a fancy lunch, escort them on a thorough tour of our plant so that they could see that we were serious about building these machines, show them a payroll being run—"five, four, three, two, one...there, you have it"—and let them do some hands-on operating of the computer.

In essence, we were immersing potential customers in a new world for a day, hoping that they would come out believing enough to buy. If we hadn't had the resources to do this, it would have taken fifteen years, or twenty, to launch the computer, instead of the five it took IBM.

The luxury of introducing a world-changing product is one that few companies can afford. Most entrepreneurs who succeed today do so by making small increments of improvement in existing products and services. If you do have a world-changer on your hands, expect to make up in time and imagination what you lack in money and organization, because you usually have to beat a path to the world's door.

It seems that there is an important role that large companies can play in the information age: they can introduce the world-changing products. Their biggest challenge is to find the vision and guts to do it, as Watson Jr.'s IBM did.

IBM's size and resources helped us to capitalize on another, more subtle opportunity. We discovered the secrets of industry leadership and we deliberately did what it took to position ourselves as the leader in the office equipment industry.

By the mid-1950s it was becoming apparent that the healthy industries in America were those that were oligopolies (industries with no more than half a dozen companies) in which one company assumed industry leadership. The "sick" industries, like coal, garments, and housing, were atomized into hundreds of small competitors with no framework to insure a healthy industry as a whole.

In the Executive School we developed, in cooperation with the American Management Association, a management game that simulated the running of a company in an oligopolistic industry. The class of executives would split into teams that ran four competing companies.

Each company started with the same balance sheet and income statement. In fifteen minutes, which simulated a quarter, each company had to make key financial decisions, such as price, expenditures for R&D, and expenditures for product and for marketing, all within available cash.

Decisions were entered in the computer. It simulated the competitive interaction of the companies and produced for each company a new quarterly balance sheet and income statement, as well as a statement showing cash available for the next round of decisions. This process went on all day, simulating five years of operations.

After running dozens of games over several years, we noticed that certain games exhibited characteristics of a sick industry in which no company could make profits. In other games, every company in the industry made large profits. We analyzed what had happened.

The conclusion was exciting. In every game exhibiting a healthy industry, there was one company that did two things:

1. It made superior management decisions, frequently by chance.

2. It raised its prices gradually but consistently, establishing a price umbrella under which all companies in the industry could also raise their prices. The industry leader made R&D and marketing expenditures, allowing it to add value to the product and command its high price.

In sick industries, the competitive compulsion was to cut the price in order to gain market share and drive competitors out of business. The result was that the lower prices yielded too little cash for all companies. No company could make significant investment in R&D and marketing to raise the value of its product to its customers.

It was duck soup for IBM to assume industry leadership and provide the price umbrella that sheltered its industry. IBM's commitment to R&D, starting way back with the $25,000 Watson Sr. borrowed in the 1920s to do R&D and education, was bedrock. Our ability to spend money on R&D and our formidable service to the customer built both the appearance and the reality of a product worth a premium price. And we were able to raise prices gradually and consistently because we had such a firm handle on finance.

Finance in Watson Jr.'s Era

As in Watson Sr.'s era, the rental policy kept our cash flow steady and predictable. There was, however, in Watson Jr.'s era, one interesting glitch.

Watson Jr., when he took over IBM, signed a consent decree that settled a government antitrust suit against IBM. One key item of the settlement was that we agreed to sell our machines if customers didn't want to rent them. The fact that we sold machines gave us an inflated profit picture and extraordinary cash flow for a number of years—instead of the twelve-month rental revenue we expected, we got the entire price of the machine in one year if the customer opted to buy.

While a relatively small percentage of customers chose to buy rather than rent, companies sprang up that bought IBM machines outright and then leased them at rates cheaper than IBM's rental rates. They could do that because they were small and had lower overhead than IBM. The impact on IBM revenue and profit was significant enough that IBM carried a warning notice in several annual reports, immediately after the statement of earnings, saying things like "...IBM's gross income and earnings showed abnormally high rates of growth, primarily because of a major increase in the level of outright sales of data processing."

In effect, IBM was liquidating fixed assets. Today, there is a mammoth liquidation of fixed assets going on in America, with a concomitant puffing up of profit and ROI. However, companies aren't blaring the story in their annual reports. As we point out later in our chapter on the economic environment, if a company has been shoring up profit and cash flow with the sale of fixed assets, sooner or later it will have sold all superfluous plant, property, and equipment and will then sink or swim based on its ability to generate cash flow from operations.

Finance was tightly controlled at the top at IBM. Corporate financial people insisted on a standardized chart of accounts and closely supervised financial decision-making throughout the corporation. If there is anything that maintains bureaucracy, it is centralized policies and procedures about finance and personnel. The acid test of delegation is how far down you let decisions be made about people and money.

In spite of this bureaucratic compulsion to centralize finance, Watson Jr. tried to push some financial responsibility down into the ranks by instituting budgeting by line managers. Managers were asked, for the first time, to take a crack at putting dollar amounts on their plans.

In the Executive School, I was doing my part to democratize finance. A continuing problem in IBM was the tension between operating executives and financial executives. It seemed to operating executives that every time they had a great idea, a financial executive was lurking nearby to point out that it would cost too much. Operating executives, not being responsible for finance, tended to give too little attention to the financial dimensions of their decisions.

I spent three years developing tools and techniques to give non-financial executives the insights they needed to handle finance confidently. Then they could communicate with financial executives and build financial integrity into their operations decisions. Two of those tools for understanding finance and making intelligent financial decisions are included in the "finance" section of this book.

The Maintenance of the Monolith

"IBM's $500 billion gamble" was the label Fortune magazine gave Watson Jr.'s second mammoth effort to introduce a major new product line, the System/360. Watson called it "a sharp departure from the concepts of the past... the most important product announcement in company history."

The announcement on April 7, 1964, ushered in a new generation of technology—called solid logic technology—to supercede the transistor, just as the transistor superceded the vacuum tube. It meant that IBM had to make its own components rather than buy them.

This vast undertaking marshalled the development effort of English and German laboratories as well as American facilities. To coordinate this internationally designed product, IBM required a new international communication system that let machines talk to machines across the ocean. That information system became the prototype for worldwide information systems that coordinated and managed manufacturing, marketing, and finance as IBM became a transnational corporation.

Manufacturing the System/360 had its problems; we recalled the headaches of cold-soldered joints encountered on the first computers as evaporators used in making semiconductors for the 360 produced metallurgical defects that slowed production. Shortages of contact tabs, copper laminate, and epoxy glass compounded the frustration.

But the greatest problem was the software. IBM learned that programming and software would cost at least as much as the 360 hardware. IBM ran squarely into the information age. While the hardware was a great success, the programming effort associated with the 360 and other products to come daunted us.

IBM has yet to solve the software problem. Bringing forth software does not lie at the heart of IBM's grand historic mission—to develop, produce, and sell machines.

By the late 1960s, IBM was blindingly successful—blindingly. I was coming to the conclusion that change and innovation would be the watchwords of successful companies of the future. But the large companies of the industrial age—in part because of their great success—would be the last to welcome sea changes in what they did and how they did it.

Even IBM, for all its growth and buzzing activity worldwide, seemed to be in a holding pattern, living out four implicit imperatives: to develop, produce, and sell machines; to grow; to be financially successful; to preserve the IBM family.

I always get restless in holding patterns—be they over airports or in corporate board rooms. So in 1970, I took early retirement from IBM and turned my attention to other organizations—non-business organizations, and smaller, entrepreneurial businesses.

Watson Jr., after a heart attack, took early retirement from IBM in 1971. One of his looming concerns toward the end of his career at IBM's helm was the limitations of a large bureaucracy. His classic statement was, "We need more wild ducks in IBM." And his managers would say, "Yes, but we have to fly in formation."

Since Watson Jr.'s retirement, IBM executives have shepherded IBM's heritage. They have done a superb job of fulfilling the imperatives that made IBM the superstar of the industrial age:

IBM executives have dominated the mainframe and personal computer market and held their own in minis and micros—they have developed, produced, and sold machines, in spades.

They have doubled the size of IBM every five or six years—they have achieved IBM's implicit imperative of growth.

They have made IBM the most profitable industrial company in the world—they have kept IBM financially successful.

And they have provided a secure career home for more than half a million people, with a turnover rate of only 2.8% a year—they have preserved the IBM family.

A new era designates new things worth doing, and insists on new ways of getting them done. Watson Jr.'s IBM, perhaps more than any company in the world, ushered in the information age. The information age management challenge—for IBM itself, for the other industrial giants, for emerging entrepreneurial companies—is to move beyond IBM as we know it.

The lessons from Watson Jr.'s IBM speak to companies aiming for prosperity in the information age: be timely; be distinctive; craft useful systems; manage cash flow; make visions that speak to the emerging needs and wants of a new day.

Chapter 2 Digest

Watson Jr.'s great personal contribution to IBM's vision was his lonely conviction, early on, that electronics was the way of the future. Against his father's intuition and advice, Watson Jr. made IBM an electronics company.

IBM's strengths in leadership, marketing, and finance carried the company through a wrenching conversion into the world of electronic computers.

On leadership: The leadership story of IBM in Watson Jr.'s era is found in the move from autocracy to bureaucracy. IBM's size and complexity meant one mind could no longer order it: policies and rules had to be instituted. That was fine with followers: people were no longer so desperate for security. World War II was over and people expected to settle into a world in which the forces of upheaval had been vanquished. They were suspicious of power concentrated in the hands of one individual. Bureaucracy, with its rules and policies designed to be uniformly applied, prevented leaders from being arbitrary. Bureaucracy was even-handed. It was timely.

The pivotal lever in the shift from autocracy to bureaucracy was IBM's management development program. The program approached leadership pragmatically—bureaucracy was a tool, not an ideology.

While Watson Jr.'s willingness to build a bureaucracy made IBM timely, his willingness to bust out of the bureaucracy when necessary allowed IBM to be distinctive. In addition to a commitment to its "three beliefs"—service to the customer, respect for the dignity of the individual, and the principle of excellence—IBM relied on systems, particularly computer systems, to manage complexity and respect individual differences more creatively than bureaucracy generally allowed.

The only way to capitalize on complexity is to order it with systems. Without systems, complexity dissolves into chaos. If there is one new insight to be learned from the Watson Jr. era by business-people today, it is that you can apply systems to leadership, marketing, and finance.

On marketing: The concept of marketing, under which sales was subsumed, was born during Watson Jr.'s era, and IBM was among its earliest midwives. Marketing is a systems story. You don't have a customer until you have a product, but you don't really have a product until you have a customer. A systems approach to an opportunity has you working on all fronts simultaneously.

IBM discovered, through computer simulations run in the IBM Executive School, the secrets of how to be an industry leader, and how an industry leader keeps an industry healthy. Every healthy industry has one company that makes superior management decisions and raises prices gradually but consistently, so that all companies in the industry can raise their prices under the umbrella established by the leader. The industry leader makes R&D, marketing, and service expenditures, allowing it to add value to the product and command its high price.

On finance: As in Watson Sr.'s era, the rental policy kept cash flow steady and predictable. There was one interesting glitch. Watson Jr. settled a government anti-trust suit against IBM with a consent decree under which he agreed to sell machines if customers didn't want to rent them. The resulting sales splurge gave IBM an inflated profit picture and extraordinary cash flow for a number of years. The impact was so significant that IBM carried a warning notice in several annual reports. In effect, IBM was liquidating fixed assets. Today, America is undergoing a mammoth liquidation of fixed assets with a concomitant puffing up of profit and ROI. But unlike IBM, most companies aren't trumpeting the story in their annual reports.

Watson Jr.'s IBM, perhaps more than any other company in the world, ushered in the information age. The information age management challenge—for IBM itself, for the other industrial giants, for emerging entrepreneurial companies—is to move beyond IBM as we know it.

The lessons from Watson Jr.'s IBM speak to companies aiming for prosperity in the information age: be timely; be distinctive; craft useful systems; manage cash flow; make visions that speak to the emerging needs and wants of a new day.

◄ CHAPTER 3 ►

Build on IBM

IBM has been a magnificent industrial age company. The acceleration of change in our time, including the epochal shift from industrial age to information age, demands timeliness and distinctiveness. The concept of corporate culture itself is dangerous; any corporation in which all the people share and perpetuate the same behaviors and values for too long is apt to fail. Don't copy an industrial age superstar and expect to succeed in the information age. Don't copy IBM— build on it.

IBM appears to be in the forefront of the information age because it is providing the hardware that allows information exchange. But in the information age, the information itself is more valuable than the vehicle that conveys it. When "CBS News" breaks a story from halfway around the world, no one asks whether CBS got it thanks to phone line, satellite, fiber optics, or pony express.

If you want to get ahead in a business, you gravitate to the revenue-generating centers, not the cost centers. For example, if you want to get ahead in a bank, you don't become a teller. A teller is a cost. You become a loan officer, because banks make money by lending money. While in the industrial age most businesses generated revenue by selling hard goods, in the information age more and more revenue comes from information and services.

For industrial companies, IBM included, information has been a cost and hard goods, a product. Increasingly, for information age companies, information is the product and machinery merely a cost—and a relatively small one at that.

IBM's industrial success, probably more than that of any other industrial age company, has ushered in the information age. It is the technologies of communication and transportation that spawned the shifting values underlying the transformation from age to age.

Communication and transportation have brought a world of multiplied options. Every person on earth has seen a jet fly overhead. Astronauts-turned-mystics paint new visions of the earth to rapt audiences. The peasant farmer with the transistor radio to his ear is no longer satisfied; he knows that there is a more comfortable life somewhere. Kids in Harlem watch "Dallas" on TV.

Expectations are shooting up exponentially. A recent *Wall Street Journal* "Review & Outlook" whimsically called for a "National Leaders Protective Association," because communications have become so rapid and so pervasive that leaders can't keep up with events. The article postulated that China's Deng Xiao Ping "must be the most puzzled of all... he's buried Mao Tse Tung, reversed the cultural revolution, introduced private markets and incentives, and even announced plans for a Shanghai stock exchange. Suddenly, he's got students in the streets demanding that he shake the place up."

When people face a variety of options, their needs and wants tend to diversify and shift toward newer options. Once they see what is possible, people pursue the new with formidable vigor. In the three decades since Roger Bannister broke the four-minute mile for the first time in recorded history, more than a dozen people have equaled or surpassed his feat.

Once satisfied, needs and wants are no longer needs and wants. Most people in richer nations are saturated with goodies and gadgets— the hard goods that were the bread and butter products of industrial age companies. The needs and wants of these people are shifting to information and services.

Bureaucracy—the management system geared to mass production and mass marketing of goods—can serve a world of relative stability. It does not equip a company to serve a world of rapid change. When their implicit purpose is to perpetuate the past, bureaucratic organizations are ill prepared to set new goals for satisfying emerging human needs and wants.

Statistics are legion showing that the large industrial bureaucracies are losing steam. Since 1980, the Fortune 500 have required 2.2

million fewer people to do their work. In 1985 alone, fledgling U.S. enterprises churned up 1.4 million new jobs. Expenditures by heavy industry for capital equipment have plummeted. It's manufacturing for a mass market that demands big investment in plant, property, and equipment. America now spends roughly the same number of dollars on Frito-Lay snack foods as it does on machine tools.

The shift to an information age does not imply that there will be no more manufacturing, just as the shift from an agricultural age to an industrial age did not herald the end of farming. But the relative importance of agriculture to the overall economy, the percentage of people who get rich through agriculture, and the number of people employed growing things diminished monumentally during the industrial age. Large companies that mass-produce and mass-market hard goods will not disappear in the information age, but their ranks will thin and their relative contribution to the economy will continue to shrink.

Large companies are engaged in massive restructuring. They are liquidating plant, property, and equipment at an unprecedented rate. They are moving out of manufacturing and into the information businesses. Takeovers are hastening the liquidation. Raiders buy a company and sell off the plant, property, and equipment that the previous management couldn't bring themselves to imagine the business without.

To move into the information age as healthy organizations, companies must resolve several overriding tensions between industrial age management assumptions and emerging information age imperatives.

Stability and Change

The tension between the habitual grasp for stability and the need for continual change plagues companies, especially large companies.

It is extremely difficult for a large company to change. IBM, for example, is hampered by its size. Its mammoth constituencies are ankle weights grounding it to the status quo. Stockholders are betting almost $100 billion on the economic success of IBM. Four hundred thousand employees trust IBM for career security and opportunity.

Some 35,000 vendors depend on IBM for significant portions of their sales. IBM does much of the work of the government by collecting taxes, providing health care, guaranteeing retirement security, and assuming other responsibilities for almost half a million IBM'ers.

It is a paradox that when you are big, you have to serve an existing society, and in doing so, compromise your ability to serve an emerging society.

Robert N. Kharasch wrote a piercing book called *The Institutional Imperative* in which he said that the driving motivation of large industrial age bureaucratic institutions is to keep doing the work going on. When your product will be sold to millions of customers, year after year, the urge to keep doing the work already going on is not too harmful. But in a rapidly shifting marketplace, in which the customer's first question is, "When can I get an update?" the quest for stability leaves you shuffling around at the starting line.

In the political sphere, preserving the work already going on is called "saving jobs."

How did new industrial age companies carry on the institutional imperative to keep doing the current work? They muscled their way into defined markets, competing for market share. Almost every business plan assumes that the company will move into a given industry with a known market and start chipping away at it in the name of competition.

The hazard to IBM of this longtime imperative is that younger companies, not so successful at what they already do, can more easily adapt their purposes to the times. And the small firms make inroads. A classic example is Apple Computer.

IBM could not come out with a personal computer because just imagining it required too great a shift in its self-concept. IBM descended on the PC market only after Apple demonstrated that a mass market existed for something radically different from anything IBM had ever made or seen itself making. IBM can continue to capture these new mass markets, if it chooses. IBM's size, power, and reputation can produce results provided the market is large enough to be served by mass production and mass marketing.

The proliferation of values, needs, and wants born of the worldwide information explosion means far fewer big established markets to shoulder your way into. While the dominant configuration of industrial age industries was oligopoly, the information age is providing so many opportunities for myriad kinds of businesses that the very idea of an industry may soon be anachronistic. Competition for market share, too, has less meaning as big, old, stable markets burst into thousands of pieces, called niches. And the big boys, like IBM, who need a mass market to make it worth their while, will find it harder to be relevant—not impossible, since there are still mass markets out there, but harder.

The stability-oriented approach to a problem is "How can we do harder or better what we've always done?" The change-oriented approach to a problem is "What can we do that's different?"

A subset of the stability/change tension is the stress between an orientation to the past and an orientation to the future. An axiom of industrial age management decision-making was "Get the facts." All facts are about the past; there are no facts about the future. If you are geared to change, you concern yourself more with your assumptions about tomorrow than your analyses of yesterday.

Extrapolation grows out of an orientation to the past. Rarely in today's world can purposes remain fixed enough to justify extending our past behavior blithely into the future. Financial planning today, for example, calls for a close look at each number and each strategy that produced it to determine what should be done next year. Extrapolating trends and projecting arbitrary percentages of improvement over last year are pallid approaches to planning.

Industry ratios are similarly suspect. Looking around to see how everybody else did in the past has limited use when you are making plans for your future.

Surveying the past to decide what not to do in the future has value. What actions failed to achieve your purposes in the past? What purposes from the past are now irrelevant?

Being poised to change when necessary is not the same as adopting the trendy. *Inc.* magazine ran a pair of stories on Kollmorgen Corporation. The first was in 1983 when Kollmorgen was "institutionalizing" some tenets of "new management." The second article came in 1987 after nine straight quarters of earnings decline at Kollmorgen, where CEO Jim Swiggett was reassessing the firm's new corporate culture. In the second article, Jim Swiggett told *Inc.*, "there's just too much oversimplification going on about these new management techniques.... We're chastened. I think that we were pushed by our organization into doing things that we now know were inappropriate— things we couldn't sustain."

To be alert to change you have to carefully monitor the environment and choose the appropriate strategy from as wide a range of options—new and old—as you can conceive. A diverse business environment calls for diverse responses. Think carefully before you set about institutionalizing anything.

IBM is vividly aware of the need for change. While reaffirming its three beliefs—respect for the dignity of the individual, service to the customer, and the principle of excellence—it strives to be better. But better at what? IBM President John Akers told his senior worldwide executive team in January of 1987, "...All these actions add up to a transformation of the IBM company—unquestionably one of the most abrupt and rapid in our history. We're not passing through a brief bad patch with the expectation of an early return to the habits of the past, to business as usual. We are changing the shape of the IBM company forever..."

The challenge for IBM, and for other companies, large and small, is to change the shape of the company, and change it again, and change it again.

Perhaps IBM's greatest challenge is to brook a change in the business of the business. IBM still primarily thinks of itself as a manufacturer of hard goods. While it recognizes that software and services already make up 42% of the information industry's revenues, IBM continues to provide software and services primarily to sell hardware.

Almost as challenging to imagine, and perhaps even more staggeringly tough for IBM to do, is to move beyond bureaucracy. Bureaucracy as a management system is geared to stability. The ordering principle of bureaucracy is structure. But in the information age, structure is being upstaged by process.

Structure and Process

The most stable structure in the world is a pyramid. The structure of hierarchical, pyramidal organization is designed to keep things running smoothly—just the way they are. It is an efficient way to employ docile people to achieve fixed goals in a stable world. To the extent that these conditions don't hold, the tension between structure and process rears its head.

People in structure-oriented companies are slotted into functional specialties—typically sales, engineering, manufacturing, finance, and personnel—where they ultimately answer to a vice president who is responsible for that activity. The assumption is that there will always be these activities, as there have been in the past. There will always be a vice president to oversee each one. People will be rewarded for the hours they spend doing these activities.

Rules and policies are an important part of a structure-oriented company. They help make sure that the same thing happens over and over, every time and everywhere.

Contrast this structure-oriented company with a company oriented to process. People tend to be organized according to the specific and changing goals of the company. The "lines of responsibility" are particular projects. Project managers shepherd the projects, and people with expertise contribute as needed.

If most of your judgment decisions involve interpreting how a policy will apply to the decision in question, your company is probably hidebound with structure. If most of your decisions require figuring out how to accomplish your part of a specific task or what specific tasks ought to be undertaken next, your company has discovered how to organize itself around the process of reaching goals.

Some organizations are instituting what appears on the surface to be the best of both worlds—they call it grid management, or matrix management. Functions are line responsibility, and projects are also line responsibility, and people situated in the grid created by the intersecting lines report to two bosses. Such expediencies or compromises sprout in times of change, when companies try to hold onto the advantages of the old system while experimenting with a new one.

There is a place for structure in organizations in the information age, but as a last resort, not a first cause. Having structure to fall back on when all else fails is like having a police force—very different from living in a police state.

Bureaucratic structure breeds specialists and clusters them. As size increases, specialization grows. When specialization grows, interfaces between the specialists grow. Managing the interfaces is a generalist's job. But generalists do not grow well in a world of specialization. In 1956, when IBM split into divisions, it suddenly needed seven presidents, not one. The Executive School was created in part to turn top-flight specialists into generalists.

In the 1950s, IBM was a model company organized along functional lines, with an occasional task force for special or emergency jobs. By the time the 1906s blew in, the traditional functional organization was causing two problems. First, there was no one except the president to manage the interfaces. Second, the interfaces were getting prickly. Specialized functions were competing ever more vigorously with each other. Engineering wanted to design a product and plop it on a dutiful sales department—after all, engineers knew where the technology was going. Sales felt that it should be in charge of deciding what engineering would design and manufacturing would build—after all, it knew what the customer wanted. Finance felt that it ought to set prices because it knew what was needed to make a profit, but sales thought surely it should set prices because it knew what the market would bear.

So IBM converted specialists into new mutations: marketing specialists and marketing teams bridged the divide between sales and engineering; manufacturing engineers mended the gap between manufacturing and engineering; pricing teams managed the interface between finance and sales.

But the increase in diversity of skills and knowledge needed to run a business—and the interfaces—grew even faster than IBM did. Slowly, in some parts of IBM, specialized departments became staff groups whose job was to provide advice to decision-makers. Decision-makers—the line organization—became project managers, program managers, task force managers, systems managers, and product managers.

IBM has created independent business units (IBUs) that are a step beyond project management and task forces in terms of autonomy. It is an open question whether IBUs can work well in IBM or any other large industrial company. The logic of selection and training in big bureaucracies does not prepare people to become entrepreneurs.

Don't confuse committees with a process orientation. With the discovery of the importance of feedback in communication, committees emerged to provide immediate feedback, communication, and an increased feeling of participation. The problem is that committees are put together to study problems. Contrast them with task forces, which are put together to achieve goals.

Information age companies are finding staffs of specialists increasingly redundant when they can tap the equivalent skill or knowledge outside the company. Goal-oriented managers, who find in-house skills and knowledge insufficient to cover the diversity of tasks and information needs in a given project, go outside. They hire consultants, contract for specialized services, tap into networks and data banks, and develop a cadre of personal contacts who can guide them to information when they need it. Information age companies can be smaller because they don't have to put everybody on the payroll. They can use experts whose role and relation to the company are determined by clear goals, called contracts.

Uniformity and Diversity

In a world of change and diversity, the ability to create healthy transactions becomes ever more important. In a world of blossoming differences, the ability to perceive and satisfy needs and wants different from your own becomes increasingly valuable.

Uniformity has been the key assumption of industrial producers and marketers. Diversity is the reality of information age people. The tension between uniformity and diversity appears in many forms.

For ordering everything from organizational structure to income distribution, the assumption of uniformity, which guided industrial age practices, falls short. When your outsiders, such as customers and vendors, are increasingly diverse, your decisions about things worth doing shift frequently. When your insiders are increasingly diverse, the way you get things done shifts regularly, too. The two irreducible jobs of management, deciding things worth doing and getting things done, are more demanding in a world of diversity.

Automation, flexible manufacturing, and artificial intelligence satisfy special needs and wants. Olivetti, for example, makes three different keyboards for their computers—to type Spanish. The Spanish keyboard sent to Spain is a little different from the Spanish keyboard shipped to Puerto Rico, which is a little different from the Spanish keyboard delivered in New York City.

Automation and artificial intelligence are also creating a world where labor and hours worked no longer relate to productivity. Distributing income on the basis of jobs and employment is increasingly tough. Already we see anomalies in commercial enterprises like those in the software industry. Much effort goes into developing an idea that gets expressed as a computer program. You can produce a program for a few dollars and sell it for a few hundred. The customer does not pay for labor, but for the creativity of the idea, its realization, and its marketing.

What values will we reward in an age where almost anything we can visualize can be readily created? Most likely we will continue to devalue hard goods because they can be made so easily through automation. We will up-value ideas and creativity, and the ability to manage creative transactions. The people who capitalize on diversity will do well in the information age.

At present, entrepreneurs seem best able to respond to proliferating needs and wants. Entrepreneurs are both fragile and resilient. They fail a lot, but they usually rise up and try again. The title of Sheldon Saltman's forthcoming book says it: *Man on a Roller Coaster: A Millionaire Three Times and Broke Four*. There is no easy way to protect entrepreneurs. If we trained them, they would be replications, rather than unique. If we selected them, they would aim to please rather than be creative sparks. If we financed them, they would avoid risk-taking and would serve the interests of their backers.

Since entrepreneurial companies are generally small, the entrepreneur has a relatively easy time interacting with customers and shifting the business of the business to meet customer needs and wants. In other words, entrepreneurs are better able to respect differences than are large unwieldy giants.

Entrepreneurs also relate better to employees. Most entrepreneurs can relate to everyone in their companies on a face-to-face basis. This means that the entrepreneur can perceive employees' needs and wants and abilities to contribute. Contrast this with a large corporation that has to reduce thousands of employees to an abstract idea called "personnel" and deal with them through policies designed to satisfy the average—the one person in ten who falls in the middle area of a bell-shaped curve.

Small companies can generally do a better job than large ones in communicating with employees and customers and can therefore change more rapidly. Large companies have come to rely more and more heavily on computer communications that flash facts and information but miss meaning and wisdom.

Computers handle data and information beautifully. Data are records of isolated events from the past, which can be delivered sequentially, geographically, etc. Information is data that human consciousness has ordered in some manner. Information implies comparison of different things, or it signals a change. "Sales of $1 million" is data. "Sales of $1 million compared with assets of $2 million" is information. So is "Sales of $1 million this year; sales of $.7 million last year."

Meaning relates information to purpose. You process data, perceive information in it, and relate the information to your individual or collective purposes. Meaning is rare in computer communications. Wisdom is rarest of all. Wisdom is data, information, and meaning related to the diversity of purposes and values of a larger community—such as humanity.

Bureaucracy is largely limited to data and information, because it insists on objectivity—on facts. In decision-making in a world of change, it is crucial to take facts and information from the past and combine them with purposes, dreams, hopes about the future—all of which people, not computers, provide. A task of decision-makers is to transform data and information into meaning and wisdom.

Closed Systems and Open Systems

When we are exposed to a vast array of ideas, values, information, and events, we can interpret all that input as chaos. Systems are needed to order diversity.

Since 1945, the mushrooming of diversity in the business environment and the acceleration of change have antiquated many systems and forced development of newer ones.

By 1950, biologists had probed so deeply that they had to create new systems to comprehend living organisms. These systems were quite different from those designed to deal with the physical world, such as machines. They were called "open systems" because anything that lives must exchange information, materials, and energy with its environment. A closed system like a machine, by contrast, is threatened by its environment; this is why we oil a machine, put covers on it, and hang out a "Do not tamper" sign.

We feel the tension between an open-systems view of a company and a closed-systems view every time we have to make a decision about "us in here and them out there."

It is no accident that the organizational model for companies in the industrial age was the machine: "build 'er right, crank 'er up, and let 'er roll." Structured like a pyramid, designed to function repetitively, the mechanistic organization worked well at doing the same job over and over in a stable, unfriendly-looking environment. Competition was the watchword of industrial age companies because it is the way closed systems relate to each other.

The information age requires that we see a company as a living organism. We must lay an open-systems viewpoint over its mechanistic compulsion—as the forebrain lies over the midbrain, adding immeasurably to its capabilities. A company can evolve open-systems characteristics: open and friendly exchanges with the environment; free flow of information between individuals inside and outside the organization; purpose derived from the environment, which is the larger system that gives meaning to the business; the encouragement of living expressions and emotions like creativity, hope, enthusiasm, and drive. Open systems are far more adept at dealing with diversity than closed systems.

Nowhere is closed-systems thinking more prevalent than "bottom-line management." When managers see sales or revenue as a given, they can only reduce costs ever lower to give a profit that is ever higher, quarter by quarter. The irreducible limit is quickly reached. In contrast, "top-line management" sees sales or revenue as a variable that can be managed upward—and the sky is the limit. Rather than devising ever more clever ways to bake a cheaper pie by shuffling costs, we bake a bigger pie by expanding marketing efforts.

Put it another way: when companies compete with each other for market share in a stable industry with a definable market, all they can see to manage are their costs and profit. They keep trying to make the machine more efficient. And they keep looking at each other to judge how well they performed.

Bottom-line management does something important: it gets things done. But top-line management adds an even more important dimension: it decides the things worth doing. Leaders of viable, growing information age companies will have to do well at both.

Top-line management—the task of generating revenue—is pure open-systems work. Subsystems find meaning in the larger systems of which they are a part. Customers—present customers and potential customers—will help you create your visions of things worth doing.

This book would be contradictory if we even suggested a few specific options for things worth doing in the future. The successful company in the information age will be able to draw from thousands of options. It's the only way that many smaller companies can be distinctive and unique. Any healthy organism must be an open system—always changing. This means that whatever it is today, it ought to be something a little (or a lot) different tomorrow.

Many management practices in the pivotal areas of leadership, marketing, and finance are holdovers from an industrial age. Don't copy them, build on them. IBM offers the best to be built on. Serve the customer, respect individuals, be timely, be distinctive, work on your systems, work on your purpose or vision, understand and manage cash flow. The industrial age is fading fast. Given that the future is where the fun is, we turn our attention to leadership, marketing, and finance—beyond IBM.

Chapter 3 Digest

The acceleration of change in our time, including the epochal shift from industrial age to information age, again demands timeliness and distinctiveness.

Technologies of communication and transportation have led to a world of multiplied options. People's values, needs, and wants are diversifying. While the dominant configuration of industrial age industries was oligopoly, the information age is providing so many opportunities for myriad kinds of businesses that the very idea of an industry may soon be anachronistic. Competition for market share, too, has less meaning as big old stable markets shatter into thousands of pieces, called niches, which speak to diverse needs and wants.

The company that brought the world into the information age will have difficulty being an information age superstar. IBM is hampered by the inertia of size; the confines of computer communication that flashes facts, but misses meaning; the quagmire of mammoth constituencies, inside and out; the logic of bureaucracy, which breeds specialists and clusters them.

There are four key tensions between industrial age management assumptions and emerging information age imperatives. They are:

1. *The tension between a habitual grasp for stability and the need for continual change.* The driving motivation of large industrial age bureaucracies was to keep doing the work going on—to be stable. IBM President John Akers said in January of 1987, "We are changing the shape of the IBM company forever." The challenge for IBM, and for other companies, large and small, is to change the shape of the company, and change it again, and change it again.

2. *The tension between structure as an ordering principle and process as an ordering principle.* If most of your judgments involve interpreting how a policy will apply to the decision in question, your company is probably hidebound with structure. If most of your judgments require figuring out how to accomplish your part of a specific task or what specific tasks ought to be undertaken next, your company has discovered how to organize itself around the process of reaching goals. Structure in organizations in the information age is useful as a last resort rather than as a first cause. Having a bureaucratic structure to fall back on when all else fails is like having a police force—very different from living in a police state.

3. *The tension between uniformity, which has been the key assumption of industrial producers and marketers, and diversity, which is the reality of information age people.* When your outsiders are increasingly diverse, your decisions about things worth doing shift frequently. When your insiders are increasingly diverse, the way you get things done shifts regularly, too. The two irreducible jobs of management, deciding things worth doing and getting things done, are more demanding in a world of diversity. At present, entrepreneurs seem best able to respond to proliferating needs and

wants. Entrepreneurs are both fragile and resilient. They fail a lot, but they usually rise up and try again. There is no easy way to protect entrepreneurs. If we trained them, they would be replications, rather than unique. If we selected them, they would aim to please rather than be creative sparks. If we financed them, they would avoid risk-taking and would serve the interests of their backers.

4. *The tension between a closed-systems view of a company (a company is like a machine) and an open-systems view of a company (a company is like a living organism).* The organizational model for companies in the industrial age was the machine: "build 'er right, crank 'er up, and let 'er roll." Structured like a pyramid, designed to function repetitively, the mechanistic organization worked well at doing the same job over and over in a stable, unfriendly-looking environment.

The information age requires that we also see a company as a living organism. We must lay over its mechanistic compulsion an open-systems point of view—as the forebrain lies over the midbrain, and adds immeasurably to its capabilities. A company can evolve open systems characteristics: open and friendly exchanges with the environment, free flow of information between individuals inside and outside the organization; purpose derived from the environment, which is the larger system that gives meaning to the business; the encouragement of living expressions and emotions like creativity, hope, and enthusiasm. Open systems are far more adept at dealing with diversity than closed systems are.

◄ P A R T I I ►

LEADERSHIP

◄ CHAPTER 4 ►

Managers and Executives

The word "management" is deceptive. It implies that there is one body of knowledge, one set of skills, one genre of systems, and one range of values that pertain to all people who "manage" other people. But there is an enormous difference between the work of a person who has just become a manager and the work of a fully capable executive.

Conventional wisdom in the industrial age defined management as "getting things done through people." In today's environment, there are two glaring inadequacies in this definition.

First, the idea that you get things done *through* people perpetuates the idea that you can command subordinates—that you can manipulate their behavior. The work of managers today is better described as getting things done *with* people.

Second, the industrial age definition of management omitted the most crucial task of the people running a business, which is the work executives do: decide things worth doing.

Managers and executives require skills, knowledge, systems, and values that allow them to do their jobs. The acquisition of these characteristics is usually a growth curve. From the time you become a new manager until you become a fully responsible executive, you will know a continual maturing of your leadership capability. Becoming an executive is a process of accretion, of expansion.

The information age is calling more and more people to develop executive capability. Entrepreneurs must do the work executives do plus the work managers do. And they usually have to meet this extraordinary challenge fast, or they fail. Within large companies, intrapreneurs face the same challenge, which is perhaps even harder for them, since they have grown up guided by the assumptions of bureaucracy.

The industrial age was built on the bureaucratic principle that the pyramid was the way to organize. The vast majority of stones in a pyramid are near the bottom; likewise, in a bureaucracy the vast majority of people—non-managers and managers—are close to the bottom. Things worth doing is the last thing on the minds of people in the body of the pyramid. The job is to get things done.

When managers become executives, they suddenly bump into a whole new pyramid. It's an inverted pyramid perched atop the one they know. (See Figure 1 in Appendix A.) This second pyramid represents the larger environment. It is composed of a new, formidable set of constituencies whose interests must be respected. An executive must not only satisfy the interests of all the people getting things done in the lower pyramid, but also must explore the upper pyramid— those people whose needs and wants will indicate what things are worth doing.

The executive sits where the two points of the pyramids join. Every executive at that critical nexus feels the heavy weight of both pyramids.

If you are a fully capable executive, you can handle the job. You have within you all the manager's capabilities to get things done, and you've added a new constellation of abilities that allow you to decide things worth doing—the primary work of the executive. In the industrial age, the executive was one in a thousand people. Pyramids don't require many stones at the top.

The information age is flattening pyramids. That does not mean there is less to do, that the crucial capabilities of certain managers and executives can be eliminated or ignored, or that you don't have to be as good as before to be a manager or executive.

On the contrary, the flattening of pyramids means that more and more people can and must acquire the whole spectrum of abilities and values of the fully capable executive—and the spectrum continues to widen. For one thing, the information age business environment is more complex than it used to be. The executive who was running a stable company in a stable market didn't have the same challenge to decide things worth doing that executives in our turbulent environment have now.

Moreover, people are becoming more and more sophisticated—more and more mature. A low spot in a hierarchy, in which workers do nothing but what they are told to do, was acceptable early in the industrial age when many people were newly off boats and farms, and safety and security were profound values. Today achievement and self-fulfillment motivate more workers. The whole leadership system, based on maturity of people in business, is rising. Non-managers are doing work that only managers used to do; managers are doing work once the exclusive bailiwick of executives. Executive work continues to develop and mature as well, to address the complexity of an information age environment and the achievement and self-fulfillment needs of an information age workforce.

As more people within a company develop executive characteristics, they shore up the tiny intersection of the two pyramids. An executive can meet the challenge of a tumultuous environment not only by growing himself or herself, but by nurturing growth in other people in the company as well.

Since the mid-1950s, when we started studying and experimenting with how people grow from non-manager to manager to executive, we've learned a lot about the growth and development of leaders. We now know that as you mature, from the time you become a new manager to the time you become a fully capable executive, you acquire broader skills and knowledge. You learn to create and manage ever more complex systems. You come to understand and embrace an ever wider range of values.

In this chapter, we will talk about the capabilities you must acquire when you become a manager, the capacities you add as you become an executive, and how you can accelerate growth and development—your own, and your people's.

A Manager's Skill and Knowledge

A new manager needs to know the business. If you are a new manager, you have to integrate, frequently for the first time in your life, all you know about your specialty with the needs of your company.

As a non-manager, your larger environment—your context—is your trade or professional specialty—engineering, accounting, whatever. That is the primary environment you identify with. You read professional journals, go to professional society meetings, and hang out with people who do what you do. When you become a manager, your context shifts to the company you work for. Your most relevant work environment becomes your company. You need to learn as much as you can about the business of the business.

Moreover, you need to learn how your particular specialty applies to the business of the business. For example, if you're an IBM engineer, newly promoted into manager ranks, you have to take a new look at your professional expertise. You have to learn about IBM's technical needs and practices and experiences. You need to combine your engineering insight with IBM's engineering needs. And you must understand IBM's beliefs, policies, procedures, and practices. This is not to say that they are totally unfamiliar to you. You've probably been promoted precisely because you've already begun to identify with your company's needs, beliefs, etc. Much of the growth process from non-manager to manager, and especially from manager to executive, is a gradual enlarging of identification with the company. One reason entrepreneurs grow so fast is that they have total identification with their enterprise right from the start.

If you are a new manager who does not have a profession, you have a special challenge when you become a manager. Your relevant environment has been school, family, or community, which probably had little relation to your job. For you, learning to identify with any work-related community like a company is a new experience. IBM dealt with this problem by creating the "IBM family." It built community by such unusual means as opening country clubs for the enjoyment of all employees. A non-manager could identify with the IBM community and find meaning in it.

The most important thing a new manager must learn is leadership. Leadership is not a mystical quality you have to be born with. The essence of leadership is communication, motivation, and commitment. These can be learned and taught.

There are three elements that constitute the bull's-eye of communication. First, communication depends on differences. If there is no difference, there is nothing to communicate. Within a company, there will be differences in experience, in knowledge of the company, in skill, in interests. Second, communication is complete only when there is feedback. You have not communicated if you say only, "Now hear this. Now do that." In a company, feedback must include feelings as well as thoughts, attitudes as well as facts. Thoughts and facts do not generate human energy: feelings and emotions do. Finally, communication is effective only when there is something worth communicating.

Motivation isn't a black box, but it is subtle. The crucial fact about motivation is that you can't motivate anybody—they can only motivate themselves. You work on yourself, the job, and the environment, not the person carrying out the task. As industrial psychologist Frederick Herzberg showed, you must look beyond "hygiene factors:" Things like pay, hours, and benefits de-motivate if they are bad, but do not motivate most people even if they are very good. Look instead to achievement factors that can be built into your management system.

Commitment stems from agreement. Agreement is the only lasting authority there is. If you and I agree to something, I'm committed to it and you're committed to it. The more we crystallize the agreement and make it important, the more we are committed to it. One way to crystallize an agreement is to draw up a document we both sign. Contracts have power because both parties agree. Commitment occurs when you identify your own purposes with the purposes of a larger community, like a company. Commitment comes of free choice by free people.

Communication speaks to the mind, motivation grows out of the emotions, and commitment springs from the spirit. The leader who can address all of these elements of a human being is often called charismatic. "Charisma" is one of those funny words that we use to cover up ignorance. We recognize good leaders but we don't know why they're good. So we simply say they've got charisma, and we aren't sure what we've said. In truth, we're talking about these three things: communication, motivation, and commitment.

There is a management technique that systematically allows a manager to teach communication, stimulate motivation, and inspire commitment. This is the joint task of creating results or goals to be achieved by the people who create them. When a manager and a non-manager sit down face to face and create desired results that, when achieved, will satisfy both the non-manager's purposes and the high-level purposes of the company, you have the best opportunity there is for communication, motivation, and commitment.

Nothing is more worthwhile to communicate than the job results to be achieved—it is the heart of why you are all there. Many of the usual things communicated within companies, such as who got promoted or the new policy for dealing with tardiness, are pale communications compared to goals to be achieved.

The joint job of creating goals motivates because people have a chance to say what turns them on and what doesn't. They are given some choice in aspects of what they want to achieve. Choice is motivational. When your company adopts a purpose that you suggest, you are excited, because now you are working on something you created.

Agreeing to goals allows a manager to manage the work and not the worker. When results to be achieved are clear, activity can be delegated. Clear goals will determine the nature of the activity needed to achieve them. With them, managers can delegate to the person best able to decide what activity is appropriate—the person charged with achieving the result. This is freeing, and freedom motivates the vast majority of today's people. We don't like people breathing down our necks, needling us to do things that don't make sense to us.

Agreeing to achieve results is the only authority that lasts. Coercion will work for a while, but in the long run you will get rebellion—active rebellion like strikes and even sabotage, or passive rebellion like listlessness or "in-plant retirement."

I (Kate) remember a large foundry whose workers even had a name for that passive rebellion. I was having coffee after working with a maintenance crew to fix a machine that had gone down in mid-shift for lack of obvious preventive maintenance. I asked a couple of mill-wrights why, since they foresaw this problem, they had let it happen. One of them, a big guy called "Red," said, "Kate, when a new guy comes into this plant, we watch him. At first, he'll try to do things and he'll make suggestions and he'll tell them things that are wrong, and nothing comes of it. He finally realizes that his job is to do what he is told. That's when he develops 'the attitude.' Once you get 'the attitude,' you don't try anymore."

When people feel forced to serve purposes that are not their own, they don't work, they merely serve time. "The attitude" undercut productivity in a lot of industrial age companies. It was the downside of the mechanistic nature of bureaucracy.

Of course, some people managed to climb above "the attitude." One is Ron Duensing, now Senior Electrical Engineer at GM's Central Foundry in Danville, Illinois, in charge of 200 managers and non-managers. He is one of those leaders who raises everybody's level of leadership capability.

I (Kate) met Ron Duensing when I was selling centrifugal blast equipment for Wheelabrator-Frye and he was in charge of maintenance for all of Central Foundry Danville's "Wheelabrators" and a half-dozen other types of equipment. Centrifugal blast equipment is cannibalistic—it chews sand and scale off castings, but devours itself while doing the job. Most companies had trouble scheduling the preventive maintenance needed to keep their Wheelabrators in good shape, and so they limped along with 60% to 70% uptime. Ron's twenty-one Wheelabrators, however, chugged along like a phalanx of overgrown dishwashers—at 98% uptime. I made it my business to find out how Ron operated as a manager of people. I spent hours talking with him.

The people who work for Ron plan, execute, and evaluate their own work. The complete cybernetic cycle of planning, executing, and evaluating is not reserved for Ron alone.

Here's a bit of the story, in Ron's words. "Every year we get together as a group, and make a list of all the projects people think we need to do, or want to do. We try to put them into perspective—what might shut us down if we don't do it? We assign some dollars to the projects. You can't do every job you write down. I try to make sure we include a few of the fun ones. You've got to give people an opportunity to create and have fun.

"People get the whole job—they plan it, they do it, and they evaluate it. If you give responsibility and not authority you're a dead duck. I write down when the job's going to be done. They make a commitment to get it done on time. I make a commitment to get them the time, tools, and materials they'll need and the training if they'll need it. My word is my bond. Their word is their bond.

"Sure, I get mistakes. But I get people's heads as well as their bodies. I came out of the hourly ranks and I know how it feels when people think just because you're not wearing a white shirt you're stupid. I tell people, 'Don't be afraid to be creative. Control your destiny. No one will discipline you for an honest mistake. I'll go out the gate for you if anybody gives you trouble for an honest mistake.' We capture the mistakes for future knowledge. If somebody screws up, we go through it logically and decide what could be done differently in a similar situation next time.

"Once you get people thinking like this, you'd be amazed at the things they do. I've got electricians developing software. I've got a millwright who's in charge of five miles of conveyors, all computer-controlled. He's surveying, listing jobs, determining the manpower needed to keep them up and the material needed to replace worn out parts, and he schedules the work. He will evaluate his own job.

"You spend most of your life on the job—you have to get pleasure out of it. My biggest enjoyment in my job is watching people grow when you give them authority and responsibility. I watch people who used to be meek and mild and now they're animals! They're three steps ahead of you. They raise hell. I love it."

Ron is a master at getting things done with people. He's a legend in his own plant. He foments communication, motivation, and commitment by allowing his people to commit to get projects done, to do them in their own way, and to evaluate their work.

The activity of jointly creating results to be achieved with the people who will achieve them operationally builds common purpose. Managers like Ron Duensing foster common purpose for their particular area of the company. The executive's job is to make sure the purposes of all areas draw from and contribute to an overall company purpose—what things are worth doing for the whole company.

Executive Skill and Knowledge

Capable executives are skillful at creating, communicating, and maintaining common purpose for the entire company. If the executive does not do this job, it goes undone. Sometimes, the executive's job is called policy-making. We aren't using that term because it can mean different things to different people—anything from "ROI will be 20% next year" to "Don't smoke in the bathrooms."

Purpose answers the question, "What is the business of our business?" If you have a company, you have implicitly decided to do some things and not others. An executive must always have a clear grasp of why the business is there. If the executive is fuzzy about what the business is trying to do, then people in both upper and lower pyramids also will be confused.

As an executive, you create purpose by integrating the varied interests of the people in the lower pyramid with the myriad interests of the people in the upper pyramid. Your personal dreams and imagination contribute to corporate purpose, too. Formulating purpose is a very creative activity; you deal with differences on a grand scale.

An executive cannot create a lofty purpose and let it wave out there in the breeze. To communicate and maintain the purpose you've created requires chunking down purpose into concrete desired results. These specific high-level results, when achieved, move the company in the direction of purpose. Goals make purpose operational. Until you translate purpose into specific results that you plan to achieve with your managers, it's just a tale, told by an executive, full of sound and fury, signifying nothing.

As an executive, you cannot achieve all of these desired goals alone—your management team will work with the non-managers to make them happen. Therefore others must have a hand in creating these high-level goals. Agreement is as important here as it was for the manager exercising leadership. You don't forget all you knew about leadership. You apply the kind of leadership that promotes motivation, communication, and commitment in the process of setting goals with your management team.

The joint creation of high-level goals links executives and managers. It is primarily through this process that the executive can understand and integrate the needs and enthusiasm of the people in the lower pyramid.

Warren Olsen is a good example of a manager-turned-entrepreneur who learned fast how to be an executive. He has done a tremendous job of growing his company by growing his people, and vice versa. When I (Kate) met him in 1978 he had just quit his job, mortgaged his house, and, with two partners, bought Metalmasters, an aluminum die-casting foundry. The partners paid $400,000 for the company, $350,000 of which was debt to the previous owners. It had been losing money for five years. Warren became president of the little sixteen-person operation. In September 1987, he sold his interest in the business for $20 million. The company was doing $60 million in annual sales, with four plants, 800 people, and a good profit and cash flow.

Warren describes how the company grew: "We didn't have salesmen. We took engineers who had the communication skills and aggressiveness and put them in the field. If anything stood out in getting those people to grow, it was that they knew they could take a shot at new things. One of our guys couldn't get us into the party balloon business by himself, but he could go out to a potential customer and commit us to a new method of manufacturing—if that's what it took to get the sale. He knew he could come back and say, 'Here's what I had to do,' and we'd say, 'Okay, we'll find a way to do it.' Most of the time, of course, he'd be able to check with us before making a commitment, but sometimes you're in front of the customer and the deal's going down and you've got to get it.

"Sometimes somebody would make a mistake—commit us to something too expensive to make for the price he quoted. We'd have to go back to the purchasing agent and say, 'Sorry, we made a mistake.' Sometimes this would get the purchasing person bent out of shape. But I found that every single time we got into a problem with a customer, it was an opportunity. If we played the game right—if we were willing to commit the time to make things right—we'd come out smelling like a hero.

"It was this way that we kept expanding into new niches—we got forced by our customers and the commitments our people made that we stood behind. We didn't sit down in a darkened room, a little triumvirate of partners at the top, and say, 'You know, there's a big business in control machines. Why don't we, over the next five years, go for 20% of that market.' We were growing too fast for that. Our salespeople would go for an order and we'd find a way to make it, or we'd buy it outside until we could rev up the capacity inside. We kept expanding into our border areas—you know, the bigger your light the more darkness you light up. The key thing is to have expertise in your people. If you've got that, you can go buy machines and a building and go do it.

"We grew that expertise in our inside people the same way we grew it in our field people. We had a philosophy—if somebody wanted to do a job, let them do it. The cream rose to the top. When people gained the respect of their supervisors and other people by competent behavior, good judgment, and avoiding stupid mistakes, we'd let them expand their responsibility. And we'd reward them. We paid people 30% more than the going rate and expected 100% more. And we'd think nothing of giving a $30,000 bonus to somebody making a salary of $50,000. Like Al McGuire used to tell his basketball team, I'd tell everybody, 'If you're going to play, we'll all go downtown together.'

"There were always opportunities for people to try new things because we were growing and our salespeople were always coming back with these new projects. Say, for example, Ford came to us and said, 'This is what we want, can you handle it?' We'd have our staff in the meeting, down to the first-line managers. They were the ones who could say why we couldn't handle it. We'd say, 'What would it take?' Individuals would say, 'Well, we need this and this and this. People would think about it, and pipe up which part of it they would take responsibility for. We'd pencil the sucker out and have at it."

As people grow from managers to executives, their jobs involve more and more monitoring of the environment. How does an executive monitor the upper pyramid? Usually, if you are an executive, you read voraciously, participate in conferences about the social, economic, and political environment, bring in consultants, and form a network with people who can keep you up to date in various arenas. Many executives, particularly in smaller companies, personally stay in touch with a number of customers. For instance, Warren Olsen, president of the little foundry that flourished, didn't make cold calls himself after the first couple of years, but he talked to customers on the phone every day and he made sales calls.

An executive knows how to ask discerning questions—the questions that bring you close to the essence of an area of expertise or reality as it relates to your business. Good executives have to be good generalists. You develop little techniques like asking several people in a field, "Besides you, who knows the most about this field?" or, "Where do you get your best information?" When you hear the same name, or newsletter, or whatever a few times, you know you're getting close to the bull's-eye. Robert Mueller, former chairman of Arthur

D. Little, mentions in his book *Corporate Networking* that he keeps a "GWRK" Rolodex—Guys and Gals Who Really Know.

Where does imagination come from—that ingredient of purpose that allows you to marry the diverse needs of all those constituencies with the things that personally inspire and motivate you? You don't get imagination, you grow it.

You grow imagination in a climate of freedom. In the industrial age, that climate existed only when you were sitting on top, free at last of the institutional imperative. There were, here and there, pockets of freedom in companies. These pockets were created by a specific task so new that rules and practices had not yet had time to grow, or by a single person who somehow managed to be so valuable that he or she could break some of the rules. Imagination could breathe a little in those pockets. Executives, who resist acculturation and insist on being their unique selves, often rise to the top by creating and/or moving through these pockets of freedom.

Today, executives are deliberately creating pockets of freedom in companies. They are recognizing that the pockets are not anomalies in structure that need to be plugged, but opportunities for creativity and growth that need to be opened up.

In the joint formulation of desired results—high-level goals between executives and managers and lower-level goals between managers and non-managers—people within the organization begin to ask questions once reserved for the few at the top: "What do I want to do that turns me on? How can I accomplish my purposes and the purposes of this company, too?"

Systems and Values: The Growth Curve from Manager to Executive

From the time you first become a manager until you are a fully capable executive, the diversity you perceive and order continues to swell. For example, as a fresh new manager you may have ten people whose efforts you coordinate, and one executive to whom you report. As an executive, you may have 3000 people in your company, another 80,000 customers, 2000 stockholders, a handful of bankers, several dozen relevant government agencies, and a society at large of somewhere between 240 million and 5 billion, depending on your range of vision. In short, as you grow, so does the diversity you manage.

A system is a tool to order diversity. As you grow from manager to executive, the systems you must create and manage become ever more complex. The values you must draw from to deal with all this complexity and diversity broaden throughout your career.

How do you design a system? It's a creative act. You've got to realize that you're dealing with complexity. It looks chaotic at first. Ask yourself, "What am I trying to do?" You have to examine purpose; purpose gives meaning to a system. Then you have to begin looking at pieces of that chaos and say, "Does this have any relationship to that purpose?" You begin grouping pieces that look like each other, and then you ask, "What relationship do these pieces have to one another, and what relationship to the purpose?" And you start discovering all those relationships of each part to the purpose. Gradually, after a lot of sweat and tears, you design a system that to your satisfaction gives meaning to all that complexity. When you have accomplished this, you can relate any piece of that system to the overall purpose and to the other parts of the system.

The Mobley Matrix format, described in Chapter 10, is a system for understanding the meaning of every piece of financial data as it relates to your total financial picture. Devising the format took two years of thinking and asking questions of experts. It took another three years to develop the Mobley Matrix computer-based financial management system mentioned in Chapter 11. That system has seventy-two variables. For any decision or plan the user enters, the computer solves all seventy-two equations simultaneously. Without a computer, you couldn't manage a mathematical system of this complexity.

Any system is a model that gives meaning to a great variety of individual ideas, events, or facts. Being a model, it is not the real thing. But by using such a model, the real thing can be more easily achieved. Using a Mobley Matrix program, for example, won't guarantee you a 20% ROI, but it can outline for you the most efficient way to get there, given your unique situation and capabilities. And it will guarantee that if you accomplish your plans, the ROI will be there.

The simplest system is cause and effect. Systems theory suggests that most systems are more complex than "A causes B." Building a system requires us to do two things. First, we have to explore how

"B" does, or ought to, affect "A"—in other words, put feedback into the system. Second, we must explore what other influences should be considered to make the system more representative of the reality it is designed to illuminate, thus introducing variables "C," "D," "E," and so on. Some of these variables may affect "A" or "B" directly, some may affect the process that causes "A" to influence "B." In effect, we have added a multitude of causes and effects that better represent a real world of enormous diversity and complexity. When systems contain hundreds or thousands of variables, as in the Apollo mission, the digital computer is an essential tool for handling all the interactions.

As a new manager, you usually have to make a piece of the machine work—you have to get things done. Your decisions generally require choosing between two, or a few, variables. For example, in dozens of cases every week, you must make a judgment about the degree of control you're going to exercise over your non-managers. You can't do that well unless you have a system that says that there are two things operating against each other: one is the need for freedom and creativity and the other is the need for a certain amount of order through control. Now, if you get ideological and apply some principle across the board, you will impose too much control on some people or give too much freedom to others. But if you recognize both needs that are in tension, and you know your purpose in a given situation, you can apply the right judgment as to where the balance is. You're aware that there's a cost to fixing mistakes, as well as a cost to keeping control. Overcontrolling costs: it costs to create and maintain controls. Further, overcontrolling produces resentment, reduces motivation, and dehumanizes people. Undercontrolling costs: in errors created, morale deflated due to low confidence in management, the drag of inefficiency.

The system you create must monitor, formally or informally, both the cost of control and the cost of fixing errors. The time, energy, and cost of keeping controls should roughly equal the time, energy, and cost of correcting errors that occur with that degree of control. (See Figure 2 in Appendix A.) With each human being, this balance will be different. As your people grow, they are likely to want and be able to handle more freedom.

Executives create systems that must deal with the company as a whole, not just one of its parts, and must relate the company in a meaningful way to its economic, social, and political environment. Three systems described in this book are suggestive of helpful executive-level tools. These systems deal with the complexity and diversity an executive must integrate. Chapter 5 outlines a leadership system; Chapter 8 describes an open system for marketing management; Chapters 10 and 11 describe a financial system. Just as your systems must handle more diversity as you grow from manager to executive, so your values must accommodate ever more diversity. Harlan Cleveland, in the introduction to his book, *The Knowledge Executive*, says, "I have come to believe that the art of executive leadership is above all a taste for paradox, a talent for ambiguity, the capacity to hold contradictory propositions comfortably in a mind that relishes complexity."

Perhaps more than any other single value, respect for differences characterizes executives. Executives love differences. In our discussion about diversity with General Bill Creech, whose management system for the Air Force's Tactical Air Command we use as illustration in Chapter 5, we asked whether he sees the world as black and white or in shades of gray. He said, "No," adding, "I see it in rich shades of color. And the colors have hues."

Executives especially take delight in their own uniqueness. I (Lou) first became aware of this crucial fact about executives when the Education and Testing Service (ETS) approached us in IBM about creating a test to determine which middle managers ought to be promoted to executives. We thought, "Won't that be great, to have something nice and objective." Fourteen companies, including IBM, put in money and let their executives be studied. After three years of work, the ETS people came back to us empty-handed. They said that they could not make a test that would predict executive ability.

I bored in to find out why. Testing absolutely depends on the bell-shaped curve. Tests look for patterns, for "average" behaviors. It turns out that good executives consistently fall out on the attenuated ends of the bell curve. They are the people who defy the norm and insist on being different. You can't test for them because they are all different from each other, and vigorously different from anything that looks average.

Abraham Maslow, the developmental psychologist, created a very widely referenced typology of the stages of human growth and development. He called it the hierarchy of needs. At the bottom of the hierarchy were the needs for safety, security, and belonging. Further up the hierarchy were the needs for achievement and self-fulfillment. Growth to each successive rung of this hierarchy required adequate satisfaction of the needs beneath it.

A more recent statistical study, the Values and Lifestyles (VALS) Program discussed at length in Chapter 9, updates Maslow's typology by introducing a group of Emulators between Belongers and Achievers, and by adding to these outer-directed values a parallel group of inner-directed values called Societally Conscious, Experiential, and I-Am-Me. The intermediate levels of maturity have thus become more diversified.

The top phase of what these people call psychological maturity— Maslow's self-actualized group and what VALS calls the Integrateds —describe the characteristics many executives seem to have. These characteristics were illuminated by a study on mentally healthy people by Soley of the Menninger Foundation. The findings listed five characteristics of such people:

1. They treat others as individuals, by identifying with, accepting, and understanding them.

2. They are flexible under both internal and external stress.

3. They obtain pleasure from many sources.

4. They see and accept self-limitations.

5. They use capacities to fulfill personal needs in carrying out productive tasks.

What developmental psychologists like Maslow called needs and wants, the VALS people call values and lifestyles. The word "value" is fuzzy—it is used interchangeably in our society with words like morals, ethics, beliefs, religion, lifestyles, needs, and wants. When we use the term "value" in this book, we mean simply what one feels has importance and what influences action.

Researchers on values clarification, as well as the IBM-funded $5 million Harvard study on Technology and Society led by Emmanuel Mesthene, concluded that if we hope to find out what people hold to be important, we're wise to look more to the "process of valuing" than to any particular "structure of values." When we consider the "process of valuing," we pay close attention to how we change the relative importance of things to us as we grow and mature.

New managers have to make the machine run. As a new manager, you will tend to value what lets you get things done: focus, patterns, specialization, competition within a closed system, knowing the facts. As you grow into executive work, you have to decide what is worth doing, given the needs and wants of your insiders and your outsiders. So you will tend to add values like vision, general knowledge, distinctiveness, diversity, cooperation, your own intuition. As you mature from manager to executive, you are constantly engaged in a "process of valuing."

Achievement-oriented managers are oriented to means. How can I get things done? Integrated executives are oriented to ends. What things are worth doing? The manager looks for categories to put things in. What policy does this fit into? The executive creates new categories. What policies, goals, or results are needed to achieve the purposes of the business? Managers work on specialized tasks; executives work at generalized purposes.

As a manager, you tend to look for likenesses or patterns; you want to put like things together so that you know what you're dealing with. Executives do this, too, but they also look for differences. Managers see a difference as a problem that calls for eliminating the offending difference. The executive sees a difference as an opportunity that calls for creative change or a new way of integrating unlike things.

Managers tend to be "either/or" people; when two ideas or options conflict, the manager acts decisively by rejecting one and approving the other. Executives tend to be "both/and" people; when two ideas or options conflict, the executive explores the good and bad features of both, puts all the good features together, and forms a third idea or option that is better than either of the first two. Key words of managers are "yes, but"; key words of executives are "if only..."

The executive wants to be distinctive, tries to make the company distinctive. In contrast to patterning, the executive is looking for different ways to do things: creative acts, new opportunities for making the purpose of the company more relevant to its larger environment.

Managers typically see the world as a multiplicity of closed systems; each person, each department, each company is seen as a self-contained entity, always watching out for number one. Individuals in our society have learned in sports, in grades, in job-getting, in job performance, that you must be better than all the rest to be a winner; the manager, being an achiever, wants to win in well-defined games, with clear rules.

But as you grow, you discover that there are other ways to relate to those outsiders, ways that frequently produce better results than competition. You find opportunities in cooperation. You learn that open systems offer greater opportunities for growth and development. You play win-lose when the closed system view is appropriate, and play win-win when the open system view of a situation is appropriate. Knowing which is appropriate requires judgment. When this judgment is developed, you have acquired one more characteristic of the executive.

If you're a manager, you need to focus because you have a job to do that requires that you work on a part of the company, not the total company. There are a hundred other managers working in other parts of the company who are focusing on different things. Executive vision, on the other hand, starts with divergent thinking. You scan inside the company, outside the company, and inside yourself for factors bearing on your decision. Once the decision is made, it must be implemented. This is when convergent thinking, or focus, is necessary. Creative executive decisions require both divergent thinking and convergent thinking.

Managers like a degree of stability and structure. When you first become a manager, you have lots to learn about the way your industry, your company, your department *is*. If all those things keep changing, how can you learn what the "is" is?

We depend on managers to maintain a certain amount of stability in a company and to give it a certain degree of structure; they provide the skeleton. To a great extent, managers tend to be good bureaucrats. To maintain stability, it's important to get facts about the past, because that is how the future should be in a stable world. So when you're a manager, getting the facts is important to you.

As you become more experienced, you discover the importance of human feelings and emotions, the utility of gut feelings and hunch, your own acceptance of certain kinds of intuition. You are interested not only in "what is" but in "what it is becoming." You make judgments about the future, and you have no facts to fall back on. As you add subjective realities to your fine-tuned objective ones, you grow toward executive decision-making.

How does this growth happen? Does your acquisition of broader values lead you to seek broader responsibility? Or does responding to opportunities for more responsibility cause your values to mature? For most people, it's not either/or, but a system, where both influence each: responsibility and experience tug at your spectrum of values; larger values impel you to seek larger responsibility and experience.

Leadership Development

How does a person grow into executive work? A friendly little device to help think about leadership development is to think of the five fingers of growth. The thumb is self-development. The single most important factor in a person's development is that the individual assumes responsibility for his or her own growth and development. The thumb makes it possible for the other four fingers to operate effectively.

The other four fingers, in order of effectiveness, are:

1. the boss

2. the job itself

3. in-company training

4. out-of-company experience

The index finger points the way. If you are a person's boss, you will be a supremely influential teacher, for better or for worse. Learning occurs at the time of felt need and clear relevance. The perfect opportunity to help a person who works with you to grow comes when that person says, "Boss, I need help." The way that you think about a problem, and the way you act to solve problems and make decisions, have enormous impact on those who look to you for leadership. Most skills needed on the job have never been taught in school.

People learn goal-setting, planning, problem-solving, and decision-making for the first time from their leaders on the job. Ron Duensing of General Motors helps his people grow by walking through problem-solving with them. He lets people make mistakes, and makes the analysis of the mistake a learning experience. A good boss, like Ron, can make a world of difference in a person's life.

The middle finger represents the job itself. If you snickered here, then you, too, recognize that jobs are often not structured in ways that promote growth and fulfillment. On the job, people learn by doing—by being handed a tool and taught to use it if they don't know how. In school, by contrast, they were taught how to use tools, in case they should ever have them.

The job provides the felt need and clear relevance that most other educational experiences lack: communication about real life ideas, motivation from real life purposes, and commitment to a real life organization. People can grow fast if they have the opportunity to commit to clear purposes, the freedom to achieve results in ways that make sense to them, the chance to go for more responsibility when they're ready, and counseling when needed.

It's a good idea to promote people who have already performed well at the level you're promoting them to because their boss gave them the opportunity to do it—to grow into their future job while doing their current job. Then you're not guessing about capability. This is a different approach from the traditional bureaucratic job specifications imposed by both management and labor unions, which insist that you precisely define a job, stick a person in it, and don't dare let him or her do a job that is part of some other job description.

Take, for example, a woman running a machine. After she becomes proficient, her boss says, "Why don't you also check the quality of your work? That way you don't have to wait for a quality control person to come around with calipers. Here's how to do it." So she does that for a while, and when the time comes, her boss can help her to add the job of keeping a record of her work—and now she's counting inventory. Her boss might then ask her to do some broader work in inventory control. When it comes time to promote somebody to inventory control manager, she is a fine choice.

That new inventory control manager can continue to grow by taking broader responsibility as she is ready for it. In her job as inventory control manager, for example, she may offer input into decisions about the acquisition of new equipment. So she learns about fixed assets and depreciation schedules and begins to help make decisions about long-term investments. From there, it's an easy path to learning about how to get financing for those fixed assets. Before she knows it, she's studying questions of debt versus equity, the interests of bankers and stockholders, and the cost of capital in relation to ROI. In other words, she embarks on executive work.

The ring finger represents in-company training. Classroom sessions are useful for group orientation of new hires, job instruction training, general education, and other purposes where lectures, discussions, demonstrations, and simulations can provide useful information or experience. New managers want and need a certain amount of didactic instruction about what is. Executives hate didactic instruction, but often find simulations of situations about which they have to make judgments very useful.

The pinky finger represents out-of-company experience. This is where self-development can really happen. Learning and growth opportunities abound. A person can enroll without asking anyone's permission. It is easy to find opportunities for leadership in community organizations. People can experiment, learn lots from their leadership mistakes, and still be loved for volunteering.

Adults can grow a lot after they leave school. Most growth is likely to come through organizational activity. We have roughly identified three phases of career growth to illustrate adult growth. From a trade or professional specialty, through the manager experience of supervising others, to major responsibility as an executive leader—growth continues. Each stage may require ten or twenty years.

The flattening of pyramids in the information age is moving companies towards the three-tier organization—executives, managers, and non-managers. This usually means that the "span of control" broadens—leaders lead larger numbers of people. The more this is true, the more the leaders are forced to delegate the activity that achieves results. Moreover, non-managers will do more of what managers used to do, and managers will do more of what executives used to do. And executives? They will do a whole lot more of what executives did only infrequently in the industrial age—they'll continually be deciding what things are worth doing.

Compressed pyramids and the diffusing of leadership skills throughout companies herald a democratization of leadership. Everybody can have leadership roles at times on an ad-hoc basis, or by rotation of the leadership function. Who leads may depend on the job to be done and a person's capability and enthusiasm for doing it.

In the industrial age, we saw jobs as stationary. People moved through them as they grew. In the information age, we may see people moving through ever-expanding competence and capability, and we'll continue to upgrade the requirements of jobs to keep up with the maturity and interests of people.

One of the best managers I (Lou) had in IBM was Dr. Dwayne Orton. When he was the director of all IBM education, I was his assistant. He was one of my mentors. Dr. Orton, in addition to his responsibility for providing educational opportunities for all IBM employees, was IBM's public speaker. He publicized the management philosophy of Watson Sr. At the end of many speeches, Dwayne Orton closed with the words of Edwin Markham:

> *We're blind until we see, that in the human plan,*
> *Nothing is worth the making, if it does not make the man.*
> *Why build these cities glorious, if man unbuilded goes?*
> *In vain we build the world, unless the builder also grows.*

Chapter 4 Digest

The word "management" is deceptive. It implies that there is one body of knowledge, one set of skills, one genre of systems, and one range of values that pertain to all people who "manage" other people. But in fact, the acquisition of these executive capabilities is usually a growth curve. From the time you become a new manager until you become a fully responsible executive, you will know a continual maturing of your leadership capability. Becoming an executive is a process of accretion, of expansion.

The most important thing a new manager must learn is leadership. Leadership is not a mystical quality you have to be born with. The essence of leadership is communication, motivation, and commitment. These can be learned.

On communication: First, communication depends on differences. If there is no difference, there is nothing to communicate. Second, communication is complete only when there is feedback. Feedback should include feelings as well as thoughts, attitudes as well as facts. Finally, communication is effective only when there is something worth communicating.

On motivation: You can't motivate people—only they can motivate themselves. You work on yourself, the job, and the environment, not the other person.

On commitment: Commitment stems from agreement, the only lasting authority there is. Contracts have power because both parties agree. Commitment occurs when you identify your own purposes with the purposes of a larger community, such as a company.

Communication speaks to the mind, motivation grows out of the emotions, and commitment springs from the spirit. The leader who can address all these elements of a human being is often called charismatic.

The industrial age was built on the bureaucratic principle that the pyramid was the way to organize. For people in the body of the pyramid—non-managers and managers—the job is to get things done. When managers become executives, they suddenly bump into a whole new pyramid. It's an inverted pyramid perched atop the one they know. This second pyramid represents the larger environment—customers, vendors, lenders, stockholders, government, society at large—those people whose needs and wants will indicate the things worth doing. The critical nexus of those two pyramids is where the executive sits.

The information age is flattening pyramids. This means that more and more people can and must acquire the whole spectrum of capabilities and values of the fully capable executive—and the spectrum continues to widen. The executive who was running a stable company in a stable market didn't have the same challenge to decide the things worth doing that executives in our turbulent environment have.

The most important job of the executive is to create, communicate, and maintain common purpose for the entire company. If the executive doesn't do this job, it goes undone. You create purpose by integrating the varied interests of the people in the lower pyramid with the myriad interests of the people in the upper pyramid. Your personal dreams and imagination contribute to corporate purpose, too.

From the time you first become a manager until you are a fully capable executive, the diversity you perceive and order continues to swell. A system is a tool to order diversity. As you grow, the systems you must create and manage become ever more complex.

A systems approach to the management issue of control and freedom calls for optimizing the two. There's a cost to fixing mistakes as well as a cost to keeping control. Overcontrolling costs: it produces resentment, reduces motivation, and dehumanizes people. Undercontrolling costs: in errors created, morale deflated due to low confidence in management, the drag of inefficiency. Your system must monitor both costs, and the cost of keeping controls should roughly equal the cost of correcting errors that occur with that degree of control.

Just as your systems must handle more diversity as you grow from manager to executive, so your values must accommodate ever more diversity. Perhaps more than any other single value, respect for differences characterizes executives. Executives especially delight in their own uniqueness.

As a new manager, you will tend to value what lets you get things done: focus, patterns, specialization, competition within a closed system, knowing the facts. As you grow into executive work, and have to decide what is worth doing, given the needs and wants of your insiders and your outsiders, you will tend to add values such as vision, general knowledge, distinctiveness, diversity, cooperation, and your own intuition. As you mature from manager to executive, you are constantly engaged in a "process of valuing."

In the industrial age, we saw jobs as stationary. People moved through them as they grew. In the information age, we may see people moving through ever-expanding competence and capability, and we'll continually upgrade the requirements of jobs to keep up with the maturity and interests of people.

◄ CHAPTER 5 ►

A Teleocratic Management System

Much management literature focuses on the need to be nice to people. The central message is that organizational problems of motivation, communication, and commitment can be solved if people are only nice to each other. The premise is: better people—better corporation.

A pyramidal organization is designed to make command easy and clear. Most workers today take to command like ducks take to oil spills. So everybody is trying hard to learn how to be nice—in a structure that militates against niceness.

People are bustling off to personal growth experiences to learn how to be nice. Two things happen regularly. They come back and say, "Gee, that was great, but I wish my boss had gone." Or they come back with a desire to be better but have to fight the urge to be bitter, because the job/boss/union/company/bureaucracy doesn't allow them to do or be all the lovely things they've experienced.

If you want a better garden, you don't start carving open your seeds and rearranging their insides so they grow nicely. Rather, you water, fertilize, and weed. You operate on the environment, not the living organism. (Genetic engineering may change all that someday, and in the 2001 edition of this book we may have to find another analogy. More likely, we'll be working on a book describing the shift from an information age to a bioengineering age.) In a company, the management system is the environment in which people grow, or don't grow.

Being nice is necessary but not sufficient. A company must have an effective management system.

W. Edwards Deming, management guru noted for his work with Japanese industry, and more recently with American companies such as Ford Motor Company, insists that management's job is to constantly improve systems. He is often mistakenly assumed to have gone to Japan and encouraged everybody to be nice to people by forming quality circles. In fact, Dr. Deming did hard systems work. He'll tell you that quality circles are often management's hope for an easy way out. In his latest book, *Out of the Crisis*, he describes the statistical methods for productivity and quality that are strict analytical tools for uncovering and solving systems problems.

I (Kate) have heard Dr. Deming thunder at executives in seminar after seminar, "The supposition is prevalent that there would be no problems in production or in service if only our workers would do their jobs in the way they were taught. Pleasant dreams. The workers are handicapped by the system, and the system belongs to management."

In his books and seminars, Dr. Deming focuses primarily on the internal workings of a company—on getting things done. This has been the most urgent industrial age job, and Dr. Deming's clients have been primarily industrial companies. But Dr. Deming recognizes the crucial task of deciding things worth doing. He'll talk to you about systems approaches to marketing if you ask him.

Constant improvement of a system means constant change—little is hammered down. Constant improvement of systems implies that management works harder on process than on structure.

Without an adequate management system, politics prevails. If there is no management system—no clear articulation of things worth doing or a way of getting them done—a company becomes a chaotic political milieu burning up everybody's energy toward the end of achieving nothing. This is okay if you want to be a club: it's fine for a social system to have no purpose, but the participants ought to know that the ordering principle will be a political process and the people with the most money, power, or persuasiveness will usually have their way.

Laissez-faire management promotes politics in a company, as different purposes emerge and competition among them blossoms. It is no improvement over strict hierarchical management, which relies on coercion to order activity around purposes conceived at the top.

A management system must be timely. Autocratic management systems were timely for Watson Sr.'s era. Bureaucratic management systems were timely in Watson Jr.'s day. An information age management system must allow executives and managers to decide things worth doing in an effervescent environment, and must allow things to get done with an increasingly sophisticated workforce. In this chapter, we will describe in detail one management system designed to deal with a changing environment and with workers motivated by the opportunity for achievement and actualization. It is a management system based on commonality of purpose. We call it a "teleocratic" management system. "Teleos" is the Greek word for purpose. This system is surely not the only way to answer the information age exigencies of changing environment and challenging employees, but it is far and away the best we know.

General Bill Creech, retired commander of the U.S. Air Force's Tactical Air Command (TAC), built a management system based on shared purpose. Under his leadership, from 1978 to his retirement in 1984, productivity leapt 80%, while the retention of people went from a historic low to an all-time high. In effect, with Bill Creech's management system, people were working harder while expressing satisfaction by staying with the organization. Today, Bill's work is being drawn on throughout the Department of Defense, and Bill, who is based in Henderson, Nevada, consults with a number of organizations, both public and private.

The key ingredients of a management system ordered by common purpose are: purpose (often called vision or mission); results (often called goals or objectives); activities (often called plans and programs); problem-solving and decision-making (often called supervision).

Purpose

Purpose is the business of the business. Corporate purpose defines the relation of a company to its larger environment, and therefore gives meaning to everything that goes on inside the company.

A corporate purpose statement communicates the distinctiveness of a company; it differentiates it from all other organizations. Since a corporation is an economic institution, there should be something in the corporate purpose statement that addresses its economic purpose.

How do you formulate a purpose? You first ask, "Why should this organization exist?"

Bill Creech wasn't running a corporation, he was running a segment of the Department of Defense, a very large segment. He had a budget in the billions, 180,000 people, and twice as many planes as all U.S. commercial airlines put together. As with all Pentagon commanders, Bill's purpose at the highest level was decided by Congress and passed down by the President and the Secretary of Defense. In effect, Congress decided the direction of things worth doing for TAC. A direction or purpose for TAC was to provide "the strategic air defense of the United States."

It's not enough for you as an executive to have corporate purpose in your head. The first thing you do with your idea of purpose is to make a clear statement of that purpose. You try out the statement on your key insiders, and maybe on some of your key outsiders. They will ask questions and give you feedback. Perhaps that feedback will suggest that you modify your purpose statement somewhat.

Once you have a purpose statement, you have a direction. But a lofty purpose statement hanging out in the air is useless. The executive's job is to work with managers to translate purpose into high-level results or goals. In a teleocratic management system, the joint effort of making purpose concrete allows everybody who identifies with the company to come to identify with the purpose: the company purpose becomes common purpose.

Bill Creech describes the way he handled communicating and getting feedback on purpose and creating goals: "I started developing and articulating a philosophy of command, establishing overarching principles and goals, so we could all share the same purpose. I was very careful to have our people in on the architecture of it, through an interactive and iterative process, where I would set down what we were trying to do and invite comments from all levels of the workforce about how we could go about it."

Results (also called Goals or Objectives)

The word "result," while humble, generically describes precisely the way purpose is chunked down and made meaningful and operational in a healthy management system. While we use the words "result" and "goal" interchangeably, we prefer the word "result" because it describes the end product of activity. All too often when people write "goals," they use strong verbs to describe an activity they *plan* to do, not the result that such activity will produce. A good result statement contains lots of nouns and adjectives to vividly describe the state of affairs that will be true on the achievement date.

A result or goal is a subset of purpose. It is like a milepost as you move along the direction that your purpose describes. What we call results, Bill Creech calls goals.

It's important to document the results you set—we call the documentation a "result form." There are several key elements that make a result form complete. They are: a result statement; a result date; criteria for evaluation; a commitment section (to show who agrees to make this result happen), and a "next decision" section. (See Figure 3 in Appendix A for the result form that we use, which has a place for all these elements on one page.)

A result statement is typically a sentence that states what will exist that does not exist now. It answers the question, "What will be true when we reach this milepost that is not true now?" Results you set tell you what your purpose means to you in concrete terms over the next quarter (or the next year, or the next five years).

Clear results or goals tell people what a company's purpose is far more convincingly than noble speeches at retirement dinners, friendly words from the CEO in the house organ, or rousing statements on company brochures.

An example of a result, or goal, for TAC was, "Each assigned plane flies at least twenty sorties per month." Bill Creech emphasizes that you want goals to be quantifiable whenever possible. He says, "Your all-embracing purpose is a direction. You define and articulate it— you give it meaning—through your goals. Goals are results that people can understand and work towards. To the greatest extent possible, you want goals that can be measured. If you're dependent on subjective assessment rather than objective appraisal, you're in trouble."

Once you have a result statement, you need to make sure that you will know whether or not the goal has been achieved when the scheduled achievement date comes. Criteria are standards for evaluation. The easiest criteria are quantitative—things that can be measured. A quantitative criterion might be, "Spare parts for planes arrive in an average of eight minutes."

While many of your goals lend themselves to quantitative criteria, a few do not. Descriptive criteria that flesh out the result statement can be useful in these instances. A descriptive criterion might be "Every pilot keeps track of his or her own schedule."

Finally, when you have to make criteria for intangible things such as morale or motivation, you may select judgmental criteria—but you have to decide in advance whose judgment will apply. A judgment criterion would be, "On the result evaluation date, Joe will decide if pilots feel more confident of their ability to maneuver their planes under combat conditions than they do today."

The criteria for a goal generally suggest a next echelon of results—sub-goals. These sub-goals probably deserve result forms of their own, complete with dates, criteria for evaluation, and agreement by one or more people.

The key to a teleocratic management system—a management system based on common purpose—is agreement.

Responsibility emerges when two or more people have agreed that a result is worth achieving and have agreed to see it accomplished. They may not do all the work involved, but they do assume accountability for the goal. Accountability should be fixed on individuals, not committees. Committees can be involved, but actual responsibility must rest with specific individuals whose agreement to and accountability for the result make evaluation appropriate and achievement likely.

Criteria are extremely important because they are the sole basis for valid standards of evaluation. Lacking prior agreement among people, you face the problem of who is going to evaluate whom and by what standard—who is going to make the rules after the game has been played? The objective of the evaluation is that the people who set the goal evaluate its execution according to their prior agreed-upon standards. This works because the group has agreed upon the criteria for evaluation, in advance of doing the work. And the people don't evaluate each other, they evaluate job performance.

Who is really responsible for the achievement of a result? The result form should describe the responsibilities of two, three, or maybe four people committed to the attainment of the particular result. It is useful for two people who have a vertical relationship to each other in the structure of the company, such as a president and vice president, to take responsibility for a result. Two people at different levels of an organization create a linking pin in the agreement process. Such linking pins between levels of an organization's structure hold the levels together.

The people who put their names on the result form have the responsibility. They know it clearly—they do the planning, they do the executing, and they do the evaluating. For work to be satisfying, the worker must do all three.

This discipline means that every result is operationalized by a full cybernetic cycle, carried out by the people whose names are on the result form. You don't give one bunch of people the responsibility for planning and another bunch the responsibility for doing. Peter Drucker said the greatest mistake that management has ever made is separating planners from doers. We go one step further: you don't separate evaluators from doers, either. Frequently, management reserves to itself the function of evaluating and expects everybody else to just plan and do. That breaks the cybernetic cycle just as seriously as when you separate the planning from the doing.

The final piece of a result form, the "next decision" section, closes the loop and initiates the next cycle. You ask yourselves questions such as "Is there any part of this goal we have not achieved?" or "What is the next result we want to go for?" Every system that defines a continuing process must have a provision for moving from one phase to another.

A management system should be an ongoing process of managing, or it is worse than useless. Beware of "programs," which are usually another bundle of work laid on top of the work that must be done. A management system *is* the way work gets done, or it is not a management system.

Each of the elements of this process is critical. Many MBO (management by objectives) programs have failed because, as applied, they usually ignored one or more of these elements. MBO is often just another form of command: "This year, Joe, your objective is..." and misses the key element of agreement. Often, too, objectives are stated with no criteria for evaluation, which means they risk myriad interpretations, especially at a time when somebody is about to be held accountable for not achieving one. (Memory generally distorts in the favor of the person doing the remembering.) Often, an evaluation is never scheduled to take place, just as there is rarely a formal system for monitoring whether or not commands have been carried out. The objective simply fades away in the bustle of everyday putting out of fires, or in the inertia of the institutional imperative—as everybody keeps doing the work already going on.

A management system of goals and sub-goals creates a hierarchy of purpose. This hierarchy of purpose is a beautiful method of defining and communicating the purpose of an organization. An outsider, or an insider, reading the purpose statement and several levels of results would really understand what the purpose means.

How many echelons of results you create is a balancing act. You can spend all your time documenting work and no time doing it. As Bill Creech puts it, "You don't chunk down to a nauseous degree. If everything is important, nothing is."

Activity (or Plans and Programs)

When you reach agreement on goals, you can delegate activity. Goal-setting is a liberating management system. Once people agree to a desired result, they are free to get there any way they wish.

That's what a job is, anyway. The person who gets the job done is usually the person who knows the most about how to do it. Otherwise he or she wouldn't have the job in the first place. The person responsible for receiving the results says, "I'm concerned about the end product. I don't care how you get there. I know that you'll be concerned about the infinite ways that you can figure out to get there. Be creative, be free, just satisfy our contract of having this result on that date."

This is extremely motivational because anything that increases freedom is motivational. Freedom is the greatest environment there is for motivation for most people. There are some people who really do not want to be free, but they're in the minority, typically 10% or less of today's workers. With those people, a manager may want to exercise the old command and control most of the time.

Bill Creech did some radical delegating of activity. He says, "Each squadron had goals and then I let each squadron do its own schedule, which was a radical notion in a centralized system—a top-down approach doesn't like that. But they could fly as much in May as they wanted and as much in December as they wanted, and they could fly any amount on any day. They were masters of their own destiny. All I held them to was coming out at the end of the year with the overall agreed right number of average sorties a month. This is output oriented. A lot of management schools will give you depth to the ninth decimal point on how one controls all the inputs. You regulate and stipulate and write this and write that, demand this and demand that, then you accept the output because the model of input is so brilliant, that this has to be the greatest output that can be produced. My concept was, 'Hey, this is the output we want, gang. You're responsible.' They were responsible within some broad limits. Obviously the game has some rules and some boundaries, like, you don't fly over your parents' house and do an air show. But within those broad limits, they had wide autonomy.

"I'll never forget a conversation I had with one of the sergeants out in the field. He said, 'I really like squadron scheduling,' and I said, 'I do, too. Why do you like it?' And he said, 'It lets us live with our own mistakes.' Then he smiled and said, 'And we make fewer all the time.' If the guy who makes the rules is not the guy who has to live with them, he can perpetuate the dumbest set of rules and regulations in the world."

You can draw a schematic of this management system that we've been developing. (See Figure 4 in Appendix A.) Activity—documented by plans—shows on the lines between the results. Activities move us from where we are to where we ought to be. We call the vector that points toward purpose, designates results, and acknowledges planned activity the "ought line." It is interesting to see that when you fill in activities on the lines in the hierarchy of purpose chart and turn it on its side, you have a PERT (Program Evaluation and Review Technique) chart. (See Figure 5 in Appendix A.) A PERT chart is one of the most powerful management tools developed in the 1960s. It connects activities and results for a program (in PERT language, results are called "events"). PERT gives precise control over every part of a job to ensure timely performance. The hierarchy of purpose does this for a company.

Problem-Solving and Decision-Making

While purpose, results, and planned activities define the "ought" line, real life inevitably carries us in other directions. This deviation between the "is" and the "ought" is what is classically called a "problem."

Problems can be solved only when there is clear agreement about the "ought," clear perceptions about the "is," and therefore a clear definition of the deviation between the two. When you know these three things, problems are three-fourths solved. Problems in companies typically don't get solved because there has not been prior agreement about the "ought."

Decision-making is making the "is" coincide with the "ought." Once a problem is defined, it is relatively easy to make a decision. Either you modify the "ought," you correct the "is," or you change both so that they coincide. When problems are well-defined, decision-making can be a lot of fun.

How well a company performs with this management system is measured by Return on Investment (ROI). In Chapter 11, we cover ROI in depth, but we want to show here how the financial measure, ROI, can help you to evaluate the effectiveness of your management system. The formula for ROI is: sales/assets x net/sales = net/assets, also called ROI. When the sales/assets ratio is good, you know that the upper portion of the ought line—purpose and high-level results— is being formulated well: you are doing a good job of deciding things worth doing and therefore generating plenty of sales, given the resources (assets) at your disposal. When the net/sales ratio is good, you know that you are doing a good job of getting things done: you are doing well at setting and achieving low-level results and problem-solving and decision-making; because you are operating efficiently, you are able to generate a healthy net profit. Put another way, the components of ROI tell you how well you are doing at top-line management (deciding things worth doing) as well as bottom-line management (getting things done). (See Figure 6 in Appendix A to see net/sales and sales/assets added to the management system chart.)

Where do you begin to build a management system ordered by common purpose? If you are just starting a new company, you obviously have some purpose in mind for its existence and can start creating results that lead you toward that purpose. If, however, you are in a going company, don't wait for a perfect purpose before you start making results within the organization; results will condition purpose. Don't wait to solve problems until the "ought" line is crystal clear—trying to figure out what the deviation is between an "is" and an "ought" will help you figure out what the "ought" ought to be.

This is the nature of systems. Since systems illuminate interconnectedness, you can work on them anywhere you can get a toehold, and your work on any part of the system will have some—although perhaps small—salubrious effect on the rest of the system.

The teleocratic management system does not blot out bureaucracy. The elements of structure and command that define a bureaucratic management system still have a place in organizations. But in today's environment, with today's workers, that place is rarely the day-to-day ordering principle for getting things done. Structure and command are what you fall back on when the process of agreement fails and you have to act right away. They are a last resort, not a first cause.

When you fail to reach agreement on common purpose over and over with a specific person, you both may conclude that since mutual interests cannot be satisfied, that person is in the wrong job, or perhaps the wrong company. No one will be taken by surprise at the suggestion that a change of assignment is in order.

This teleocratic management system gives teeth to niceness. You cannot do this system without listening to people because they're participating in setting their results. You cannot provide a healthier environment for motivation than the opportunity to help create results and the freedom to achieve them in whatever way makes sense. There is no more effective way to inspire commitment than to give people the opportunity to achieve their own purposes while simultaneously achieving the purposes of a larger community of which they choose to become a part.

What if two people cannot agree on a result? They go to their boss: they get a mediator. When two people can't agree, they have to go outside their own system. Usually if you have a well-established set of results from the top down, the mediation is already there. In other words, a result or a purpose will mediate whether you do "A" or "B" at the lower level. If you don't have that overall purpose, "A" is just as good as "B." What happens depends on who can yell the loudest, or whose box is higher on the chart, or who has more stripes on his or her sleeve. This is not nice.

Needs and wants satisfied are no longer needs and wants. A well-

designed management system provides opportunity for human growth
—the opportunity to conceive and then satisfy new interests and
purposes.

When you want people to grow, you don't protect them from risk,
you give them enlarged opportunity. You don't shield them from their
larger environment, you expose them. You don't hide from them the
responsibilities of the job above them, you involve them in it.

When we thought of companies as machines, such ideas were
anathema. You minimized risk, exposure to a hostile environment,
and crossing over of responsibilities. If the E hammer in your piano
started wandering over to hit the D and F strings you would rush to
restore it immediately to its original design. So, in the industrial age,
we struggled to identify which slot people fit in and kept them there.
In that system, a person fitted into a certain job box. That person
could be promoted to a higher box or transferred to a different box,
but never could he or she occupy any box he or she pleased. You
might have promoted the E hammer and made it an F hammer so
that it then hit only the F string, but never could it be an E/F hammer. Over the long haul, this rigidity makes for an efficient machine—
and a dead organism.

A machine is a system that is designed to produce a fixed result.
Its parts are standard and unchanging. The machine asks no questions. It is predictable and controllable. It has no feelings. Its efficiency is measured by how well it performs its function. Being nice
to a machine means keeping it running.

A human system is not a machine. Results and purposes are as
varied as the different people who make up a human system. People
are different from each other. They are always changing and growing. People are not predictable or controllable. They have feelings.
The meaning of a human system is determined by the commonality
of purpose of the people who choose to be part of it.

There is a fear, a hold-over from industrial days when companies
were supposed to be like machines, that people acting like people
will create chaos—without structure and command, how will leaders
maintain control? Bill Creech speaks to that issue: "I maintained co-
herence and control through that shared purpose which I worked very
hard to attain and maintain and also through those goals which spoke
for themselves. I am convinced that I had far more control the day I
left TAC than the day I arrived."

The core of being profoundly nice to human beings in a system is to respect differences among them. IBM called it "respecting the dignity of the individual."

Every person in a company has a set of different individual purposes. Each one has joined the company believing that something in his or her own set of purposes can best be achieved by being a part of this company. Good leaders have the skill to formulate, with their people, such a common purpose. Warren Bennis and Burt Nanus, in their book *Leaders*, put it well: "A vision [purpose] cannot be established in an organization by edict, or by the exercise of power or coercion. It is more an act of persuasion, of creating an enthusiastic and dedicated commitment to a vision because it is right for the times, right for the organization, and right for the people who are working in it."

In this chapter we have outlined a management system ordered by common purpose. We've said that this system is right for our times: that it speaks to the values of information age workers, and allows the flexibility necessary in a rapidly changing business environment. In the next chapter we'll expand on the values shift that is erupting in our midst. We'll zero in on its implications for leadership. First, we'll spend a few pages on historical perspective. We'll cover broadly the roots of the societal values that made bureaucratic leadership appropriate for its time. Then we'll delve into how our world is changing and how teleocratic leadership speaks to values aborning in the information age. In essence, in this chapter we offered a tool; in the next chapter we'll describe its conceptual underpinnings.

Chapter 5 Digest

Much management literature focuses on the need to be nice to people. The central message is that organizational problems of motivation, communication, and commitment can be solved if people are only nice to each other. The premise is: better people—better corporation.

A pyramidal organization is designed to make command easy and clear. Most workers today take to commands like ducks take to oil spills. So everybody is trying hard to learn how to be nice—in a structure that militates against niceness.

Being nice is necessary but not sufficient. A company needs an effective management system.

A management system must be timely. A management system for the information age must allow executives and managers to decide things worth doing in an effervescent environment, and must allow things to get done with an increasingly sophisticated workforce. A teleocratic management system—a management system based on common purpose—does this. ("Teleocratic" comes from the Greek "teleos," meaning purpose.)

The key ingredients of a teleocratic management system are:

1. *Purpose (often called vision or mission).* A teleocratic system makes sure the company purpose is a common one throughout the company. A purpose statement communicates the distinctiveness of a company in its relation to its larger environment.

   But a lofty purpose statement hanging out in the air is useless. The executive's job is to work with managers to translate purpose into high-level results or goals. In a teleocratic management system, the joint effort of making purpose concrete allows everybody who identifies with the company to come to identify with the purpose: the company purpose becomes common purpose.

2. *Results (often called goals or objectives).* Like mileposts as you move toward your purpose, results should be quantifiable if possible. When two or more people agree that a result is worth achieving and that they will see it accomplished, responsibility emerges. These agreements provide the glue for an organization's structure. The system of goals and sub-goals creates a hierarchy of purpose. A hierarchy of clearly articulated goals tells people what a company's purpose is much more convincingly than noble statements on company brochures and rousing speeches at retirement dinners.

3. *Activities (often called plans and programs).* Once people agree to a result, this management system lets them go after the result any way they wish. Freedom is the best environment for motivating most information age people.

4. *Problem-solving and decision-making (often called supervision).* Purpose, goals, and plans define the "ought" for a company, but real life

invariably carries people in other directions. The deviation between the "is" and the "ought" is a "problem." In decision-making the "is" is made to coincide with the "ought." You modify the "ought," correct the "is," or change both.

The teleocratic management system does not blot out bureaucracy. The elements of structure and command that define a bureaucratic management system still have a place in organizations. But in today's environment, with today's workers, that place is rarely the day-to-day ordering principle for getting things done. Structure and command are what you fall back on when the process of agreement fails and you have to act right away. They are a last resort, not a first cause.

A teleocratic management system gives teeth to niceness. You cannot use this system without listening to people, because they're participating in setting their goals. You cannot provide a healthier environment for motivation than the opportunity to help create results and the freedom to achieve them in whatever way makes sense. Nothing more effectively inspires commitment than giving people the opportunity to achieve their own purposes while simultaneously achieving the purposes of a larger community of which they chose to become a part.

◄ CHAPTER 6 ►

Beyond Autocracy and Bureaucracy: Teleocratic Leadership

Autocratic leadership worked in Watson Sr.'s world. The business environment was stable, therefore corporate purpose could be stable. A company could declare: we make cash registers, or cars, or soap that floats—period. The internal operation of a company was not too complex for the business to be ordered in one person's mind. People were anxious for safety and security and belonging—they were happy to work in a paternalistic system where they were told what to do and were taken care of.

Bureaucratic leadership worked in Watson Jr.'s world—the business environment was relatively stable and therefore corporate purpose was relatively stable. A company might diversify, but each division knew precisely what business it was in, and what industry that business fit into. Since one person couldn't order a business as large and complex as many businesses had become, activity was ordered by rules and policies. People wanted fairness, predictability, and security, with some opportunity for achievement. They were happy to have benefits, which are a modern, depersonalized sort of paternalism. They were somewhat willing to be told what to do, either directly or by their job description.

The information age business environment is one of rapid change. A company whose purpose does not evolve or change will probably be obsolete within two to five years of the establishment of that purpose. Deciding things worth doing is not a one-time task but an ongoing process. For a company to grow, many people in the company must continually exchange with the larger environment and contribute to the formulation of corporate purpose. Workers in the information age tend to value achievement and self-fulfillment. People can satisfy these needs if they are simultaneously achieving their own purposes and achieving the purposes of a larger community they feel a part of, such as their company. Teleocratic leadership—leadership ordered by common purpose—is appropriate to a complex, changing business environment and mature workers. It is leadership that is future-oriented, ever relevant, nonritualized, non-habitual, always thinking, and always human.

Teleocratic Leadership in Action: SAIC

SAIC (Science Applications International Corporation) is a wildly successful company whose leadership is ordered by common purpose. Founded by Bob Beyster in 1969, SAIC has grown from one lone nuclear physicist in San Diego to a company of 7600 people with annual revenues of $650 million.

Precisely how does this company decide things worth doing and get things done? Wayne Gilbert, an SAIC vice president, explains, "Bob Beyster founded this company on the theory that if you get good people and allow them to work on things they want to work on, and reward them according to results, they'll do good work.

"We have a small, austere corporate staff, and we have a line organization that can resort to autocratic control if needed, such as when something has to be done quickly. Our marketing function is decentralized over the entire company. At SAIC, people bring in the work they want to do. If it's a big job that takes fifty to sixty people, sometimes some people are wage-earners for that project, assigned to it by the line manager. But by and large, people can pick their own projects. They're not forced to do work they don't want to do."

At SAIC, purpose is generally not conceived at the top and handed down through the hierarchy. Rather, purpose is born throughout the company as workers go out, interact with customers, determine what things are worth doing for those customers, and bring the work home —work they themselves are interested in and enthusiastic about. In this way, individual purpose is served and corporate purpose, acutely responsive to the business environment, is continually created.

The whole leadership system at SAIC is buttressed by the fact that SAIC is an employee-owned company. Stock is widely distributed; Bob Beyster is the largest shareholder with only 3% of the stock. So when SAIC workers achieve their purposes, and build and achieve corporate purposes, they themselves enjoy the financial rewards of their work.

Pat Shea is a research scientist with one of SAIC's 250 small, autonomous divisions. He explains in detail how work is decided on, and done:

"If I have an idea that I think is saleable, I go talk to the people I think would be the best people to work on it. I ask them if they have time and want to do it. When I submit a proposal to a customer, it includes the names of the key individuals who have agreed to do the job. Sometimes the customer will pay for the prototype. Sometimes we need some internal funding for the project, too. If so, I have to show our inside people that the project will make money for SAIC.

"People like me are the ones in the scientific trenches. We consider ourselves to be at 'the bleeding edge'—where things get cut. We find the customer and build the contract. By the time SAIC commits to a job, the people who want to do it have already agreed to a statement of work. People will work extra hours to meet our commitments. We are the work that we do. What we're selling is our brains. If we want to do more exciting creative work in the future, we know we have to do a good job on the work we're doing now.

"The way we grow this company is by having good people who go out and find more good people. You have to have work for them when they arrive—so we grow. And we're always looking for new customers. Our company's strength is in doing prototypes—the kind of stuff you couldn't make money mass marketing. So once you do a job for a customer, you have to find something new to do. I like the fact that the entire complexion of this company changes every few years—customers, projects, technology. And we're employee-owned. It's nice to know your work will reflect on your financial future. Our stock price has been following the same exponential growth as our company."

SAIC's management system works in today's environment and speaks to the values of today's workers. It makes sense, when you think about it. But it represents what amounts to a cataclysmic shift in values, which has taken place in one short generation—ours.

Good leaders have a sense of history. In the latter part of this chapter, we will take a condensed look at the history of the values that gave rise to bureaucratic leadership, and relate the key elements of bureaucracy to those historic values. Next, we'll outline how values appear to be shifting, and relate teleocratic leadership—leadership ordered by common purpose—to the emerging values.

The diagram in Figure 7 in Appendix A outlines the key elements of the two systems we'll cover, and shows how they relate to each other. Note the large plus sign in the center of the figure. It's there to show that the new does not replace the old, but adds to it. The structures and logic of bureaucracy are not obsolete, ready to be tossed on the junk heap of history. Rather, they make a skeleton that you can fall back on when circumstances call for it. As you mature as a leader, your spectrum of value options broadens—you have a larger array of responses to choose among as situations present themselves. A teleocratic leader will sometimes be bureaucratic, sometimes even autocratic—just not most of the time.

Whence Bureaucracy?

Bureaucracy is a management system geared to stable values and purposes. It's a management system ordered by structure, classically portrayed by the organization diagram: a pyramid of boxes connected by lines showing who reports to whom. It assumes a hierarchy of role, power, wealth, and planning and control. Authority is vested in position. Rules and policies, which codify the past, are the guidelines for decisions about the future. A rigid structure, clear job descriptions at every level, and behavior guided primarily by rules and policies keep a company stable; they ensure that you keep doing what you've always done. How did bureaucracy emerge as a management system? What values did it grow out of?

From the time of Aristotle until the Renaissance and Reformation, practically nobody in Western civilization expected change. The thinking was that God created the world as it is and it is therefore perfect. People might try to understand the world but certainly should not try to change it.

This was the theological grounding for the idea that stability is good, and the idea was with us for more than a thousand years. You expected your life to be pretty much like the life of your parents, which was pretty much like the life of their parents. You had your "proper station in life" into which you were born, and everybody's station was neatly ordered by "the chain of being," a theological concept that ranked all beings, starting with God, moving down through the various levels of angels, the Pope, the hierarchy of the clergy, and finally laymen. The term "laymen" meant "untutored fools." Your theology told you this structure was good, was God's will. Your common sense told you things don't change much.

Until about the fifteenth century, the measure of progress and wealth was the rate at which plants and animals grew. About all people could do was to fight over who got the most of what. Most people had no idea that they themselves could create wealth, or ideas, or things. When science was born in the fifteenth century, the first scientists were also theologians, educated by the church. So they built their science upon the theological foundation that God created the earth but is apart from the created secular order and controls it. This assumption, labelled "the Newtonian worldview," or "mechanistic determinism," made a machine of the universe, including the human role in it. All machines need external control. If God sees something about the machine that is not quite right, He reaches in and makes a change or adjustment and gets back out again. This is called a miracle.

Classical science built upon the structural description of the "way it is." It sees the universe, including people, as basically materialistic in nature, consisting of finite material particles, however small, existing in or moving throughout empty space. If we could learn the nature of these particles of matter, and the way they moved one with respect to the other, then we would understand how the universe was structured.

Since the rightness and importance of stability and structure became prevailing and valued assumptions of both theology and science, they greatly influenced the nature of leadership. With fixed purposes and a world that is stable, structure becomes very important in social ordering: structure arranges things as they ought to be and keeps them that way. If the structure is right, it should last a thousand years. The way to solve big problems is to restructure.

While in medieval times people had their "proper station in life," in the industrial age people had specialized skills or professions which were their sole lifetime career and for which they were specially trained. Within a company, they would fit into specified boxes on the organization chart. These boxes defined precise channels of authority and communication, and carried detailed job descriptions to which people were matched, or retrained until an adequate match to the job was nailed down.

In a bureaucratic structure, power, role, wealth, and planning and control are a function of your place in the hierarchy. In medieval days, if you were born a serf, you expected to live as a serf and die as a serf. If you wanted the role of king, you had to be born into the royal family. In a modern bureaucracy, you may move up through the hierarchy, box by box, but you still fill the role described by your box exclusively: you don't expect to do vice-presidential work on this project today and technician work on that project tomorrow.

Power must be hierarchical in a bureaucracy—people at the top have the most power and those at the bottom have the least. The major instrumentality of power is wealth. People at the top should have the most; people at the bottom should have the least. How else can people at the top maintain their power and keep the whole thing stable?

We explain events and solve problems in a mechanistic universe by cause and effect. A cause and effect approach—a rational, objective approach—to problem analysis and solution rests on two basic assumptions. The first assumption is that cause and effect operates in one direction only and is not reversible. "A" may cause "B," but "B" cannot cause "A." In other words, cause must always precede effect. In a bureaucracy, when something goes wrong the first inclination is to find out what caused it. What led to this sad state of affairs? Who's to blame? Simple cause and effect assumptions beget these questions.

The second assumption is that time is a framework within which other variables operate. In a machine-like organization, operating sequentially in time, with stability accepted as the order of things, we orient to the past. Our watchwords are "Get the facts." Facts come only from the past; there are no facts about the future. In a stable world, facts can help you make good decisions about the future, because the future is likely to be more of the same.

The cause-precedes-effect logic of bureaucracy vests authority in position. Why? If people are to function properly in the machine, then obviously their behavior must be caused by a higher authority in the hierarchy—someone closer to the top, where purpose is established. Since purpose is fixed in a stable world, authority can be easily associated with hierarchical position.

When those in authority, in the name of social order, seek to perpetuate the past, they train the young to understand the past. They try to convince the young that they must adjust to the demands of the stable social order. Toward this end, and to control people's behavior, rules and laws are formulated, sanctified, and enforced. And so the original assumption about social order, namely that it is stable, is a self-fulfilling prophecy. This predilection in the larger society reinforces the bureaucratic management system, which perpetuates the past through rules and policies.

Why Teleocracy?

The Newtonian world view, which allowed unprecedented alacrity in getting things done, carried the seeds of its own diminution within itself. Coupled with the disciplines of autocratic and bureaucratic leadership, it spawned the industrial age explosion of technology. That technology—particularly the technologies of communication and transportation—proffered a tidal wave of new value choices to everybody. And as people fanned out in all directions, pouncing on new ideas, inventing new values, and conceiving new purposes, change, not stability, became the evident way of the world.

Alvin Toffler, in his book *Future Shock*, probably did more than any other individual to bring into crisp focus for an entire society the fact that the world isn't stable anymore. We no longer speak of the rate of change, but of its acceleration—the rate of the rate of change. As Kenneth Boulding, economist and social thinker, observes, "The world of today... is as different from the world in which I was born as that world was from Julius Caesar's. I was born in the middle of human history, to date, roughly. Almost as much has happened since I was born as happened before."

Science itself is being washed by a revolution. The modern relativistic physicists, building upon the insights of Einstein, demonstrated that energy is more fundamental than matter. Material particles, or structures, are explained in terms of energy equations. Quantum mechanics deals with mass and energy interchangeably. It rests on probabilistic mathematics in which time, mass, and space are united as— or equal to—energy. Velocity relates space to time, as in miles per hour. The famous equation $E = mc^2$ relates energy to mass and velocity. Energy is pure process.

Even the laws of thermodynamics, which posit an inevitable increase in entropy, must now also include the reality of life, which is a decrease in entropy. Living matter seems to be an energy sink or absorber of energy; life converts energy to higher forms of organization with less entropy, rather than more. An ordering principle or purpose appears to be at work in the universe along with the disordering principle.

The life sciences have come alive in the past few decades. As they shrugged off the rigid cause-and-effect logic that was so good at describing machines but so poor at representing life, they made great strides. Profound insights came when living organisms were seen as part of interactive systems where everything causes, or at least influences, everything else.

While machines can pound along, day after day, with minimal input from the outside world, living things must be free to continually exchange energy, information, and materials with their larger environment as a price of life. Organic freedom, rather than mechanistic determinism, characterizes living systems. General systems theorists, like Von Bertalanffy, called the type of systems that living things are, "open systems."

Many philosophers and theologians have interpreted the observations of the relativistic physicists to suggest newer, broader worldviews. Two twentieth century giants were Alfred North Whitehead and Teilhard de Chardin. Both were philosophers and theologians; both interpreted the meaning of the new science.

Whitehead drew from the physical and mathematical sciences and framed a process philosophy; de Chardin drew from the biological sciences and spoke to theology. For the process philosophers and theologians, reality is less about "isness," and more about "becomingness"—more about process and less about structure than we believed in the past.

The psychologists drew from these insights and added new thinking to the analytic and behavioral schools of psychology, which had adhered to classical science's imperative of objectivity. They took on the task of considering human consciousness and purposes. Human beings tend to be inspired by the pull of what might be, rather than the push of what has been. Humanistic psychology deals with human feelings and emotions, and concerns itself with growth and change— with "becomingness," rather than "isness." Transpersonal psychology goes beyond humanistic psychology and considers human purpose and the spiritual dimensions of life.

Augmenting all of these currents of change was the discovery by many westerners of ancient eastern religious concepts, such as the yin/yang concept of differences, organized by the elegant complex system of the I Ching. Westerners were taught to make dualisms out of everything important in life—by the church, to embrace good and reject evil; by schools, to learn to recognize the true and despise the false; and by governments, to obey the lawful right and eschew the unlawful wrong. But in eastern thinking everything contains its opposite and depends on its opposite for meaning.

All of these forces are cross-pollinating in western society, and it is by the vigor of such reinforcing motifs that cultures change. One new idea flying in over the transom won't do it, but massive new thinking in science, theology, philosophy, and psychology conspire to change the way we look at the world and ourselves. And as we see ourselves and our world differently, we act in ways that make it more so. Just as people's idea that the world was stable kept it stable, our notion that life is change makes change our reality.

Teleocratic Leadership in the Information Age

In a changing world, purpose becomes a process. Corporate purpose is no longer stable; it continually evolves. Teleocratic leadership draws on the characteristics of bureaucratic leadership and overlays them with characteristics that foster the continual creating and implementing of common purpose.

The structures made concrete by organization charts and job descriptions blur and soften, and networks emerge as better ways to get things done most of the time. A task force is an example of a network in action. It forms, it does its job, it dissolves. It is oriented toward a clear result, or purpose, that everybody identifies with. At SAIC, for example, a group of people agree to do a project; they agree because they want to do that work. When it's done, they go on to another project, very likely with a new set of co-workers.

Rather than fixing people in their proper roles in the structure with leaders at the top, networks permit roles to change, rotate, modify, grow, appear, and disappear. This includes the role of the leader, since leadership gravitates to the individuals in the network who can do the best job of creating common purpose. If Pat Shea can rally a group of SAIC people around his idea, and convince a customer that it meets the customer's purpose, he's got a project. Leaders tend to be generalists, able to think beyond their own area of specialization. They tend to possess problem-solving and decision-making skills.

Power, then, is no longer concentrated permanently at the top of a pyramid but is diffused to the places it is needed in the network. More power to more people does not necessarily weaken an organization. (Look at the United States, the greatest experiment in the democratization of power in history.) The democratic ideal has rarely worked in management because we've tried to introduce it without management systems geared to order diverse purposes.

Since wealth is the key instrument of power, it gravitates to those who can create and maintain common purpose. A lot of experimentation is going on right now to discover ways to reward achievement by both individuals and groups. Bonus plans, for example, are being devised right and left to overcome the rigidity of fixed salary schedules, which blindly reward time served. SAIC, for instance, rewards individual achievement with stock and cash bonuses.

Planning and control cannot be precisely located in a network because everybody who does a job will do the planning, the execution, and the evaluating of that job. Control in a network tends to be self-control. SAIC people want to honor their commitments to customers and to each other, and they want to ensure that they'll continue to have the opportunity to do the work they love. Nobody has to stand over them with a stick.

If leadership in the information age is anything, it is the creation, articulation, and implementation of common purpose. The leader is the author of purpose. Authority is associated with purpose. It is associated with position only as a last resort, and only for the short term.

Knowledge of the past is essential when the world doesn't change very much. The consequence of this new world view is an orientation toward the future, and there are no facts about the future.

Vision, imagination, and intuition move to the heart of decision-making in a changing world. We've been ashamed to use the word "intuitive" in polite circles in the past. It's not acceptable in the world of mechanistic determinism because it doesn't fit into a rational framework. When we're setting results or purposes, vision becomes interesting and useful. It's oriented to what might be, instead of to what was.

The single most valuable outcome of creating and maintaining clear purposes and concrete goals is the dedication and drive that these ideas generate. People are not energized by their analyses of facts about the past or present. People get excited about their visions of what might be. Such visions come from the passions, the feelings, and the emotions that galvanize thoughts. It is human energy that translates thoughts, vision, and imagination into action so that "what might be" becomes "what is."

In a world chock full of people with diverse values, creative interactions become easy to do. For an interaction (or a transaction) to create new value in the world, both parties to it must get more than they give. This is only possible if the parties are different from each other. (We cover this idea at some length in the marketing section of this book.) With people becoming more delightedly different every day, the opportunities for transactions that create new wealth are more abundant every day.

Whereas many leaders' decisions in the industrial age were centered on historic costs, leaders in the information age must consider new value that can be created. For example, market value of a company, which estimates future streams of earnings, eclipses book value, which reflects historic costs.

Leadership based on common purpose is leadership that can create new value for, and with, many diverse people.

The bureaucratic management system has been remarkably productive. It created the greatest technology and the highest standard of material living the world has ever known. We now possess the capability to make manifest almost anything we set our mind to. With the affluence generated by technology, we can now afford to move into higher levels of self-fulfillment. The purposes of technology and the quality of life are becoming questions with new importance.

When the means to achieve chosen purposes were limited, it did not matter greatly what choices about purpose were made. But now that our ability to get things done has been developed to such a high degree of effectiveness, it is extremely important that the choices we make regarding things worth doing be made well—because we are very likely to be able to achieve our purposes.

Marketing is a process of deciding things worth doing for customers. In our next three chapters, we'll cover marketing in the information age. In Chapter 7, we'll talk about top-line management—the creation of revenue, which is upstaging the controlling of costs. In Chapter 8, we'll talk about an open-systems approach to marketing. In Chapter 9, we'll look at shifting values again, from a different perspective, as we focus on "The New Customer."

Chapter 6 Digest

Autocratic leadership worked in Watson Sr.'s world. The business environment was stable, so corporate purpose could be stable. The internal operation of a company could be ordered in one person's mind. People were anxious for safety and security and belonging—they were happy to work in a paternalistic system where they were told what to do and were taken care of.

Bureaucratic leadership worked in Watson Jr.'s world—the business environment was relatively stable and so corporate purpose could be relatively stable. Rules and policies ordered the more complex operations of a company. People wanted fairness, predictability, and some opportunity for achievement; they were happy to have benefits—a modern, depersonalized sort of paternalism. They were somewhat willing to be told what to do, either directly or by their job description.

The information age business environment is one of rapid change.

A company whose purpose does not evolve or change will probably be obsolete within two to five years of the establishment of that purpose. Deciding things worth doing is not a one-time task but an ongoing process, which requires many people in the company to continually exchange information with the larger environment so they can contribute to the formulation of corporate purpose.

Teleocratic leadership—leadership ordered by common purpose— is appropriate to a complex, changing business environment and mature workers. Workers in the information age tend to value achievement and self-fulfillment. People satisfy these needs if they simultaneously achieve their own purposes and the purposes of a larger community, such as their company.

Whence bureaucracy? Societal values spawn leadership styles. Some of the historic values that buttressed bureaucracy included: the world is stable and that's good; the universe works like a machine; cause-and-effect analysis is the way to solve problems. These values led to managerial preoccupation with the structure of the company (to keep things stable); clear hierarchies of role, power, wealth, and planning and control (to keep the machine running smoothly, every cog in place); authority of position (no doubt about who causes what to happen when). Rules and policies hammered down the past, and the assumption that the world is stable became a self-fulfilling prophecy.

New forces influence our values in the information age. The modern relativistic physicists, building upon the insights of Einstein, demonstrated that energy is more fundamental than matter. The life sciences shrugged off rigid cause-and-effect logic to view living organisms as part of interactive systems where everything causes, or at least influences, everything else. Philosophers and theologians began to see reality less as "isness," and more as "becomingness"—less as structure and more as process—than we have believed in the past. Humanistic psychologists drew from these insights and added new thinking to the analytic and behavioral schools of psychology—thinking that emphasizes human consciousness and purposes.

All of these forces are cross-pollinating in western society, and it is by the vigor of such reinforcing motifs that cultures change. One new idea flying in over the transom won't do it, but massive new thinking in science, theology, philosophy, and psychology conspire to change the way we look at the world and ourselves. And as we see ourselves and our world differently, we act in ways that make it more so. Just as people's idea that the world was stable kept it stable, our notion that life is change makes change our reality.

When purpose changes, networks replace strict functional hierarchies as the way to get things done most of the time. A task force is an example of a network in action. It forms, it does its job, it dissolves. It is oriented toward a clear result, or purpose, that everybody identifies with.

Roles are more fluid. Leadership gravitates to those who do the best job of creating purpose. Power is diffused to the places it's needed to get the job done. Fixed salary schedules that blindly reward time served give way to bonus plans that reward achievement. Control tends to be self-control.

The bureaucratic management system has been remarkably productive. It has created the greatest technology the world has ever known. We now possess the capability to make manifest almost anything we set our mind to.

When the means to achieve chosen purposes were limited, it did not matter greatly what choices were made about purpose. But now it is extremely important that the choices we make regarding things worth doing be made well—because we very likely will be able to achieve our purposes.

◄ PART III ►

MARKETING

◄ CHAPTER 7 ►

Top-Line Management

J. B. Say, the French economist, laid down the rule for bottom-line management in the industrial age: "Lower costs in order to raise profit." This was reasonable advice when industries, markets, and products were stable. It is not reasonable advice in a business environment of rapid change.

Information age companies will pay much more attention to management of the top line. The top line is sales, or revenue.

In stable industries with well-defined markets, the industrial age company could only go for a bigger piece of the well-defined pie. That pie generally grew only as fast as the population grew. The classic way for a company to widen its share of a targeted market was to cut costs and cut prices. Your share of that market couldn't get too big, either, because monopoly was bad; government deemed competition necessary to keep prices reasonable for consumers.

If your only option in the quest for profit and cash flow is to reduce costs, sooner or later you will run out of steam. You will find that no amount of imagination and creativity will allow you to cut costs below a certain irreducible limit. On the other hand, if you shift your imagination and creativity to generating revenue, there is no limit to what you can do.

The information age, with its proliferating needs and wants, its diverse people, its multivaried markets, intensifies the focus on revenue. No longer are we situated in a marketing environment subdivided into rotund segments that support monoliths and "Mom and Pop" stores, with relatively little room for anything in between. Mar-

115

keting in the information age is a whole new world, abounding with opportunities to expand sales.

What is the information age imperative for the legions of new small companies, the throngs of new mid-sized companies—which were probably small not so long ago—and the more entrepreneurial units and joint ventures of larger companies? The new imperative is not to lower costs to offer a set value to the customer. It is rather to constantly expand that value to the customer—and even increase prices—at a given cost.

Efficiency was a powerful imperative in the industrial age. Getting things done remains important in the information age, but it is not as vital as deciding which things are worth doing. Why be 100% efficient at producing what the customer does not want? Your company would be better off if it were just half so efficient; it would then have fewer unwanted products sitting on its shelves.

If you decide to go the old industrial age route of muscling into a fixed market with a lower-priced product, you risk being undercut by one or more of the other players. Here's the good side: as long as your target is relatively stable, statistics on subindustry classifications can provide you with a pretty good fix on the size of your market and how well you are penetrating it.

Ball Transfer Systems, Inc., in Pittsburgh, for example, is a little company that wanted a piece of the stable ball transfer market. It decided to sell a top quality product for a lower price. Ball transfers are a special type of ball bearing used in conveyors. By looking at the Standard Industry Classification codes of the U.S. Department of Commerce and the Thomas Register, and by talking with a sampling of users, the president of Ball Transfer Systems was able to judge the market's size and estimate how many competitors he had. He got inexpensive space in a business incubator, developed an automatic assembly machine which demolished labor costs, and sold, sold, sold!

After a number of months in business, Ball's president did another thing that was usual in the industrial age: he slightly improved the product. He developed an automatic driving tool and used self-threading fasteners for his ball transfers so that one person instead of two could install the product, and in half the time. By saving his customers time and money, he won a bigger share of the ball transfer market. He recognizes, however, that he can't rest for a minute. He'll have to continue to innovate and/or diversify as newer technologies or competitors squeeze his market.

Other ways that you can add small increments of improvement to known products or services include bundling a group of known and proven products together. You also can adopt value-added retailing, where nuances of customer value preferences are detected, and bits of service or information or small complementary products are added to standard products to expedite their sale. For example, a jump rope accompanies an aerobics tape; a real estate company offers a buyer's protection plan that guarantees expensive items like your roof, furnace, and hot water heater for the first year you own your house; software is buttressed by a toll-free number you can call when you get into trouble.

If you plan to make a small increment of change in a known product or service, you have to ask yourself how much improvement, of what kind, and how fast. Your challenge is to make strategic judgments about the incremental change that the customer will be willing to risk. Any modification will require you to get the prospective customer's attention by persuasion, education, advertising, promotion, or some combination of these marketing efforts.

In the industrial age, companies introduced new products in two ways—product first marketing and customer first marketing. Both were risky. They still work in the information age, and they are still risky, but they do offer luscious rewards if you can pull them off. Each method starts with half of the ingredients necessary to generate revenue: one starts with a product or service, the other with a customer.

Product-First Marketing

If you build a better mousetrap, you may stand there aghast as the world thunders by right past your doorstep. If you have a terrific product or service, your job is only half done. Innovation is complete only when someone other than you and your company puts value on the product or service. They do this by buying it, and they won't buy it unless they know about it, understand it, can get it, can use it, can get satisfaction from it, and can afford it.

The more innovative your baby is, the greater the risk that you

won't be able to sell it. One of the greatest challenges is that a radically new beast often requires a radically new marketing approach.
So when you test market, you test not only your product but all the
elements of innovation—the marketing elements as well as the product or service itself.

For example, with a novel product or service, the old, hallowed
market surveys often are not useful. It's hard to ask people if they
want or need something it never occurred to them to want or need.
For example, the 3M Company, after much internal foot-dragging,
developed, produced, and distributed "Post-It Notes." Only after you
use the little buggers do you discover that you can't live without them.

Du Pont, like most large industrial age companies, followed the
product-first concept of marketing. Over twenty-five years, they invested about $700 million dollars to develop Kevlar—the fiber that is
stronger but more flexible than steel. They then started looking for
customers, and for ways to use this remarkable product that the customers could not resist. They believed that such a long-term, high
investment approach, followed by a massive effort to fight their way
into the marketplace, was essential for pioneers of new technology.
In the early 1980s, however, Richard Heckert, chairman of Du Pont,
thought that there might be another way. He named a group to search
in universities and industry around the world for good thinking about
marketing processes. Out of this research came a new "Strategic Marketing Process" which is essentially customer-first marketing.

Wayne Smith, international marketing manager for Kevlar, says,
"We used to invent a product that we thought was super and say,
'Here it is, world, go buy it.' In other words, we used to say, 'Here's
the answer! What are the questions?' Now we say, 'Dear customer,
what are your needs?' We make what we can sell. The Strategic Marketing Process lets people operating at the customer interface bring
the customers' needs into the existing Du Pont management system—
it lets our marketing people get our management people on their team.

"This approach has helped our Kevlar effort. While we already had
the product, our saying to customers, 'What do you want?' made a
difference in the whole tone and responsiveness of our marketplace that
was measurable. It made a significant difference in the bottom line."

In the information age, one of the key roles for large companies
will be to instigate the industry-creating breakthroughs in products
and services; they can best stand the cost and take the risk.

If, however, you do decide to do product-first marketing, before going to the expense and trouble of renting an office, finding capital, or even incorporating, make sure you have something customers are willing to buy. You can reduce your risk by first making sure that you can generate sales. You can always form a company once you have sales, because you have cash flow. Testing the water was harder to do in the industrial age because typically a large investment was required to develop, produce, and stock a tangible product. But if your product is information or a service that you think you can sell, such upfront investment is often not required. You need only bear the expense of selling it, which could even be as little as your own effort.

Robin Deutsch, of Washington, D.C., can neither sing nor play an instrument, but she found a way to perform with area rock bands, a long-time dream of hers. She had studied sign language, and so she began to offer her services to sign for deaf patrons during performances. "It's not as if there was a great clamor from the deaf community for signed concerts," she said. "But when I started doing them, people loved it. Word got around. I just kept taking the next step, and I created a demand where there was none."

Smaller companies may prefer customer-first marketing to product-first marketing. It's comforting to think that if you can supply, someone will surely buy. But customer-first marketing carries risk, too. If you have the customers but not the product, you still have only half the job done.

Customer-First Marketing

The most important thing to remember if you plan to do customer-first marketing is that customers—not markets—buy. You know markets second-hand and through statistics; you know customers first-hand, in face-to-face interaction with unique individuals. Only in this way can you discover what the customer really wants to buy. This is the way you deliver value to the customer.

Traditional marketing thinking says, "Hire a marketing consultant, do a lot of market research, and strategize your market activity." Very few small companies have the resources to do it this way, and they can't stand the risk of being wrong.

Alternative customer-finding strategy, which is probably even more productive in many cases, consists of homey little activities such as talking to people, going to trade shows, hitting the public library, getting somebody with some knowledge of an area you're interested in on your board.

Irwin Selinger, CEO of Graham-Field, Inc., in Hauppauge, N.Y., founded two successful medical products companies. His first company, Surgicot, Inc., was the result of some determined customer-first marketing. He says, "I worked for six months as a volunteer at the Montefiore Hospital Medical Center in the Bronx to try to see what need we could make a product line to fill. I found one. We developed a sterilization indicator system—there was nothing like it on the market. We grew that company from literally zero dollars in sales to $25 million in sales and sold it to Squibb."

Today, Irwin's second company is still producing products that customers ask for. All their electronic diagnostic equipment, for example, comes with a toll-free number right on the product. One individual takes those calls which often start out, "Why can't you make...?" Irwin says, "A couple of winters ago it was especially cold and we kept getting calls from emergency room nurses who would say, 'I wish your thermometers could take low temperature readings. In these cold winters we have homeless people whose temperatures go down into the eighties.' So now we have the only thermometer on the market that can take hypothermia temperatures."

If you're up for customer-first marketing, we suggest that you not worry too much about having technical expertise to find and fill a need or want. A real expert in a field is often slowed by the paradigms of the profession and his or her own skills and knowledge. Specialists are often bound by prevailing standards. People outside a special field aren't afraid to be innovative. They are often more free to make radical and significant innovations.

Automation of the farm was not achieved by farmers but by city folks; International Harvester was founded by an industrialist, John Deere by a blacksmith. The most successful commercial product for schools was not innovated by educators; it was the school bus, introduced to the schools by the automobile companies. Significant innovations are often made by hobbyists.

There is yet another way to market—a way that is less risky than product-first or customer-first marketing. Reduce your risk by doing both at the same time. You don't have a product until you have a customer. Nor do you have a customer until you have a product. The strategy of creating both the hen and the egg is better than trying to decide which comes first. We call this lower-risk, both-come-first strategy "integrative marketing."

Integrative Marketing

One of the deepest pitfalls of management in the industrial age was the misguided search for first causes. Since Isaac Newton, science assumed that if something happens, then something else before it had to make it happen. Cause precedes effect. To managers, this meant that if you wanted a certain effect, you had to first create the cause that would produce that effect. The assumption was that you can know precisely what causes what and how.

"Product-first" marketing assumes that you obviously can't sell something until you have that something to sell; how else can the customer know what you are selling? This frequently means a large investment of time and money before you can market the perfect product. You assume, of course, that you know all along exactly what customers want or need. The product is seen as the "first cause," and customer demand follows as the effect. In the industrial age, this was a fairly safe assumption. There were, after all, existing industries comprised of many companies that served proven needs. Effect followed cause for all of them; a new entrant in an industry could expect a similar effect, given a similar cause. Moreover, needs and wants did not change very much from year to year. Business was competition as usual.

But that stable world of standard industries, companies competing within industries, and uniform and predictable customer needs and wants, vanished. With customers growing ever more diverse, products started to go through dozens of engineering changes to satisfy those customers. Eventually whole new models were introduced every year to satisfy changing interests. It occurred to many companies that if they started with the customer and saw the market as "first cause," then they would know better what to produce. This is what Du Pont did; it shifted to "customer-first" marketing.

In a rapidly changing world, the old cause-and-effect logic is not so useful. The modern systems view moves beyond cause-and-effect and sees interacting factors as mutually causative, so that each continues to be modified as a result of the other, and both interacting elements experience continual growth and change. "A" may cause "B," but "B" also causes "A."

Both product and customer can be developed at the same time. This is a concept of integrative marketing.

A west coast specialty engineering firm does integrative marketing beautifully. An engineer may pencil out a rough sketch of a product on the back of a napkin over coffee with a customer. The engineer goes away and puts together a rough sketch of the design. Then it's back to the customer for feedback. The next stage may be a rough prototype, followed by further input from the customer. Then the customer may agree to fund the building of the actual prototype. More feedback. When producer and customer agree that they've got what they want, the customer issues the contract for the final product. And then, of course, six months later, another coffee and another napkin may start the process of upgrading the product to meet new needs.

Management Geared to Integrative Marketing

Muscling into mass markets, making small incremental improvements in known products and services, customer-first marketing, and product-first marketing all are holdovers from the days when mass markets were plentiful. The bureaucratic industrial age management system accommodated these approaches to marketing.

When business meant mass production and mass selling, it was reasonable for a company to ordain functional specialists, cluster them, and give them their own vice presidents who answered to the general manager, the only generalist in the place. Such bureaucratic "functional organizations" typically had four functions: engineering, manufacturing, sales, and finance. These functions nicely divided up the job of satisfying the common industrial age mission: "to develop, produce, and sell a product at a profit." Whenever there was a problem that involved two of these groups, the overworked general manager had to get involved.

As products and services have shorter and shorter life cycles because of today's effervescent marketplace, the line organization must be more flexible and dynamic than the old functional organization allowed.

Marketing itself was born when the first breach of that strict clustering of specialists took place. Some companies, like IBM, began to see that salespeople were people-oriented and engineers were technology-oriented and both orientations were necessary to provide an up-to-date product to customers. The combination of technical expertise and people skills is rarely found in one human being. So companies started putting salespeople and engineers together on "marketing teams." They found these teams effective in pleasing customers, and they found that people on the teams grew in leadership maturity. Everybody benefited from creative, interdisciplinary work.

Integrative marketing calls for teams that combine the talents of salespeople and engineers. But when creativity and the ability to respond to rapid change are important, marketing requires even more talents. If you produce a product, manufacturing must be able to make it at a cost the financial people deem sufficiently low to make a profit. So manufacturing people must be part of the marketing team, too.

As top-line management upstages bottom-line management, it becomes increasingly evident that many companies should be reorganized into product or project task forces, where achievable goals can be set, achieved, and set again—over and over. The whole idea of an organization based on a structure of top-down control shifts to a concept of creative interactions in a changing marketplace. Functional specialists deserve advisory or staff status to support a new task force line organization.

It is not uncommon today to find organizations, alert to rapidly changing marketing opportunities, continually involved in creating, managing, and dissolving time-limited task forces. Such companies have more than integrated marketing; they have integrated management led by integrated executives. These companies don't spend a lot of time trying to determine exactly how they stand compared to industry averages; they're too busy constantly improving. They measure performance, not by their share of shifting markets, but by improvements in operating cash flow and return on investment.

How Fast Can the Top Line Grow?

One of the most common snares of new, successful companies is the paradox that your success puts you out of business. You have plenty of customers; you deliver good products as fast as customers buy; your sales double every year. Yet you fail. How can this be? You run out of cash.

Tom Nourse, president of Nourse Associates, Inc., a San Diego consulting and investment advisory firm whose clients are institutional investors, conducted extensive studies of how fast companies can grow. He found that the average company with a sales growth greater than about 20% a year will have great difficulty generating enough cash from operations to sustain its fast growth. If your company is growing faster than 20% per year, you are likely to notice that before you get paid by your customers, you have to pay out a lot of cash to develop and produce your product or offer your service. If you make a product, you have to keep enough on hand to be sure you can ship. So your inventory grows. You have to spend cash on your sales effort, and you may have to wait thirty or sixty or ninety days after a sale is made before the customer pays you. In short, you have lots of upfront cash outlays to position your company to supply the sales, and the faster your sales are growing, the more you spend now to deliver those larger volumes of sales later.

If your sales grow faster than 20% a year, you will probably need external financing: you'll have to borrow money or sell stock. This is why fast growth can bankrupt young companies. Operating and investing activities require lots of cash if you are growing rapidly. Eventually, operating cash flow should cover these needs as well as allow for payback of debt. But if stockholders and lenders become impatient waiting for that day, they can—and do—pull the rug out from under a promising company. If you're a new entrepreneur, read Chapters 10 and 11 carefully so you can make sense of your finances. But first, if you can restrain yourself from leaping into the finance section (everybody's all-time favorite subject), read Chapters 8 and 9 to see why marketing is open-systems work and how to predict needs and wants.

Chapter 7 Digest

J. B. Say, the French economist, laid down the rule for bottom-line management in the industrial age: "Lower costs in order to raise profit." This was reasonable advice when industries, markets, and products were stable. The information age, with its proliferating needs and wants, its diverse people, its multivaried markets, intensifies the focus on revenue: the top line. The new imperative is not to lower costs to offer a set value to the customer. It is rather to constantly expand that value to the customer—and even increase prices—at a given cost.

Efficiency was a powerful imperative in the industrial age. Getting things done remains important in the information age, but it is not as vital as deciding which things are worth doing. Why be 100% efficient at producing what the customer does not want?

If you decide to go the old industrial age route of muscling into a fixed market with a lower priced product, you risk being undercut by other players.

You can step ahead of competitors by adding small increments of improvement to known products or services, but any modification will require getting your prospective customer's attention by persuasion, education, advertising, promotion, or some combination of these marketing efforts.

In the industrial age, companies introduced new products in two ways—product-first marketing and customer-first marketing. Both were risky. They still work in the information age, and they are still risky.

On product-first marketing: If you build a better mousetrap, you may stand there aghast as the world thunders right past your doorstep. If you have a terrific product or service, your job is only half done. The more innovative your baby is, the greater the risk that you won't be able to sell it. One of the biggest problems is that a radically new beast often requires a radically new marketing approach. So when you test market, you test not only your product but all the elements of innovation—the marketing elements as well as the product or service itself.

On customer-first marketing: The most important thing to remember is that customers—not markets—buy. You know markets secondhand and through statistics; you know customers first-hand, in face-to-face interaction with unique individuals.

If you're up for customer-first marketing, don't worry about having technical expertise to find and fill a need or want. A real expert in a field is often bound by prevailing standards. People outside a special field are often freer to make significant innovations.

There is yet another way to market—a way that is less risky than product-first or customer-first marketing. Reduce your risk by doing both at the same time. You don't have a product until you have a customer. Nor do you have a customer until you have a product. The strategy of creating both the hen and the egg is better than trying to decide which comes first. We call this lower-risk, both-come-first strategy "integrative marketing."

On integrative marketing: One of the deepest pitfalls of management in the industrial age was the misguided search for first causes. Cause precedes effect. To managers, this meant that if you wanted a certain effect, you had to first create the cause that would produce that effect. The assumption was that you can know precisely what causes what and how.

In a rapidly changing world, the modern systems view moves beyond cause-and-effect and sees interacting factors as mutually causative, so that each factor continues to be modified as a result of another, and both interacting elements experience continual growth and change. "A" may cause "B," but "B" also causes "A." Both product and customer can be developed at the same time. Frequent communication with feedback makes integrative marketing possible.

Management teams geared to integrative marketing, alert to rapidly changing opportunities, continually create, manage, and dissolve time-limited task forces. They don't spend a lot of time trying to determine exactly how they stand compared to industry averages; they're too busy constantly improving. They measure performance, not by their share of shifting markets, but by improvements in operating cash flow and return on investment.

How fast can the top line grow? If your sales grow faster than 20% a year, it is very difficult to produce enough operating cash flow to sustain your high sales growth. You probably will need external financing: you'll have to borrow money or sell stock. That is why fast growth can bankrupt young companies. Operating and investing activities require lots of cash if you are growing rapidly. Eventually, operating cash flow should cover these needs as well as allow for payback of debt. But if stockholders and lenders become impatient waiting for that day, they can—and do—pull the rug out from under a promising company.

◄ CHAPTER 8 ►

Open-Systems Marketing

Al Williams, president of IBM in the early 1960s, defined business: "A business is something that has customers." No transactions with customers, no business.

The exchange, or transaction, is the fundamental unit of business behavior. The crucial difference between a closed system, like a machine, and an open system, like a plant or animal, is that the living creature must exchange material, information, and energy with its environment or it dies.

The application of open-systems thinking to businesses brings several ideas to the fore: a marketing system can be based on our understanding of healthy transactions; every healthy transaction creates new wealth in the world and adds to the profit of your business; in an environment of change, a company must change or die; the idea of competition, appropriate enough for closed systems, is often a hindrance in today's business environment.

Creating New Wealth

The concept of creating value that never existed before is not easy to understand. Say we purchase a pen for $1.00. Doubtless, a great deal of cost accounting by the manufacturer showed that the pen cost a total of 50 cents to produce and that in order to make a 10-cent profit, the manufacturer should sell it to retailers for 60 cents. The retailers probably had cost accounting that showed that when they added 30 cents of their own expenses to the 60 cents cost-of-goods-sold, plus 10 cents for their profit, they could sell it to us for $1.00. But when we paid $1.00 for the pen, we had to make a profit, too. When our enjoyment of the pen is subjectively judged to exceed $1.00 of value, or when we sell our writings at a price that covers the $1.00 pen (and all other costs), we will realize our hoped-for profit. All three parties must make a profit—the manufacturer, the retailer, and the purchaser. Each transaction must yield a profit to both parties in each exchange.

Now in each transaction, both parties were convinced that the value to each was greater than the cost to each. Each party gained (profited) by more than each gave, according to their own values. When this kind of transaction takes place, wealth is created that never existed before. Two plus two can equal five.

In order for both parties to an exchange to gain more than each gives, they must differ from one another. Therefore what they value must be dissimilar. Difference is the fundamental requirement for creating new wealth in the world.

Arthur Koestler's book *The Act of Creation* uses the term "bisociation" to describe how the creative act requires that two unlike elements come together, interact, and produce a new reality distinct from either of the first two elements. Unless the two parties to a transaction differ from each other and therefore have dissimilar needs and wants, why exchange? People don't run around exchanging identical items—we give the retailer a pen, the retailer gives us an identical pen—that would be silly.

Nevertheless, the fact that differences are a prerequisite for any transaction that creates new wealth in the world is a bit unsettling in a society in which church, science, and government have emphasized embracing the good, true, and right, and urged rejecting of the evil, false, and wrong. And since most of us think ourselves to be good and true and right, we tend to deduce that those who are different from us must be evil and false and wrong.

In all of history, money, wealth, and property seem to have emerged in precisely those places where differences were allowed to interact. Such places rarely had natural resources of their own, but they found a way to mediate between those that did. From the city of

Kish, Sumeria, in 4000 B.C., to Thebes, Egypt, in 2000 B.C., to Phoenicia, Venice, Amsterdam, London, and New York, the economic centers of the world have been the cities where trade was free and people from different places with different ideas were welcomed.

Healthy Transactions

Every healthy transaction adds to the profit of a business. Too many businesspeople have interpreted free enterprise competition to mean that for them to gain in a transaction, the other party must lose. In a healthy transaction, both parties gain more than they give, and therefore new wealth is created.

Businesses teem with transactions—between salespeople and customers, managers and non-managers, the company and its stockholders, executives and bankers, purchasing agents and vendors, accountants and the Internal Revenue Service, etc. While we will focus on the transactions between a company and its customers in this chapter, the tenets of healthy transactions apply to all transactions that take place within a company, as well as all those between agents of the company and people and institutions in its larger environment.

How do you do healthy transactions, transactions in which both parties get more than they give? Morehead "Buzz" Wright, head of General Electric's Executive School in the 1950s, dealt carefully with this subject. Buzz had a strong personal interest in the meaning of love. He studied the history of love and various concepts of love—from ancient religions and the Greek philosophers, all the way to the modern psychologists. His favorite modern thinker was Erich Fromm, who wrote *The Art of Loving*. Buzz called his own approach to the business transaction "love in the marketplace."

Buzz was convinced that the best concepts of love were directly applicable to business transactions. He drew from Fromm's definition of love to identify the value dimensions and the intellectual dimensions of healthy transactions. He believed transactions can be most creative when the two parties share mutual respect and mutual knowledge.

Mutual respect, according to Buzz, carries a respect for differences as well as a requirement for trust on the part of the weaker or less knowledgeable party. It also demands responsible behavior on the part of the stronger or more knowledgeable party. Responsibility increases in direct proportion to power. Mutual respect is a value stance.

Mutual knowledge, on the other hand, is an intellectual requirement, divisible into six specific questions that both parties should know the answers to:

1. What do I give?

2. What do you give?

3. What do I get?

4. What do you get?

5. What are my alternatives?

6. What are your alternatives?

Good courses on negotiation provide the best techniques for finding the answers to these questions.

I (Lou) have since found that if I keep Buzz's principles in mind when I work with other people in a business setting, our work is more creative, more productive, and more satisfying to everybody. Buzz was one of my best teachers. I discovered through him that the real source of creativity, productivity, and profit originated in the values and intellectual dimensions of the transaction, the basic unit of behavior of business life.

One successful, eclectic entrepreneur who knows about healthy transactions is Bob Block. For the past twenty-five years he's been making deals in areas as diverse as software, cellular phones, television, and advertising. We recently created a joint venture with one of Bob's companies to market our Mobley Matrix financial software. We've found Bob to be the best partner we've ever encountered— from the very moment we sat down to negotiate the deal.

To illustrate our points about healthy transactions, we asked Bob to tell us about some of the deals he's made over the years—how he approaches transactions, and how he does so well. We've chosen three of those stories to highlight Bob's way of creating value for himself and for the people with whom he makes transactions.

In 1970, before cable TV came along, Bob formed an over-the-air pay-TV company. His plan was to buy air time from local TV stations throughout the United States. Bob wanted to own some of the stations but at the time he didn't have the cash to buy them outright. Bob narrowed his target to one of two stations in Los Angeles: Channel 22, for which the owners wanted $1.8 million, or Channel 52, whose owners wanted $1.2 million.

Bob sat down with the owners of Channel 22 and told them clearly why he preferred their station. He extolled the more convenient position of 22 on a TV dial and the clearer reception at a lower frequency. "They almost fell over," Bob recalls. "Nobody who had dealt with them had started out by telling them what their advantages were. We made a deal in twenty-four hours. We agreed that my pay-TV company would buy air time from them. And for $40,000 I got a six-year option to buy the station for $1.8 million." Bob also agreed to pay $200,000 for six years in a row to cover interest the sellers would have received had they sold out in the first year. "They were happy with the deal," Bob adds. "They got cash, and they got my pay-TV business at a time when a license for UHF-TV was a license to lose money. I was happy with the deal—I had my option to buy the station when I had the cash, and it only cost me $40,000. At the end of six years, I exercised my option. The station was worth $30 million."

"I attribute the speed of our negotiations and the quality of our relationship to the fact that I started the negotiations obviously ready to cooperate. When we sat down, I didn't try to minimize their assets."

Recently, the FCC conducted a lottery for licenses for cellular telephone rights in urban markets. Bob "sold" applications. In other words, he prepared applications on people's behalf. Bob offered his clients the option of either paying $1000 per application or $200 for each application plus $5000 "winner's fee" for each market in which they were a winner. All of Bob's clients chose the second option.

The FCC allowed applicants to form "alliances," so all of Bob's clients agreed to pool their applications in such a way that any person whose application won in a given lottery would get 50.01% ownership of that market. The rest of the alliance would divide the other 49.99%.

Bob guessed at how many applications might be submitted for each market and calculated the probabilities that members of his alliance would win. He expected to reap about half a million dollars in winner's fees.

As it turned out, Bob's alliance merged with several other alliances, so that people won in a greater number of markets, but they won a smaller percentage of each. Since they had agreed to pay Bob $5000 for each market in which they got a share, Bob got an unforeseen windfall.

Bob calculated what the merger of alliances meant to him and to his clients. Five clients won the 51%. They would each get several million for their investments of about $20,000. They were fine. His other clients would see an average return of about $250,000 on a $20,000 investment. Bob would see about $1.2 million in additional fees.

"I saw that it wasn't reasonable," Bob relates. "I was taking too large a part of their winnings. I believe that when you enter an agreement, you do so based on a set of assumptions. When your assumptions turn out to be not in line with reality, both parties should be mature enough to recognize that reality and make adjustments. You need to adjust to accommodate each other's needs in light of reality.

"So I went back to my clients and asked them to pay me $5000 for each 1% they won rather than for every market. In effect, I said to my clients, 'Since our alliance merged with others, and you won smaller pieces of more markets than we'd both anticipated when we made our deal, we'll revisit the deal so that my winner's fee represents the proportion of fee to winnings that we intended when we made the deal.' I'm confident that all of these clients will invest with me again in the future.

"I was a 'giver,' if you will, in this deal, but I've been a 'receiver' in others. I remember a deal with Sid Shlenker, who now owns the Denver Nuggets. Sid engages in healthy transactions. Sid and I had both applied for TV station licenses in Houston and Dallas/Fort Worth. When the FCC deadline for applications passed, it turned out that Sid and I were the only contenders for the licenses in both cities. Sid called me and said, 'Are you interested in negotiating?' I said, 'Sure. I'm a lover, not a warrior.' We met at the L'Ermitage Hotel in Los Angeles and in about two hours we'd fashioned a deal. We set a date to negotiate the details in Houston.

"In a nutshell, the terms of the deal gave me a substantial interest in the Houston pay-TV company. I wanted an interest in the Dallas/

Fort Worth market, but Sid said that wasn't possible because of his relationship with his partner in that market. I accepted his representation. But two days after we'd signed the deal, Sid called me and told me he'd figured out a way he could give me a piece of the Dallas/Fort Worth market after all, and he did. Sid wanted a healthy transaction. A few years later, one of Sid's deals went sour and he needed me to give up a piece of my ownership. I responded willingly, because he had shown me that he was not a taker but a partner."

Bob has been able to move gracefully from deal to deal. He can forge a good deal fast. His cooperative relationships endure over the years. Bob's skill in making healthy transactions allows him to take advantage of diverse opportunities the information age presents to creative people.

In the sluggish markets of the industrial age, you had to make relatively few deals. As the stability of mass markets gives way to ebullient, changing markets, the ability to make healthy transactions assumes protean proportions. So does the ability to spot the opportunities in the first place. For most information age companies, the imperative is not "grow or die" but "change or die." Often, the opportunity to adapt to your environment lies in shifting niches.

Stick to Your Niching

Even in the era of mass marketing, astute companies began to see opportunities to tailor their products to segments of the market. While IBM marketed general purpose punch card machines, it tried to perceive the special needs of special industries. In the late 1940s, IBM had "special industry marketing representatives." I (Lou) worked with these representatives to design and run special industry classes at the Customer Executive School in Endicott, N.Y. We offered one-week schools for retailing, banking, public utility, insurance, education, local government, manufacturing control, and other areas of specialized record keeping. IBM had discovered what is known as vertical marketing.

Vertical marketing was the forerunner of niche marketing. The expensive way to do vertical marketing was to design, produce, and sell a different machine for each different vertical market. A much cheaper way to tap vertical markets was to produce general purpose machines that could be used in many different ways by varying the procedures and programs. Dr. John von Neumann, the mathematician, showed IBM how electronic technology could give general purpose hardware wide applicability to record keeping and data-handling jobs by the use of stored programs. The computer was born.

In the computer industry today, vertical niches for low-end (less expensive) software and hardware are mostly handled by value-added resellers (VARS), rather than manufacturers themselves. Joanna Tamer, a Los Angeles-based consultant who builds distribution channels for the computer industry, emphasizes that manufacturers of low-end products can't afford their own direct sales forces in today's market. "If you load all expenses for keeping direct salespeople on the road, it costs a big company $1000 a day," Joanna explains. "The salesperson has to bring in $1.2 million a year to make it worthwhile. You can't do that selling systems that cost $20,000. The entrepreneurial VARS, on the other hand, are lean and mean. They're doing 'pull marketing,' meaning they are attracting customers by word of mouth, free seminars, selling themselves as well as the systems. They can succeed in the first year to two out if they can gross $1 million a year.

"VARS generally come out of the industries they serve and they become computer-literate, rather than vice versa. A VAR whose niche is architects, for example, is much more likely to have been an architect who learned about hardware and software than a 'techie' who mastered architecture. These VARS can offer the extensive, expensive training and hand-holding that manufacturers' reps don't do."

Niche marketing rarely means creating a niche and staying there. In this world of rapidly changing needs and wants, niche marketing is more likely to be dynamic. You continually create markets. The next market is always waiting in the wings. In the industrial age, a company produced a specific, well-defined product. In the information age, your stance shifts from "This is what we do" to "We find ways to satisfy customers." General Motors is an industrial age company producing a well-defined product in a well-defined industry. In 1985, the auto maker generated $2.19 of revenue for every dollar invested in property, plant, and equipment. By contrast, Dun and Bradstreet generated $4.60 of revenue for every dollar of property, plant and equipment. D&B can use its assets to produce whatever information the customer may want; General Motors can produce only automobiles—in case the customer may want them.

Another type of niche is a horizontal niche. In a horizontal niche, satisfying customers is everything. John Williams runs a rather renowned little software store in Washington, D.C., called "The Software Specialists." John's business depends on an installed base of customers who love and trust him and his people. This niche evolves and changes as new products come onto the market. As John puts it, "In a fast-paced environment, we make order out of chaos. When there is confusion, we make the most money. We make our money on new products, when people need lots of help. We add value—knowledge, service, and support.

"Once a product becomes a commodity, and support becomes an industry in itself—such as all the templates and training courses and books and videos that teach you how to do word processing—we move on to the next product. We stay at the crest of the wave. That's what I do. I surf for a living. It's easy to stay up there. It's hard to get up there.

"We got up there by giving people the straight scoop and it's valuable to get the straight scoop. We don't sell people stuff they don't need. When something first comes out, people say, 'Why should I buy this? How can I best make use of it?' We keep track of our individual customer's environments and needs. We keep them current. It's a question of remembering. We remember what our customers bought before, and why. Some people remember songs. I remember what software everybody has. And the people who work with me have a lot of authority and responsibility—they don't turn over fast, so customers don't have to tell their whole life story over to a new person every time they come in.

"Now I can sell high-ticket items to my installed base and they don't ask price. I can just send stuff over to some of my customers with an invoice and they'll pay it. Then they call and say 'How do I use this?'"

The Software Specialists built a beautiful niche based on attention to the customer's needs and environment, on service, and on making healthy transactions. Paradoxically, the stability of their niche stems from the fact that they can successfully ride the crest of the wave; that they are continually meeting new needs and wants; that they are constantly changing.

When you find or build a juicy niche, you always expect that somebody is going to come in and compete with you for that niche, or that the need will dry up. Your objective is to fill your niche as long as you can and be ready to move ahead to the next niche.

The U.S. Vehicle Registration Service, a two-year-old business in the Washington, D.C., area, has knitted a neat string of niches, and has plans for its next ones. Its imposing name is probably designed to suggest that it is imperious enough to accomplish the service it offers to its first niche: they will come and get your car, take it through D.C.'s nightmarish registration process (a one- to two-hour wait, standing in line, during business hours only), get it through inspection (a one- to two-hour wait, riding in line), wash it if you request, and bring it back to you, clean, shining, and legal. The company's way of getting customers is ingenious: employees put flyers on the windshields of cars with out-of-state license plates or with D.C. inspection stickers soon to expire.

Should the D.C. government ever find a way to streamline its procedures, the U.S. Vehicle Registration Service won't be out of business. The little company expanded into a second niche. They'll pick up your car, take it to a mechanic or dealer for repairs, and bring it back. Usually, they give same-day service, because the company has built relationships with repair people based on the volume of business it brings in. The company's third niche can be even more helpful. They'll get your towed car out of impoundment.

The vehicle service firm is currently gearing up for yet another niche. In Washington, the city sends out a "boot truck" that patrols the city streets, scanning license plates and attaching a "Denver boot" to any car that is known to have more than four unpaid parking tickets. Once your car gets the boot, you can't move it until you go downtown and pay your fines. The U.S. Vehicle Registration Service plans to have a bicyclist follow the boot truck, placing flyers on the windshields of the afflicted autos. The company offers to take your credit card number over the phone, then go downtown and pay the cash to get your car unbooted.

The president of this fledgling company, Nicholas Montgomery, hopes eventually to have a personalized automobile club serving an even wider array of niches, growing out of needs of automobile owners who are long on money but short on time.

A niche may grow into a new mass market. If it does, and you stay with it, your company will take on some of the characteristics of an industrial age company—it will compete for market share in a known industry. On the other hand, if you like being small and entrepreneurial, you may leave the first niche and create another one. If you have a good niche, and want to move to another, there are always larger companies willing to buy your business. You can also diversify and become a niche conglomerate, but then, of course, you have a larger company instead of a smaller one.

Mass marketing provided a hundred products to a million people who needed them; niche marketing finds ways to serve a hundred people who want one of a million different products. Many general purpose magazines went out of business when special interest magazines appeared targeting smaller markets with a specific interest or hobby. *Sports Illustrated* has moved over to make shelf space for one hundred different sports magazines, everything from *Runner's World* to *Muscle and Fitness*. You can find a dozen different publications on wrestling, alone... if you really want to.

Niching is being nudged along by both public and private movements toward deregulation. The lifting of industry regulations by agencies of the government, as well as the loosening or removal of regulating standards for professional, trade, and industry associations, has opened up a new era of creativity and expansion into new business opportunities.

Many old regulations have gone by the wayside because the categories of activities they were designed to regulate have disappeared. Industry classifications became anachronistic as companies within them became conglomerates. Professional specialties are becoming interdisciplinary (psychoneuroendocrinology, for instance—really), and traditional trade groups are losing members because the typical worker can expect several careers in a lifetime.

Often a great challenge of niche marketing is to find ways to translate a need or want for service and convenience into well-defined and identifiable product attributes. Today's market presents myriad ways to marry products, information, and services to nimbly match your company's offering to a unique need or want.

Take, for example, two decisions a potential customer might face: whether to own or rent a machine, and whether to use it himself or herself or to hire an outside operator. You can combine these options four ways, each combination suggesting a different type of business opportunity. Christopher Lovelock, in his book *Services Marketing*, illustrates that a person might want to buy a car and drive it, or buy a car and hire a chauffeur to drive, or rent a car and drive it, or hire a taxi or limousine. Four distinctly different businesses could serve the same fundamental need. The challenge is to communicate to the right customers that you offer just the right option.

Computers and communications technologies, which catalyzed all this diversity of needs and wants in the first place, can make it easier to find niches and monitor them. Computers and telecommunications often facilitate the search for prospective customers who are likely to need what you offer. Not only can electronic links match service with customer, but they can provide the continuing feedback that an open system absolutely requires.

Competition and Cooperation

One of the most significant impacts the information age is making on the process of business is the re-examination of competition. With the information explosion, the growing respect for differences, and the discovery of creativity that emerges from team effort and healthy transactions, it becomes natural to ask, "Why not cooperate rather than compete?"

In the industrial age, companies tried to satisfy huge markets where needs and wants were simple. "I need salt," the customer would say. "Where can I buy it cheapest?" The full question unconsciously being asked by mass-market customers was, "Where can I buy what everybody else has at the lowest price?" Contrast that with what information age customers seem to be asking: "What is the best product to satisfy my special need at a price I'm willing to pay?"

When two or more companies offer an identical product, they compete for customers who want that product. That is typical of industrial age markets. But in a world of rapid change and burgeoning options, two enterprises seldom offer the same product for long. If they do, at least one of them is missing the opportunity for value-added differentiation. What meaning will competition have when every company has a different product or service?

A new age cries for a new system. The company in the industrial age saw itself as a closed system. Its unfriendly environment included other companies that were seen as outright hostile, vendors of products to be bought in the open competitive market for the lowest price, and customers who looked only at price out there in the market place. These are competitive views. The information age company sees itself as an open system. It sees other companies as opportunities for joint ventures, sees vendors as companies to be assisted in supplying better products, and sees customers as people or companies with whom long-term relations are built. These are cooperative images.

In the industrial age, a company operated competitively within an industry with a fixed market, a defined industry structure, and a government-assigned industry classification code. The bargaining power of purchasing agents and salespeople was crucial. It could change your market share. Industrial age companies have aimed to reduce costs and price, to focus on a specific market segment, and to make minor differentiations in product or service.

In a more free-wheeling environment, a company may belong to one industry with one product or service and to another industry with another. With a breakthrough new product or service, it could create a new industry. Rather than haggle with customers or vendors over price, you creatively find ways to lift the value of the transaction to both parties and so increase the profits for both parties. The strategies of information age companies are more likely to be: increase value, and possibly even price, for a given cost; focus on creating new market segments or niches; differentiate product or service substantially.

In the industrial age, you looked at yourself and your customer and asked, "How can we do better what everybody else does?" In the information age, you ask, "How can we do things differently from everybody else—and do them well?" The very idea of market share is becoming an anachronism: taken to a logical extreme, your potential market is anybody who wants anything and has something you might want in return.

Amar Bhide, in his *Harvard Business Review* article, "Hustle as Strategy" (Sept.–Oct. 1986), writes of a certain obliviousness to competition in the booming financial services industry:

Strategy, its high-church theologians insist, is about outflanking competitors with big plays that yield long-term 'rents' from a sustainable advantage. It is questionable whether this proposition is itself sustainable. Strategy involves a lot more and also a lot less.

The competitive scriptures almost systematically ignore the importance of hustle and energy. While they preach strategic planning, competitive strategy and competitive advantage, they overlook the record of a surprisingly large number of very successful companies that vigorously practice a different religion. These companies don't have long-term strategic plans with an obsessive preoccupation on rivalry. They concentrate on operating details and doing things well. Hustle is their style and their strategy. They move fast, and they get it right.

In a world where there are no secrets, where innovations are quickly imitated or become obsolete, the theory of competitive advantage may have had its day. Realistically ask yourself, if all your competitors gave their strategic plans to each other, would it really make a difference?

Certainly, some of these companies talk about establishing sustainable competitive advantage, but somehow their words do not lead to the elaborate strategies that manufacturing companies, for example, may pursue. Plans consist of targets—of revenues, costs, profits, and number of employees...

In the information age, the most enthusiastic competition may be with yourself. Can you beat your own performance of yesterday? A paradox: the best way to compete may be to cooperate.

Biologists who identified the open systems characteristics of living organisms first focused on the Darwinian images of struggle and war. Early on, Darwin's "law of nature" led biologists to see competition and to play down evidence of cooperation. "Social Darwinism" suggested that survival of only the fittest was natural and right. More recently, scientists have been compiling contrary evidence. Lewis Thomas, in his lovely book *The Lives of a Cell*, says it well: "Most of the associations between the living things we know about are essentially cooperative ones, symbiotic in one degree or another; when they have the look of adversaries, it is usually a standoff relation, with one party issuing signals, warnings, flagging the other off...We do not have solitary beings. Every creature is, in some sense, connected to and dependent on the rest."

Bob Greenleaf created the executive development program for AT&T in the early 1950s. When I (Lou) was at IBM, trying to differentiate between managers and executives and figuring out how to develop one into the other, Bob was a wonderful resource for me and a good friend. He has written at length on the concept of leader as servant. Some of Bob's thinking touches on our cultural preoccupation with competition. He writes: "I believe that dominance of the culture by elements like coercive power, private gain, and survival in the competitive struggle do not make for the quality of society that is reasonable and possible with the resources we have."

Strategic alliances and joint ventures, which are springing up like daisies in the information age, are perfect demonstrations of companies cooperating to their mutual benefit.

Adam Rostoker, who manages the COMDEX conferences, the largest computer and software trade shows in the world, says, "Trade shows like COMDEX present the opportunity—and underscore the need—for strategic alliances. Hardware manufacturers and software publishers gather at COMDEX to forge marketing partnerships. Companies get together and throw money into a pot to go after the same market niche or tangential markets.

"Strategic alliances usually involve two or three companies sharing distribution channels or personal networks so that buying one company's goods or services provides incentives to buy another's. Every Aldus Pagemaker program includes a certificate that lets you get the Microsoft 'Windows' program for $30 instead of $100. There are now 200,000 Aldus Pagemakers sold, and most customers have gone on to buy 'Windows.' It's a good strategic alliance."

In essence, strategic alliances let you make more contact with the customer; one company provides an entree for the other. Adam points out another advantage to this sort of cooperation. "Strategic alliances make things better when times are good, and they can save you during lean years. The other company may be up while you're down. Take the Apple and DEC alliance. If Apple were to start to lose market share, the fact that DEC is using Macintoshes as an intelligent front end to its product lines would still move a lot of Apple equipment."

During the 1987 Miss America pageant, contestants paraded to a song called "Heart of America," which included the lines, "And now we take up the challenge/ To be the best that we can be/ 'Cause the spirit of competition/ Is American to a 'T.'" Perhaps it was, in the industrial age, but it deserves rethinking today.

In this chapter, we have looked at marketing as the function that most insists that a company be an open system—that it act like an organism, not a machine; that it energetically exchange with its environment. In an ever more variegated environment, transactions with customers require relatively more respect for differences and diversity, and relatively less reliance on statistics, demographics, and market segments that assume uniformity of customers. While there are still some big stable markets in the information age, they are fewer; and so marketing today, for more and more companies, is a process of niching, rather than constant competition in a stable market in a predictable industry structure.

In the next chapter, we'll explore what made all these changes necessary. In addition, we'll look at how some fundamental shifts in society spawned new needs and wants, creating the fastest and most profound values metamorphosis in history.

Chapter 8 Digest

Al Williams, president of IBM in the early 1960s, defined business: "A business is something that has customers." No transactions with customers, no business.

The exchange, or transaction, is the fundamental unit of business behavior. The crucial difference between a closed system, like a machine, and an open system, like a flower or an animal, is that the living creature must exchange material, information, and energy with its environment or it dies.

The application of open-systems thinking to businesses brings several ideas to the fore: a marketing system can be based on our understanding of healthy transactions; every healthy transaction creates new wealth in the world, and adds to the profit of your business; in an environment of change, a company must change or die; competition, appropriate enough for closed systems, is often a hindrance in today's business environment.

On creating new wealth: A transaction creates new wealth when both parties gain more than they give. For example, I buy a pen from you for $1.00. The pen is worth more to me than the dollar; the dollar is worth more to you than the pen. In order for both parties to an exchange to gain more than each gives, what they value must be dissimilar. Therefore, they must be different from one another. Difference is the fundamental requirement for creating new wealth in the world.

The fact that differences are a prerequisite for any transaction that creates new value in the world is a bit unsettling in a society in which church, science, and government have emphasized embracing the good, true, and right, and urged rejecting of the evil, false, and wrong. And since most of us think ourselves to be good and true and right, we tend to deduce that those who are different from us must be evil and false and wrong.

Every healthy transaction adds to a business' profit. Too many businesspeople have interpreted free enterprise competition to mean that for them to gain in a transaction, the other party must lose.

On healthy transactions: Healthy transactions require mutual respect and mutual knowledge. Mutual respect requires trust on the part of the weaker party and responsible behavior on the part of the stronger. Mutual knowledge demands that both parties know the answers to six questions:

1. What do I give?

2. What do you give?

3. What do I get?

4. What do you get?

5. What are my alternatives?

6. What are your alternatives?

As the stability of mass markets gives way to ebullient, changing markets, the ability to make healthy transactions assumes protean proportions. So does the ability to spot opportunities in the first place. For most information age companies, the imperative is not "grow or die," but "change or die." Many companies must stick to their niching.

Niche marketing rarely means creating a niche and staying there. In this world of rapidly changing needs and wants, niche marketing is more likely to be dynamic. You continually create markets. The next market is always waiting in the wings. Your stance shifts from "This is what we do" to "We find ways to satisfy customers."

Mass marketing provided a hundred products to a million people who needed them; niche marketing finds ways to serve a hundred people who want one of a million different products. Both public and private movements toward deregulation are nudging niching. Many old regulations have fallen by the wayside because the categories of activities they were designed to control disappeared. Industry classifications became anachronistic as companies became conglomerates.

With the information explosion, the growing respect for differences, and the discovery of creativity that emerges from team effort and healthy transactions, it becomes natural to ask, "Why not cooperate rather than compete?"

When two or more companies offer an identical product, they compete. In a world of rapid change and burgeoning options, if two enterprises offer the same product, at least one of them is missing the opportunity for value-added differentiation. What meaning will competition have when every company has a different product or service?

A new age cries for a new system. The company in the industrial age saw itself as a closed system. Its unfriendly environment included other companies that were seen as hostile, vendors of products to be bought in the open market for the lowest price, and customers who looked only at price out there in the market place. These are competitive views. The information age company sees itself as an open system. It sees other companies as opportunities for joint ventures, sees vendors as companies to be assisted in supplying better products, and sees customers as people or companies with whom long-term relations are built. These are cooperative images.

◄ CHAPTER 9 ►
The New Customer

No single factor caused the industrial age to emerge in the nineteenth century. The technology that grew out of science, the Protestant Reformation with its values of hard work and thrift, the invention of the corporation, the emergence of democratic government—all were contributing factors. The industrial age has created the highest level of affluence the world has ever seen. The corporation is beginning to compete with government for the position of most powerful institution of our time. No government can ignore its wealth-generating capability. It gave the mass market what it wanted and needed—the material necessities of life.

But needs and wants, once satisfied, are no longer needs and wants.

The Demassification of the Marketplace

Michael Piore and Charles Sable, after ten years of research, wrote an expansive book called *The Second Industrial Divide: Possibilities for Prosperity*. In the chapter called "The Mass-Production Economy in Crisis," they point out that more than 90% of American households are now saturated with the classic goods of mass production—TVs, refrigerators, toasters, vacuum cleaners.

As people's desire for goodies and gadgets are satiated, they turn their interest to services and information and to products enhanced by a service or some useful information.

Lands End, a catalog clothing company grossing $265 million a year, provides a toll-free service to all their customers. You can call and ask if the Goretex jacket on page 7 will coordinate with the corduroy slacks on page 60 and the tassel cap on page 19. Moreover, you can send in a swatch of material from something you already own, and Lands End will suggest things from their catalog that will look dashing with it. They'll keep track of what sizes you, and everybody you love, wear. This adds a significant new increment of information to the transaction. It also adds an opportunity for the individual customer to interact with a real live person at Lands End—a common yearning in an information-oriented economy.

Even developing countries, whose hunger for goodies and gadgets has yet to be assuaged, seem determined to leapfrog the focus on quantity of goods that captivated the industrialized nations. Communication and transportation technologies have displayed for people all over the world the emphasis on quality of life implicit in an age of services and information, and expectations to participate rise. The Small Business Administration figures that the six highest U.S. export potentials are computers and peripherals, hardware, telecommunication equipment, computer software and services, medical instruments and supplies, and electronic parts. Every one is a tool for providing services and information.

Mass production and mass marketing of goods in the industrial age flourished in a world of stable needs and wants. Social patterns, ethnic groups, demographics, statistics, the lulling predictability of a giant middle class neatly narrowed into nuclear families—these were standard tools of the industrial age marketeer. In the information age quest for customers, these relatively reliable cubbyholes are crumbling. The number of classifications that still accurately encompass millions of people dwindles every day. Certainly there are still mass markets, but they are ever fewer and farther between.

When people's basic needs and wants are satisfied, where do they go? In all directions.

In the industrial age, much marketing revolved around spotting a large, clear market and muscling your way in, usually by offering a lower price. In the information age, you've got to see what isn't there. Unless you plan to play the industrial age game, and compete in known markets with the big boys, you've got to predict needs and wants even as they are just emerging. The way to predict needs and wants is to study values. The old verse says it:

> *If you would know John Smith*
> *And what John Smith buys,*
> *You must see John Smith*
> *Through John Smith's eyes!*

To Predict Needs and Wants— Study Shifting Values

Watson Sr.'s vision for IBM came from within and without: within himself, from his own hopes and dreams and convictions; outside himself, from his perceptive scanning of his environment for existing, as well as emerging, values. Watson Jr., who saw that environment-scanning was no longer a one-person job, involved his management team in the surveillance of values. In the late 1960s, when values were in tumult, IBM spent $5 million on a Harvard study on Technology and Values. In fact, while the young people of the 60s were skewering traditional values, fourteen major research projects were conducted by corporations who were trying to determine what needs and wants might grow out of this values revolution.

One study, headed by Willis Harmon at the Stanford Research Institute (SRI), was called "The Changing Images of Man." Out of it grew an in-house project at SRI known as VALS (Values and Life Styles), headed by Arnold Mitchell and Marie Spengler. By 1987, VALS was a multimillion-dollar operation, with 135 high-powered clients ranging from CBS to Citicorp to Chrysler, all of whom were looking to the values people hold to determine what they will want and need, as well as how to get their attention.

VALS research showed that in 1983 only 11% of all Americans still held those safety and security values that created the mass markets for food, clothing, and shelter. These were the values that made autocratic and bureaucratic management necessary and appropriate. VALS labelled these people the "Need Driven."

VALS discovered that by 1983, 68% of the population held "Belonger," "Emulator," and "Achiever" values. VALS called these people

"Outer-Directed." Researchers also found that the values revolution of the sixties pushed a growing part of the population into the "Inner-Directed" category. The VALS researchers called them the "Societally-Conscious," the "Experientials," and the "I-Am-Me's." By 1983 the Inner-Directeds had grown to 19% of the population.

This left 2% of the population who had risen above it all to become "Integrated." Many good executives and successful entrepreneurs seem to belong to this 2%. Here's a larger description of each stage of the VALS typology, as the VALS researchers describe it:

The VALS typology is divided into four major categories, with a total of nine lifestyle types. These lifestyles are fitted together in what is called the VALS double hierarchy. (See Figure 8 in Appendix A.)

It should be understood from the start that these lifestyle categories are not fixed and immutable. Many people grow from one level to another as children, as adolescents, and as adults. Some very few may start at the bottom and reach the top within a lifetime. But far more common is movement of a level or two.

1. THE NEED-DRIVENS

The Need-Drivens are people so limited in resources (especially financial resources) that their lives are driven more by need than by choice. Values of the Need-Driven center around survival, safety, and security. Such people tend to be distrustful, dependent, non-planning. The Need-Driven category is divided into two lifestyles: Survivors and Sustainers.

Survivors: Survivors are the most disadvantaged in American society by reason of their extreme poverty, low education, old age, and limited access to upward mobility. Many, now infirm, once lived lifestyles associated with higher levels of the VALS hierarchy. Others are ensnared in the so-called "culture of poverty."

Sustainers: Sustainers are a group struggling at the edge of poverty. They are better off and younger than Survivors, and many have not given up hope. Their values have advanced from depression and hopelessness to expression of anger at the system, and they have developed a street-wise determination to get ahead.

2. THE OUTER-DIRECTEDS

The Outer-Directeds conduct their lives in response to signals—real or fancied—from others. Consumption, activities, attitudes are guided by what the outer-directed individual thinks others will think. Psychologically, outer-direction is a major step forward from being Need-Driven. In general, the Outer-Directeds are the happiest of Americans, being well attuned to the cultural mainstream—indeed, creating much of it.

The VALS typology defines three principal types of outer-directed people: Belongers, Emulators, and Achievers.

Belongers: Belongers constitute the large, solid, comfortable, middle-class group of Americans who are the main stabilizers of society, and the preservers and defenders of the moral status quo. Belongers tend to be conservative, conventional, nostalgic, sentimental, puritanical, and conforming. The key drive is to fit in—to belong—and not to stand out.

Emulators: Emulators are trying to burst into the upper levels of the system—to make it big. The object of their emulation is the Achiever lifestyle. In truth, many are not on the track to make them Achievers but appear not to realize this. They are ambitious, upwardly mobile, status conscious, competitive.

Achievers: Achievers include many leaders in business, the professions, and government. Competent, self-reliant, efficient, Achievers tend to be materialistic, hard working, oriented to fame and success, and comfort loving. These are the affluent people who have created the economic system in response to the American dream. As such, they are the defenders of the economic status quo.

3. THE INNER-DIRECTEDS

People called the Inner-Directeds contrast with the Outer-Directeds in that they conduct their lives primarily in accord with inner values—the needs and desires private to the individual—rather than in accord with values oriented to externals. Concern with inner growth thus is a cardinal characteristic.

It is important to recognize that, in American society today, one can hardly be profoundly Inner-Directed without having internalized Outer-Directedness through extensive and deep exposure as a child, adolescent, or adult. One implication is that inner-directed people tend not to come from need-driven or inner-directed families. Some measure of satiation with the pleasures of external things seems to be required before a person can believe in or enjoy the less visible, incorporeal pleasures of Inner-Direction.

VALS has identified three stages of Inner-Directedness: I-Am-Me, Experiential, and Societally Conscious.

I-Am-Me: This is a short-lived stage of transition from Outer- to Inner-Direction. Values from both stages are much in evidence. Typically, the I-Am-Me person is young and fiercely individualistic to the point of being narcissistic and exhibitionistic.

Experientials: As the I-Am-Me's mature psychologically, they become the Experientials. At this stage of Inner-Direction, the focus has widened from the intense egocentrism of the I-Am-Me to include other people and many social and human issues. Experientials are people who most want direct experience and vigorous involvement. They are attracted to the exotic (such as Oriental religions), to the strange (such as parapsychology), and to the natural (such as "organic" gardening and home baking).

Societally Conscious: The Societally Conscious have extended their Inner-Direction beyond the self and others to the society as a whole—in fact, sometimes to the globe or even, philosophically, to the cosmos. A profound sense of societal responsibility leads these people to support such causes as conservation, environmentalism, and consumerism. They tend to be activistic, impassioned, and knowledgeable about the world around them. Many are attracted to simple living and the natural; some have taken up lives of voluntary simplicity.

4. COMBINED OUTER- AND INNER-DIRECTED: THE INTEGRATEDS

At the pinnacle of the VALS typology is a small group called the Integrateds. These rare people have put it all together. They meld the power of Outer-Direction with the sensitivity of Inner-Direction.

They are fully mature in a psychological sense—able to see many sides of an issue, able to lead if necessary, and willing to take a secondary role if that is appropriate. They usually possess a deep sense of the fittingness of things. They tend to be self-assured, self-actualizing, self-expressive, keenly aware of issues and sentiments, and often possessed of a world perspective.

Once you've studied this VALS typology, you'll spot its application in lots of advertising efforts. A classic is the Merrill Lynch bull. Merrill Lynch wants to attract Achievers, who tend to have lots of money to invest. Originally Merrill Lynch's symbol was a thundering herd of bulls, but achievers are not enthusiastic about blending into thundering herds. So Merrill Lynch switched to the stalwart lone bull crossing a stream to the rich pasture on the other side, sheltered in a cave from the inclement environment, adroitly wending its way through a china shop—the capable individualist, making its successful way in the world.

Citicorp's ad doesn't bother with subtle images, but says straightforwardly: "Because Citicorp understands the drive to succeed...to do more than just get by...we have become the nation's largest financial services company...Citicorp, because Americans want to succeed, not just survive."

But the subject of this section is *predicting* needs and wants by studying values. A nice example of a company that studied values and then tailored a product to needs and wants is Ray Ellison Homes, Inc. This company is San Antonio's largest home builder, up from fourth place since it started subscribing to VALS research and designing houses accordingly. The builder found, for example, that more than half of San Antonio's home-buyers are Achievers, who go for features like fancy front doors, fireplaces, security systems, wet bars in the master bedroom, and energy efficiency. Achievers can afford energy inefficiency, but efficiency appeals to their affection for orderliness and control. So Ray Ellison Homes builds what most home buyers in its marketplace want.

VALS is only one cut—one way of looking at changing values. The VALS research has been exhaustive, and the companies that apply VALS typologies to their marketing efforts get impressive results. But you don't have to subscribe to VALS to discern the momentous value shifts in our time: the civil rights movement, the women's movement, the sexual revolution (and an AIDS-related counter-revolution?), the New Age movement, the resurgence of religious fundamentalism, the gay rights movement, the environmental movement...the list goes on. Each movement reflects emerging values. Some, such as the women's movement, the civil rights movement, and the gay rights movement, are specifically concerned about people's rights to increased options in their lives. And each of them spawns thousands of new needs and wants.

I (Kate) remember some of my needs and wants in my first job out of college. It was the kind of job that opened to women as a result of the women's movement: I sold heavy industrial equipment. I was always on the lookout for products that fit my unusual lifestyle. Shoes, for example, were a big problem. Nobody made decent-looking women's shoes that could also take in stride the shards of metal sprinkled over the foundry floor, climb up the perforated plate stairs, and keep traction in mini oil slicks. I would have happily paid some shoe-making entrepreneur $400 for a pair of thick-soled, low-heeled, pretty shoes. In fact, I still would.

When the courts broke up AT&T, the seven Bell regional holding companies, all of which are now Fortune 100 companies, suddenly found themselves without R&D capacity. R&D had been centered in Bell Labs, which AT&T kept. So the "Baby Bells" formed a company called Bell Communications Research, or Belcore, to develop new services that the Bell companies can offer. Jim Rothweiler is a district manager with Belcore. He and his people are working to predict needs and wants that will be served in the mid-1990s and beyond. Jim looks closely at shifting values.

One of Jim's most interesting projects grows out of the women's movement and the fact that most women who have children now hold jobs outside the home. Jim says, "Working mothers have been telling us for years that their greatest concern is the safety of their children. They say that what they want is to know how the child is during the day—is the little one happy, sad, hurt? At the end of the day, when the mother asks, 'How was your day?' the child's usual answer is 'Okay,' and that doesn't tell the mother much of anything.

"We're in the communications business, and working mothers are telling us that they desperately want to communicate with their children during the day. So we're working on a child monitor system, perhaps something like a beeper that might monitor blood pressure, brain waves, skin temperature, or some other indicator of emotional state. I'm not sure society is ready for it in the next one to two years, but I suspect we will be in the next three to five.

"If you went out and interviewed mothers and asked them, 'Do you need this electronic device that will connect you to the mental state of your child?' they would look at you like you're weird and give you a flat 'No.' But if you talk to them about their values—if you ask them what is important to them—you'll find that the mother-child bond needs massaging during the day. Working mothers say they'd pay anything for constant feedback about the well-being of their children."

Jim Rothweiler has found that to perceive emerging values and conceive new products and services, you need more—and less—than traditional research methodologies. Jim says, "The old methodologies—environmental scanning, demographics, survey research, focus groups—don't do it anymore. They'll give you a good measure of how well you're doing what you did before. They'll tell you how fast you're moving down the road you're already on. But they don't give you much insight into new directions you should go.

"Our traditional methods only tap into surface things. The future resides underneath that surface. You have to penetrate deeper into people. You have to live with your customer, or as your customer.

"I'm looking at the small business market as well as the consumer market. I have my managers go out and live with law offices, real estate agencies, securities and commodities brokerage firms, tradespeople. My managers watch the action and talk to the people. Then they come back and fit what they observed into our statistical data and analyze the whole situation. But even this face-to-face interaction isn't the best way to know the customer.

"There's an 'ethnomethodology' in which you become the customer for a while. We had a consultant in, an expert on gerontology. She had actually become an old person for a year—wore wrinkled makeup, moved into a retirement community, lived as one of the people she wanted to understand. I want to do more of this research. I want to have one of my managers go to work as a secretary in a law firm for a few months, another as a clerk in a brokerage firm. Call it shoulder-to-shoulder marketing research, or arm-in-arm—it's even better than face-to-face."

Some of the best TV comedies take their spark from shifts in values. Arthur Koestler theorized that humor is the way we deal with tension between old and new values. *All in the Family* capitalized beautifully on the tension between traditional and new values. Archie Bunker personified older values, while his son-in-law "Meathead" held emerging values. Their weekly sparring was a metaphor for the struggle that was playing itself out throughout our society in the mid-1970s.

Night Court, one of 1987's most rambunctious shows, every week paraded before judge Harry Stone several caricatures of quirky New Yorkers. From the Manhattan denizen suited in tinfoil who was building a landing strip for flying saucers (Harry's order to the bailiff: "Beam him up!") to the stunning blonde Swedish stewardesses that lusty prosecutor Dan Fielding lured to his apartment, only to learn that they were stunning blonde Swedish transvestites, *Night Court* played with every new value and lifestyle and belief system it could find.

Zen and the Art of Motorcycle Maintenance, subtitled "an Inquiry into Values," is a favorite book of ours. We both read it in the mid-1970s, when it first came out. An edition published in 1984 has a new afterword in which the author, Robert Pirsig, considers the overnight success of his book, a book that had been turned down by 121 publishers. He attributes the book's huge sales to the fact that it spoke to values emerging in society at the time it appeared. He writes:

> Culture-bearing books challenge cultural value assumptions and often do so at a time when the culture is changing in favor of their challenge. The books are not necessarily of high quality. *Uncle Tom's Cabin* was no literary masterpiece but it was a culture-bearing book. It came at a time when the entire culture was about to reject slavery. People seized upon it as a portrayal of their own new values and it became an overwhelming success.
>
> The success of *Zen and the Art of Motorcycle Maintenance* seems the result of this culture-bearing phenomenon.... The book also appeared at a time of cultural upheaval on the matter of material success. Hippies were having none of it. Conservatives were baffled. Material success was the American dream. Millions of European peas-

ants had longed for it all their lives and come to America to find it—
a world in which they and their descendants would at last have
enough. Now their spoiled descendants were throwing that whole
dream in their faces, saying it wasn't any good. What did they want?

The hippies had in mind something that they wanted, and were
calling it 'freedom,' but in the final analysis 'freedom' is a purely negative goal. It just says something is bad. Hippies weren't really offering any alternatives other than colorful short-term ones, and some
of these were looking more and more like pure degeneracy. Degeneracy can be fun but it's hard to keep up as a serious lifetime occu-
pation.

This book offers another, more serious alternative to material success. It's not so much an alternative as an expansion of the meaning
of 'success' as something larger than just getting a good job and staying out of trouble. And also something larger than mere freedom. It
gives a positive goal to work toward that does not confine. That is
the main reason for the book's success, I think. The whole culture
happened to be looking for exactly what this book has to offer. That
is the sense in which it is a culture-bearer.

This illustration about a product that speaks to a whole society may
seem to contradict our earlier emphasis on a business environment
that is diversifying. Any inconsistency disappears if you step up another systems level.

Even as we are eschewing uniformity and embracing our own
uniqueness, as a whole culture of people we are also shifting. At one
systems level, people can be roaring off in all different directions—
like the Los Angeles freeways at rush hour. Only when you rise above
that systems level can you notice that everybody is also heading the
same way, as the earth spins. And if you could keep stepping back
systems levels, you'd eventually see the movement in the spiral arms
of the Milky Way galaxy. (If you figure out how to do it, give us a
call.) The largest value shifts are sometimes the hardest to grasp; it is
difficult to stand far outside our own system to examine it, to imagine
how it might change. It's like asking a fish to think up alternatives to
water.

The value shifts taking place in our time, covered in this chapter
and in our chapter on teleocratic leadership, are molded by the people who are your prospective customers. As you seek to predict needs

and wants by studying shifting values, stay tuned as best you can to several levels of change at once.

Everything you do in marketing—from studying shifting values, to creating healthy transactions, to sticking to your niching—has one definite, clear, measurable objective—to create and enlarge sales per year. The sales figure is the most important figure in all your financial statements.

If you are in business, you are managing an economic institution. The existence of sales gives you some economics to manage. This is why marketing is important. This is why sales is important: it is the top line on your income statement. Managing sales is top-line management.

Once You've Got Sales...

If you have a good top line, you are well on your way to success: you have decided something worth doing for your customers. To judge how well you do this, compare your annual sales to your total resources for doing the job—your total assets. Your comparison can be shown as a ratio between sales and assets or sales/assets. This ratio is called your sales turnover of capital. It answers the question, "How much value do we create for the customer with the resources we have for doing the job?"

You must also create new value for your company: you must make a profit, or net income. To generate net income you must control your costs—you must manage all the transactions that affect your balance sheet. Net income measures how well you get things done. When you compare net income to sales you get your profit margin, net/sales.

Combining your top-line management success with your bottom-line management success gives a reading of overall management success, called return on investment.

We now turn to the management of finance—how to constantly improve net income (which means profitability) as well as cash flow (which means solvency) in a way that makes maximum use of all your assets.

In Chapter 10, we'll introduce a complete financial picture that includes all the dollar amounts necessary to manage a business. In

Chapter 11, we'll describe a total financial management system that relates strategies and behavior to the financial results they produce. In Chapter 12, we'll examine the changing economic environment of the information age and how it gives meaning to the economic institution called a company.

Chapter 9 Digest

Needs and wants, once satisfied, are no longer needs and wants. More than 90% of American households are now saturated with the classic goods of mass production—TVs, refrigerators, toasters, vacuum cleaners. As people's desires for goodies and gadgets are satiated, they turn their interest to services and information and to products enhanced by a service or some useful information. Even developing countries, whose hunger for goodies and gadgets has yet to be assuaged, seem determined to leapfrog the quest for quantities of goods that captivated industrialized nations. All of the top six export potentials for the United States are tools for providing services and information.

When people's basic needs and wants are satisfied, where do they go? In all directions. Diversity is a fundamental reality of the information age business environment.

Unless you plan to play the industrial age game and compete in known mass markets, you've got to predict needs and wants even as they are just emerging. The way to predict needs and wants is to study shifting values.

A preeminent study of shifting values was conducted by the Stanford Research Institute (SRI). Called VALS (for Values and Life Styles), the study finds that only 11% of Americans still hold those safety and security values that responded so well to mass marketing. These were also the values that made autocratic and bureaucratic management necessary and appropriate.

VALS subdivides the rest of society into a number of categories with labels such as "Achiever" and "Societally Conscious" and "Integrated," each with different values and lifestyles. Marketers study these characteristics and order both advertising and product development according to a constellation of values. Companies have found VALS data of great benefit.

Once you've studied this VALS typology, you'll spot its application in lots of advertising efforts. A classic is the Merrill Lynch bull. Merrill Lynch wants to attract achievers, who tend to have lots of money to invest. Originally Merrill Lynch's symbol was a thundering herd of bulls, but achievers are not enthusiastic about blending into thundering herds. So Merrill Lynch switched to the stalwart lone bull—crossing a stream to the rich pasture on the other side, sheltered in a cave from the inclement environment, adroitly wending its way through a china shop—the capable individualist, making its successful way in the world.

You need more—and less—than traditional research methodologies for finding what customers value. Traditional marketing methodologies, such as environmental scanning, demographics, and survey research will tell you how well you're doing what you've done in the past, but don't provide much insight into wants and needs just beyond your horizon. To perceive shifting values, try living with your customer. More than face-to-face, it's "arm-in-arm" marketing research.

As you seek to predict needs and wants by studying shifting values, stay tuned as best you can to several levels of change at once. Even as we are eschewing uniformity and embracing our own uniqueness, as a whole culture of people we are also shifting. At one systems level, people can be roaring off in all different directions—like the Los Angeles freeways at rush hour. Only when you rise above that systems level can you notice that everybody is also heading the same way, as the earth spins. The largest value shifts are sometimes the hardest to grasp; it is difficult to stand far outside our own system to examine it, to imagine how it might change. It's like asking a fish to think up alternatives to water.

◄ PART IV ►

FINANCE

◄ CHAPTER 10 ►

The Total Financial System

Most of us view financial statements as unrelated reports measuring discrete areas of our businesses. We sense that there ought to be some juicy meaning in them somewhere—after all, they're measuring the very guts of our businesses—but the meaning eludes most of us.

It doesn't elude everybody. Corporate raiders, for example, have it all figured out. They have designed integrative systems that pull together fragmented data and give them meaning. Many people to day who are profiting handsomely because of their ability to make sense of financial information have no formal training in accounting or finance. T. Boone Pickens was a geology major in college. Carl Icahn majored in philosophy and went to medical school. These people don't get lost in the details of accounting definitions and protocols because they never learned them in the first place.

The meaning of financial data doesn't have to elude anybody.

In keeping with a bureaucratic mindset, the typical organization in the industrial age designated financial specialists. The treasurer watched cash. The controller watched income. The CEO kept an eye on the balance sheet, and tried to manage the business with input from the specialists. Fractionated data fed a fractionated management effort. That's not good enough anymore.

The information age calls for generalists. Entrepreneurs have no choice but to know it all. A management team is most powerful if all of its members understand the business whole.

Financial data interrelate. Like a jigsaw puzzle, if you know how to arrange the pieces, the big picture becomes immediately clear. Here's how the jigsaw works.

A balance sheet measures the status or structure of property at a specific time. It is like a snapshot. Annual reports are obliged to show that snapshot for the beginning date and ending date of the fiscal year covered by the report. What you actually see is the ending balance sheets of last year and the year before. What last year ended with, this year begins with. Only recently have both balance sheets been shown. Outsiders demanded some record of how things changed. Financial reports presented to most businesspeople today fail to show clearly what happened during the twelve months between those two shapshots.

During the period of time bracketed by two balance sheets in an annual report, a business engages in multitudinous transactions. Most of those transactions have two parts—a promise part and a fulfillment part; a commitment part and a settlement part. These two parts of a transaction are usually separated by time. In fact, if all transactions were initiated and concluded in the same breath, balance sheets would not be necessary, except perhaps to show that net worth equals cash. At every moment you would know precisely what you have—with no unfilled promises, no long-term investments.

Most often, one part of the transaction is cash, and the other part is not cash (we call it non-cash). For example, a customer agrees to buy your product. That's a sale, and it is non-cash. Sometime later, perhaps thirty days later, the customer pays you. That's a collection, and it is cash.

Sometimes, it takes a number of periods for parts of a transaction to be completed. For example, you invest in a machine. That's a cash outlay. Every year for the next ten years, you depreciate the machine. Each of those depreciation charges is a non-cash expense.

Some transactions affect both net income, or profit, and cash at the same time. In a cash sale, for example, the promise to buy and the fulfillment, or payment, come at the same time.

About 5% of the transactions of a business in a given year affect neither income nor cash, but do affect two accounts on the balance sheet. We call these balance sheet adjustments. A stock dividend, for example, is a balance sheet adjustment because it affects neither income nor cash, but does affect capital and retained earnings.

In addition to a balance sheet, businesspeople generally receive an income statement. An income statement measures the non-cash part of transactions. This is important. You can't spend profit. The income statement records only the non-cash promises, commitments, and non-cash cost allocations you make to generate sales. It tells you half of the story of a business' activity.

Seeing only half of all transactions in a business is like trying to judge distance with one eye closed while shooting the rapids. It's never easy, and the closer you get to the big jagged rocks, the more distressing the imprecision becomes.

If you want to see both the non-cash and cash parts of transactions you've got to have a direct cash statement in addition to the income statement. The cash statement is the missing link in almost everybody's financial puzzle.

Don't confuse a real, true, and useful cash statement with a funds flow statement, also called "sources and uses" or "sources and applications of funds" statement. These statements simply subtract one balance sheet from another and present you with the difference. There are also hybrid statements out there that mix cash data with such non-cash data as depreciation. If you submit your taxes on the so-called "cash basis," you probably use your confusing hybrid statement for internal management purposes as well. It's treacherous going. You need a direct cash statement that shows what goes in and out of the bank.

Once you have a direct cash statement, you're ready to put the puzzle together—to see your business whole.

MCI Communications Corporation is the first company we have seen to publish a direct cash statement in their annual report. MCI did this for the first time in 1986, because, as then Chief Financial Officer Bill Conway put it, "We're on the leading edge." Bill has since gone on to become a partner in the Carlyle Group, a merchant bank based in Washington, D.C. He is convinced that Wall Street will become increasingly attuned to cash flow. Moreover, he says, "A business can recover from anything but running out of cash. You can handle a manufacturing mistake, even a regulatory mistake, but you can't run out of cash."

We agree that MCI is on the leading edge in financial reporting. To illustrate how the total financial system works, we've taken MCI's annual report for the fiscal year ending December 31, 1986 and formatted their financial data to make interconnections clear. All major accounts are here, shorn of supporting detail and free of the slowing underbrush of intermediate totals. (See page 165.)

The first column of the report shows MCI's balance sheet on December 31, 1985, which is also the beginning balance sheet for the fiscal year ending December 31, 1986. The second column, the balance sheet adjustment statement, shows the transactions that affected the balance sheet but did not affect income or cash. The third column, the income statement, shows all non-cash parts of transactions affecting income that took place during 1986. The sums of all cash parts of transactions fall into their categories in the fourth column, the cash statement. Column five shows the status of the property at the end of 1986, the ending balance sheet.

Vertically, the income statement adds and subtracts to yield net income at the bottom—the famous, or infamous, bottom line. The cash statement adds and subtracts vertically to show the net change in cash at the top of the cash statement. But note—and this is the beauty of this system—each line also adds and subtracts horizontally, so that you can easily see how each balance sheet item changed during the year because of activity in income, cash, and balance sheet adjustments.

Take accounts receivable. They totaled $422 million at the beginning of the year at MCI. Sales added $3,592 million to the money owed to MCI, but collections subtracted $3,513 million from the money owed. Due to acquisition, in 1986 MCI increased its receivables by $66 million shown as a balance sheet adjustment. So the new status of accounts receivable on December 31, 1986 was $567 million (422 + 66 + 3,592 − 3,513 = 567).

The horizontal flow-in-time picture of a business that this format highlights gives meaning to financial data. These are numbers you can do something about! Balance sheets and income statements are not divergent documents but subsets of the total financial system. The balance sheet adjustment and cash statements complete the system. Finance appears chaotic and unmanageable only until a system like this one makes sense of it. In the next chapter, we'll focus on how to manage each account in the system. But first, it's worthwhile to take a closer look at the meaning in each statement—each vertical column.

Mobley Matrix for MCI Corporation, 1986*

BEGINNING BALANCE SHEET 12/31/85		BALANCE SHEET ADJUSTMENTS		INCOME STATEMENT		CASH STATEMENT		ENDING BALANCE SHEET 12/31/86	
ASSETS								ASSETS	
CASH	853		0			CHANGE IN CASH	− 75	CASH	778
RECEIVABLES	422	ADJUSTMENT	+ 66	SALES	3592	COLLECTIONS	3513	RECEIVABLES	567
INVENTORY	0		0	COST-OF-GOODS-SOLD	0	PRODUCTION	0	INVENTORY	0
OTHER CURRENT	87		0	AMORTIZATION	33	PREPAYMENT	0	OTHER CURRENT	54
GROSS FIXED	4164	ADJUSTMENT	+ 164			INVESTMENT	956	GROSS FIXED	5284
ACCUM								ACCUM	
DEPRECIATION	1119	ADJUSTMENT	− 4	DEPRECIATION	451			DEPRECIATION	1574
NET FIXED	3045							NET FIXED	3710
OTHER LONG TERM	103	ADJUSTMENT	52	OTHER AMORT	6	OTHER INVESTMENT	0	OTHER LONG TERM	149
TOTAL ASSETS	4510	TOTAL ADJUST	278					TOTAL ASSETS	5258
LIABILITIES & NETWORTH								LIABILITIES & NETWORTH	
TAXES DUE	18	ADJUSTMENT	+ 51	TAXES	− 32	TAXES PAID	18	TAXES DUE	19
PAYABLES	767	ADJUSTMENT	− 353	EXPENSES	3546	DISBURSEMENTS	3037	PAYABLES	923
DEBT	2152	ADJUSTMENT	+ 165			BORROW/-PAYBACK	467	DEBT	2784
OTHER LIABILITIES	255	ADJUSTMENT	+ 39	OTHER EXPENSES	36	RECEIVE/-PAYBACK	− 60	OTHER LIABILITIES	270
CAPITAL	819	ADJUSTMENT	+ 376			PAID IN/-OUT	16	CAPITAL	1211
RETAIN EARNINGS	499		0	NET INCOME	− 448	DIVIDENDS	0	RETAIN EARNINGS	51
TOTAL LIAB & NW	4510	TOTAL ADJUST	278					TOTAL LIAB & NW	5258

The first column of the report shows MCI's balance sheet for 12/31/85. The second column, the balance sheet adjustment statement, shows the transactions that affected the balance sheet but not income or cash. The third column shows the income statement. The fourth column shows a direct cash statement. The balance sheet for 12/31/86 shows the status of MCI's property at the end of the year, given all of the activity during the year.

The income statement adds and subtracts vertically to show net income at the bottom of the income statement. The cash statement adds and subtracts vertically to show the net change in cash at the top of the cash statement. Each line also adds and subtracts horizontally, so that you can easily see how each balance sheet item was changed during the year because of income, cash, and balance sheet activity.

For example, take accounts receivable. At the beginning of the year, MCI's accounts receivable were $422 million. Sales added $3592 million to the money owed to MCI, but collections subtracted $3513 million from the money owed. Due to acquisition, in 1986 MCI increased its receivables by $66 million shown as a balance sheet adjustment. So the new status of accounts receivable on 12/31/86 was $567 million (422 + 66 + 3592 − 3513 = 567).

*Units: Millions.

The Balance Sheet—The "Where Gots" and the "Where Gones"

It took 400 years from the time that the church sanctioned private property until the corporation was invented. The corporation allows a group of people to own a collection of things. The relationship of people to things is called property and the record of property is called a balance sheet.

The balance sheet was the first accounting document to evolve. In the early days of mercantilism, investors in a ship and crew had a long wait for the eventual sale of the cargo, which, they hoped, would yield them a profit. Since human memory could not be depended on then any more than now, the law required a record of the status of property. The form of our present day balance sheets is much like those seawater-stained documents of the 1400s. Even now, in bad years, saltwater droplets occasionally appear on financial reports.

Balance sheets describe what things a company owns and who put up the money to get them. The things are called assets, and they are listed in order of liquidity. The people who put up the money are called, obscurely, liabilities and net worth, and they are listed in order of claim. Vendors yet to be paid, local and federal governments due money next April, stockholders, lending institutions—all of these groups provide money to acquire the assets of a company. This is property—the connecting of people to things. Balance sheets balance because the same dollars show up twice. Assets equal liabilities and net worth because the "where gots" equal the "where gones." What does MCI's beginning balance sheet on December 31, 1985 tell us? Look at each item.

> *Cash.* This is checkbook money. It can include marketable securities and other near-cash items. MCI shows $853 million in cash on their beginning balance sheet. Keeping too much cash in the bank is usually a sign that a company hasn't yet found a way to invest this cash productively in its business. Ideally, a company's cash balance is just large enough to prevent checks from bouncing.

> *Accounts Receivable.* This shows that MCI's customers owed them $422 million on December 31, 1985. The sales have been

made, but the cash has not been collected. If MCI's receivables get too high, they will be financing their customers and denying themselves the use of that cash. If their receivables get too low, customers will object that they are pressed too hard for payment. MCI's receivables are just right when they maintain happy customers with collections that are as fast as possible.

Inventory. MCI is an information age company. They have chosen to stay out of the business of manufacturing telecommunications equipment. They buy or rent what they need, but they don't sell hardware. MCI has no inventory. If a company has inventory, the balance sheet figure shows what it has paid for the inventory on hand. Inventory, of course, has not yet been sold. If inventory gets too high, the company will tie up too much cash in inventory; if it gets too low, they will miss deliveries. Theoretically, the best inventory is just-in-time.

Other current assets. These $87 million represent all of MCI's short-term assets that are not cash, receivables, or inventory. A prepaid insurance policy, for example, is an "other current asset."

Gross fixed assets. Also called property, plant, and equipment, this account shows the value of the long-term tangible things that MCI has acquired. These assets make up MCI's global communications network. Like inventory, fixed assets are valued on the balance sheet at what they originally cost. On MCI's beginning balance sheet, gross fixed assets are valued at $4,164 million. A company should not keep property just because it has it. The corporate leadership should be convinced that the property's current contribution to profit and cash is larger than the cost of keeping it. Otherwise it should be sold or written off.

Accumulated depreciation. When MCI bought the various pieces of property included in $4,164 million of gross fixed assets shown on the beginning balance sheet, it assumed that each piece of property would last for a number of years. So it only allocated a portion of the original cost of the property to the cost of doing business every year. The income statement shows that MCI allocated $451 million to the cost of doing business in 1986. In past years, MCI had depreciated a total of $1,119 million of the gross fixed assets. When you add accumulated depreciation to the $451 million and a write-off balance sheet adjustment of $4 million, you get a new accumulated depreciation on the ending balance sheet of $1,574 million.

Net fixed assets. Subtracting MCI's accumulated depreciation from its gross fixed assets gives $3,045 million of net fixed assets for the end of 1985.

Other assets. This figure shows the value of intangible things MCI has acquired that have a long-term value. Typical intangible assets are items such as start-up costs, patents, franchise acquisition costs, and goodwill. MCI's long-term intangible assets, mainly acquired rights for right-of-ways for fiber optic cables, cost $103 million up to December 31, 1985.

Taxes due. On December 31, 1985, MCI owed $18 million in taxes for the previous year. Lots of companies spend an inordinate amount of management time trying to avoid paying taxes. The tax tail shouldn't wag the company dog.

Accounts payable. MCI owes $767 million to vendors and employees for purchases or commitments not yet paid for on December 31, 1985. MCI should make sure that vendors are not unhappy—they are almost as important as employees. MCI is keeping vendors waiting in spite of a large cash balance with which they could pay those vendors. Keeping vendors waiting as long as possible is standard operating procedure in most American companies. Often, it is not a good strategy. Chapter Eleven, on financial strategy, shows why not.

Debt. This is the amount due to banks or other lending institutions or individuals. More and more, companies look to debt rather than equity for cash. This is a function of the relative cost of debt and equity, and a sign of our times. One reason debt is cheaper is that the government pays part of interest costs. How? Interest payments reduce net income and, there-fore, reduce taxes. We'll inspect both sources of capital—debt and equity—from several angles in the chapter on the economic environment. A company should be sure that it will be able to generate enough operating cash flow to cover new debt obli-gations. MCI's total debt on December 31, 1985 was $2,152 million.

Other liabilities. This is the value of obligations, short- and long-term, that will require satisfaction someday, excepting current taxes due, payables, and debt. Possible entries here are endless, the impact on operations generally small. Other liabilities could include deferred taxes, lease obligations, and pension fund reserves. MCI's other liabilities were $255 mil-lion as of December 31, 1985. Like debt and equity, this source of funds must be used productively because it carries a cost.

Capital. This is the amount stockholders—owners—served up in the hope of return some day, in the form of dividends, ap-preciation of the stock, or both. MCI has attracted $819 mil-lion from stockholders who were willing to risk their cash on MCI's future stream of earnings. Many companies today are buying back their own stock with cash they generate from op-erations. This stock is called treasury stock. Companies have been doing this because in recent years debt has been a much cheaper way to raise capital than has equity.

Retained earnings. So far, MCI's stockholders' risk has paid off. With that $819 million in capital that they invested in the business, MCI by December 31, 1985 had generated $499 mil-lion of retained earnings. Retained earnings represent the to-tal amount of net income (or losses) accumulated to date that has not been paid out in dividends. Stockholders of many young companies, like MCI, expect to see reward, not from dividends, but from a rising stock price. MCI, and companies like it who pay no dividends, can put maximum cash to work building their business. In 1986, MCI sat on its cash. As the cash statement shows, the firm paid no dividends.

There you have it—the structure of MCI's property on December 31, 1985. It's useful to know how you stand. Like the skeleton of our bodies, balance sheets give us something to hang a whole lot of activity on. As we said earlier, balance sheets were born in the era of mercantilism to protect outsiders looking into a business from insiders who might take advantage of them. Balance sheets were not designed to help decision-making insiders manage the transactions that make or break a business.

The Income Statement—
The Non-Cash Parts of Transactions

The first statement to evolve that attempted to record the process of conducting transactions was the income statement. With the rise of the large corporation in the twentieth century, we saw for the first time executives who were not owners of the companies they ran. They were managing businesses larger and more complex than the world had ever seen. These executives needed more information than balance sheets gave them. Absentee owners, meanwhile, wanted fuller disclosure of what went on in their companies than balance sheets offered. The income statement took a first step toward describing the activity and decisions within a business.

For a company's decision-makers, the income statement is not sufficient to manage the company, but it is a very important start. The income statement shows you the non-cash half of operating transactions. Seeing half of all your transactions is like having half a loaf—better than none, but don't invite the neighbors in for a party.

The income statement is useful because it lets you see how your long-term approach to business is netting out. It is an abstraction that attributes portions of decisions from the past and the present to the cost of generating sales revenue in one specific period. (Only in an abstraction can you have "portions of decisions.") The income statement answers the question, "What did our sales in this period cost us?"

Like all good abstractions, the income statement is simultaneously powerful and dangerous. It can give you a valuable insight into a complex reality. But if you don't know the parameters of the abstraction, you can follow your interpretation over a cliff. Of all the financial misinterpretations lying in wait for innocent non-financial businesspeople, the deadliest is confusing income with cash. Many signals lead us to believe income is something we can slap on the counter at the drugstore. Textbooks and courses tell us, "Dividends are paid out of income," "Income retained in the business is part of cash flow," "The company is so profitable, it should pay us higher wages." Dollar signs appearing next to the numbers on the income statement whisper "spendable" to many of us. But you can spend only cash. Cash is money that went into or came out of your bank account.

The income statement is a record of promises: for instance, expenses are promises that you'll pay your vendors cash someday; sales are promises that your customer will pay you cash someday. The income statement is also a record of how fast assets are being used. A dollar value on the income statement for depreciation, for instance, does not reflect any exchange of cash. It simply is a way to show how much value a tangible asset, such as a machine, has lost by being used during the period.

To explore more fully what the income statement tells us, and doesn't tell us, let's take a look at MCI's income statement, item by item, for the twelve-month period from December 31, 1985 to December 31, 1986.

Sales. This non-cash value, also called revenue, is the value of goods or services customers bought. This is the record of promises to pay. MCI's customers promised to pay $3,592 million during this period. When customers actually pay, the cash they send will appear as collections on MCI's cash statement. When there is a cash sale, the promise to pay shows up as a sale on the income statement, and the cash that changes hands shows up as a collection on the cash statement.

Cost-of-goods-sold (CGS). MCI does not have CGS because it has no inventory. Companies that sell inventory show cost-of-goods-sold on their income statement. This non-cash figure represents what came out of MCI's inventory during the year.

The original cost to a company of all items shipped during this period is CGS. Don't confuse CGS with additions to inventory, an account which is sometimes labelled "cost-of-goods." Confusing what went out with what went in leaves you mystified as to what you have. If the company's business is selling a product (as opposed to selling a service as MCI does), CGS becomes the most important figure to control. It determines, more than anything else, what profit will be.

Amortization and depreciation. These abstract concepts are the most difficult accounting inventions to understand. Say MCI makes an investment that is going to have value for some time, such as $100,000 for a communication unit (a fixed asset). MCI incurs this cost so that it can make or support sales. The cost must be spread over the years that the asset will be used. If the $100,000 communication unit is to last five years, then $20,000 will be allocated to each of these years as a cost of generating sales. This allocation is called depreciation. In fact, MCI will allocate the same amount every year if it chooses "straight line depreciation." It can also choose "accelerated depreciation," which assumes the machine loses more value in early years, and less in later years.

Conceptually, amortization and depreciation are the same. While depreciation covers tangible assets, amortization covers intangible assets, such as patents and copyrights. In both cases, a company pays cash to acquire something that will have value for several years. A portion of the original value of the asset will be subtracted from revenue each year. MCI's total amortization for its fiscal year ending December 31, 1986 was $33 million for other current assets and $6 million for long-term other assets. Its depreciation was $451 million.

Taxes. This amount is the taxes that a company expects to pay, given its profit for the period. MCI, because of a net loss of income, has no tax liability for 1986. Even better, they received a deferred income tax benefit that reduced their loss.

Expenses. These are promises MCI has made to pay vendors, employees, landlords, etc. These are typically the costs associated with the day-to-day operations of the company. During this period, MCI made promises to pay $3,546 million. Operating expenses divide into two classes. You ought to know how your chips fall. There are fixed expenses, also called G&A (general and administrative)—costs such as rent and executive salaries that don't vary with sales but vary with the size of the company measured by the value of its assets. There are variable expenses (also called "cost of sales") such as commissions or shipping costs, which do vary with sales volume in a given period. To manage these costs, you compare variable expenses to sales, and fixed expenses to assets. Chapter 11 covers this in depth.

Other expenses. This is a catchall for all expenses not listed elsewhere. It also accounts for income that doesn't come from operations, such as interest income, which is considered a negative expense. The $36 million showing on MCI's income statement as other expenses is the difference between its income from interest on its cash, and the interest paid on debt.

Net income. This is the non-cash measure of the newly created wealth of the company. MCI "took a bath" in 1986, losing $448 million. Taking a bath means that the company's leaders sacrificed profitability during this period for the sake of long-term goals. They restructured the company by eliminating unprofitable operations and acquiring more profitable ventures. This is gutsy in a world that demands quarter-to-quarter profit improvements.

Few non-executives realize that consistent striving for quarter-to-quarter profits severely limits a company's efforts to do anything bold or creative for the long-term health of the company. That $448 million took a big chunk out of MCI's retained earnings. Management decided it was best to get it all out of the way and show only a single year of what unsophisticated outsiders might view as "poor performance." As the chief financial officer put it, "When you take a bath you want to get very clean."

It can be argued that income information—"near-cash" as it is sometimes called—was adequate to run a company in the industrial age. In a stable world, if you make a decision and see what happens, and then make the same decision again and see similar results, and again and again, you can begin to manage simply from your feel for the way things work. But the world isn't stable anymore. You or your vendors or your customers can go into and out of business within a year.

The Cash Statement—The Missing Link

David Birch, M.I.T. professor and president of Cognetics, Inc., in Cambridge, Massachusetts, has compiled an eighteen-year history of 12 million businesses—how they formed, evolved, died. He shows that in any given region, 50% of all businesses in place in 1983 will have been replaced by different businesses by 1988: the "half-life" of a company is five years. Dun and Bradstreet reports that 61,232 businesses failed in 1986. Frequently, they were showing a profit at their demise. Most of them ran out of cash. Thousands more scaled back innovations-in-progress because they didn't have the cash to fund the R&D or marketing they once thought they could handle.

What the world needs now is cash information. Cash information is current. Cash doesn't reflect what things were worth five years ago. Cash information doesn't assume you can sell everything in your inventory tomorrow. Cash information tells lenders whether you can pay them back. Cash information tells you whether you can buy a truck today and still make payroll next week. And cash information is what lets you see that other half of your transactions.

When you can see both the non-cash and cash parts of transactions, both promise and fulfillment, commitment and settlement, you can manage the process of doing business. Recall the principle of equifinality, a fundamental tenet of general systems theory, which states that it doesn't matter so much where you start, the process you engage in is most important in determining where you end up. Cash and income information together tell the basic story of what went on in MCI during 1986.

Cash information is a black box for most businesspeople. Once you have it, you can make sense of your transactions and therefore control your business and create the ending position you want.

A direct cash statement, remember, chronicles what flows in and out of the bank. Since MCI shows a direct cash statement in their annual report for 1986, we can see MCI's whole story during 1986 for every balance sheet account. We see why the numbers changed from beginning position to ending position. For instance, we know from MCI's annual report that beginning accounts receivable was $422 million. Sales increased it during the year by $3,592 million. But collections decreased it by $3,513 million. MCI's balance sheet adjustment for receivables must have been +$66 million ($422 + x + 3,592 − 3,513 = 567; x = 66$). The same procedure holds for every other item on the balance sheet adjustment statement.

Here are the accounts on MCI's cash statement:

Change in cash. The change in cash results from subtracting all the cash paid out by MCI from all the cash collected by MCI. Positioned at the top of the cash statement, it accounts for the change in the cash balance from the beginning balance sheet to the ending balance sheet. This figure determines MCI's solvency. To survive, a business must be both profitable and solvent. MCI had a change in cash of minus $75 million that decreased its cash balance from $853 million to $778 million.

Collections. MCI collected $3,513 million in cash from customers during this year. This figure is usually a company's largest inflow of cash.

Production. This is all the cash that a company spends during a period to produce inventory. The big cash outlay for production is usually for direct labor. With no inventory, MCI has no production.

Prepayment. This is the most common cash transaction that increases other current assets. Sometimes there are advantages to paying early for something—you might get a discount, for instance. MCI prepaid nothing during this year.

Investment. This $956 million covers the cash purchases of fixed assets—the money MCI took out of its bank account to buy plant, property, or equipment. Every cash outlay for an investment should be made without studying its implications for payback, ROI, and cash flow.

Other investments. This is the cash a company spends during this period for long-term intangible assets, such as capitalized R&D or organization expense. It also covers the purchase of securities. MCI made no cash investments in long-term intangible assets.

Taxes paid. This is the total of all checks that pay any form of taxes. MCI paid the $18 million they'd accrued last year.

Disbursements. This covers all of the checks issued to MCI's vendors for previous purchases and others that had been carried as accounts payable. Also, a cash purchase is recorded here as well as in the sales account on the income statement. MCI paid out $3,037 million during this year.

Borrowing and payback of debt (shown on the cash statement as borrow/payback). This covers all the cash received during this period as a result of borrowing. It also covers cash MCI uses to pay off loans. This is a payback. MCI borrowed $467 million in cash this year.

Receiving other cash and payback of other liabilities (shown on the cash statement as receive/payback). This is cash received that creates a new liability and/or cash paid to discharge a liability. The net figure shown on MCI's cash statement is a $60 million payback. This number consists of a cash inflow from other income of $47 million subtracted from a cash outflow of $107 million interest on their debt.

Paid-in capital and paid-out capital (shown on the cash statement as paid in/out capital). This is cash received from or paid to stockholders which affect the company's capital holdings. MCI's capital was increased by $16 million from employees for stock ownership.

Dividends. This covers cash payments issued to stockholders as dividends. A cash withdrawal by owners would also be listed here. MCI paid no dividends during this year. Many stockholders today do not want dividends; they want appreciation when they sell their stock.

A statement that shows what cash came into and went out of your company is called a "direct cash statement." Without a direct cash statement, it is very difficult to manage your cash.

Cash flow management is extremely important.

The direct cash statement can be broken down into three types of accounts that cover the three basic categories of activity involving cash:

1. *Operating accounts.* These are the accounts that show the cash that flows in and out of your company as a result of the operations—your buying and selling activity. Cash flow from operations, also called operating cash flow (OCF), is the cash you generate internally in your business.

   MCI's operating accounts were: collections ($3,513 million), prepayment (0), taxes paid ($18 million), interest, which is a part of the receive/payback for other liabilities item ($107 million), and disbursements ($3,037 million). Production is also an operating account, but since MCI has no inventory, it has no production account. You can calculate MCI's operating cash flow (OCF) for the year by totalling these cash outflows and inflows. It was $351 million (3,513 − 18 − 3,037 − 107 = 351).

2. *Investing accounts.* These accounts cover the cash that you spend when you invest in tangible assets, such as a plant, property and equipment, and intangible assets, such as patents and copyrights.

   MCI's investing accounts are: investment in fixed assets ($956 million) and other investments ($0). MCI's cash outflow for investments is reduced by an inflow of cash of $47 million, which is accounted for in the receive/payback item on their cash statement. The $47 million is a cash inflow, which was subtracted from a cash outflow for interest of $107 million, resulting in the number you see in the receive/payback item on the cash statement of $60 million. MCI's investing cash flow (ICF) was $909 million (956 − 47 = 909).

3. *Financing accounts.* If you don't generate enough cash flow from your operations to cover all your operating and invest-

ing cash needs, you have to go outside for more cash. You have to take on debt or sell stock (equity). Cash you get from outside your company is called financing cash flow (FCF). MCI did not generate enough cash flow from operations to cover operating and investing activity, so the company chose to get financing to make up the difference. It could have drawn down its cash but decided to keep a large supply on hand because, as controller Doug Maine put it, "We want to be braced in case an opportunity for acquisition comes up. And you never want to get caught short of cash." MCI ended the year with a cash balance of $778 million. The accounts that represent MCI's financing activity are: borrow/payback of debt ($467 million), paid in/out capital ($16 million), and dividends ($0). MCI's financing cash flow totaled $483 million (467 + 16 = 483).

Knowing what your operating cash flow, investing cash flow, and financing cash flow are lets you manage cash flow in your business. Operating cash flow (OCF) is the lifeblood of a company. A business can get money in only three ways—operations, debt, and equity. As we said earlier, if you can't cover your operating cash needs and investing cash needs out of operating cash flow, you'll have to go outside for financing. But lenders and stockholders will let you have their money only if they are convinced you will be able to generate cash from operations over the long haul. Operating cash flow is the key.

MCI's summary cash flow for 1986 was investing cash flow ($909 million), minus operating cash flow ($351 million), minus withdrawal from cash ($75 million), equals financing cash flow ($483 million).

The Balance Sheet Adjustment Statement

The balance sheet adjustment statement is next to the beginning balance sheet in MCI's financial report. It covers those rare transactions that affect neither income nor cash but still affect the balance sheet.

In 1986, MCI executives did a lot of restructuring. They reduced their workforce by 15%; they consolidated their operations to position them for the post-equal-access market for telecommunications. These restructuring moves, together with the acquisition of Satellite Business Systems from IBM, account for practically all of the entries in the balance sheet adjustment column of MCI's financial report.

When a company restructures, it changes the numbers on its balance sheet. In an acquisition, values on the balance sheet of one company must be transferred to the balance sheet of the other company. When such transactions do not involve cash and do not affect income, they must be recorded on the balance sheet adjustment statement.

For example, MCI gave IBM $376 million worth of stock for Satellite Business Systems. This, together with $16 million of stock sold to MCI employees for cash, fully explains how MCI's capital increased from $819 million to $1,211 million (819 + 376 + 16 = 1211). MCI also acquired from IBM $66 million in receivables, and $52 million in other assets; both show as balance sheet adjustments for other assets.

The other items in MCI's balance sheet adjustment statement are summaries of adjustments to each account. The details of all the numbers that contributed to the summary numbers are explained in the notes of MCI's annual reports. We won't try to list them all here.

All balance sheet adjustments require that two entries be made in the balance sheet adjustment statement. This reflects the traditional concept of double entry bookkeeping. Insist that balance sheet adjustments be accompanied by footnotes whenever you are in a position to do so because most "creative accounting" takes place with balance sheet adjustments.

The Mobley Matrix

There you have it: all parts of MCI's financial story as they relate to each other—how they total up, net out, where value came from and where it went. Also, you follow the flow-in-time of MCI's transactions—how MCI got from there to here. You see both the structure of assets and liabilities and net worth, as well as the process of how they changed over time. The format is one of the tools I (Lou) developed to teach finance fast in the IBM Executive School. My students dubbed it The Mobley Matrix. I thought the name was rather catchy and kept it.

In this chapter, we've tried to make financial data easy to read and understand so that you can use it as the powerful management tool it can be. We've distilled the essence of a financial system. While we've used MCI's financial information as an illustration, the system applies to anybody who has a balance sheet. Each account we've defined will have supporting data. These subsystems are important. Somebody has to manage each of them, but nobody needs to get lost in them.

Like the report you get after your physical exam giving your weight, height, cholesterol level, triglyceride level, etc., a clear, concise and comprehensive financial report is only a beginning. It offers the opportunity to make smart decisions about future behavior. If you really understand what your health report is telling you, you won't glance at it, and then, elated or dejected, put it in the bottom drawer hoping for good results next year. You'll make decisions about how to eat, sleep, exercise—whatever—so you get the reports you want in the future. Likewise, a good financial report offers the opportunity to make astute decisions about future strategies.

Understanding what financial data means is the launching pad. The wild blue yonder is knowing what to do about it. See Chapter 11.

Chapter 10 Digest

In keeping with a bureaucratic mindset, the industrial age organization bred financial specialists. The treasurer watched cash. The controller watched income. The CEO kept an eye on the balance sheet, and tried to manage the business with input from the specialists. Fractionated data fed a fractionated management effort. That's not good enough anymore. The information age calls for generalists. Entrepreneurs have no choice but to know it all. A management team is most powerful if all its members understand the business whole. This chapter distills the essence of the financial system so that financial data can be used as powerful management tools.

Financial data interrelate. Like a jigsaw puzzle, if you know how to arrange the pieces, the big picture becomes immediately clear. Here's how the jigsaw works:

A balance sheet shows the structure of property at a specific time. It's like a snapshot. Annual reports display that snapshot for the beginning date and ending date of the fiscal year. During the period of time bracketed by two balance sheets in an annual report, a business engages in many transactions. Usually, a transaction will have two parts: a non-cash part, and a cash part. For example, a customer agrees to buy your product. That's a sale, and it is non-cash. Sometime later, perhaps thirty days later, the customer pays you. That's a collection, and it is cash.

An income statement shows the non-cash part of transactions. Of all the financial misinterpretations lying in wait for innocent nonfinancial businesspeople, the deadliest is confusing income with cash. You can't spend profit.

Seeing only half of all transactions in a business is like trying to judge distance with one eye closed while shooting the rapids. It's never easy, and the closer you get to the big jagged rocks, the more distressing the imprecision becomes. To see both the non-cash and cash parts of transactions you've got to have a direct cash statement, too.

A direct cash statement allows you to format financial information so you can easily see how each item in the balance sheet at the beginning of a period is affected by both income and cash parts of transactions to give you your new balance sheet at the end of the period. For example: beginning accounts receivable plus sales minus collections equals ending accounts receivable. This format was dubbed "the Mobley Matrix" by IBM executives. We use MCI's financial data to illustrate the Mobley Matrix system because MCI is on the leading edge in financial reporting: it publishes a direct cash statement in its annual report. (See MCI's Mobley Matrix financial report earlier in this chapter.)

The horizontal flow-in-time picture of a business that this format highlights gives meaning to financial data. These are numbers you can do something about!

◄ CHAPTER 11 ►

Financial Strategy— Managing and Planning Profit, Cash, and Assets

Once you have a coherent system for understanding what past financial data are telling you, you can ask, "What can I do about this in the future?"

You can fine-tune your financial system like you can fine-tune your car. A fine-tuned financial system is balanced and optimally efficient in achieving your purposes. In a balanced system, every piece of the system makes an appropriate contribution to the whole. In practical terms, this means that there is a "just right" number for every item in the system, as shown on the Mobley Matrix. No item should be too large or too small.

You're dealing with a complex system. The Matrix shows sixty numbers. Each column in the Matrix must be managed, as well as each horizontal line, as well as each individual item. This chapter will tell you how to optimize each piece of the total financial system of a business.

The Mobley Matrix computer program described at the end of this chapter is a financial management and planning tool that allows you to decide on the "just right" numbers quickly and easily with the help of your personal computer. The management considerations that you must weigh, covered in this chapter, are vital whether you have electronic help or not. We describe a bit of the math (some of it separated out as figures so you can study it or not, as you choose) should you not have software to do it for you.

The story of People Express Airline displays as vividly as any company's story in recent memory how unbalanced financial strategies can do you in. Stellar performance in some areas of People Express not only failed to compensate for sub-optimum performance in other areas, but actually contributed to the instability of the total system.

In a nutshell, here's the financial story of People Express, taken directly from its annual reports from 1982 to 1985 and processed through the Mobley Matrix program.

Don Burr, CEO of People Express, was a marketing whiz. His formidable marketing effort generated more than a 70% average increase in sales revenue for each of his last three full years in business. But to generate these sales, he bought more airplanes. To buy more airplanes, he borrowed more money, and to service those sales and that debt, his operating expenses mushroomed so that his profit and cash flow were inadequate to keep the business aloft for the long haul.

In 1984, People Express spent $240 million on additional planes but generated only $6 million in operating cash flow. So Don Burr sold $92 million in additional stock, borrowed $95 million, and drew down $49 million from his cash balance. In 1985, he bought an additional $187 million of flight equipment on borrowed money, increasing his total outstanding debt by the end of 1985 to half a billion dollars. In the two-year period, maintenance costs rose from $8 million to $121 million. All operating expenses rose from 82% of sales in 1983 to 86% in 1984 to 89% in 1985. Interest expense on debt rose from $10 million in 1983 to $60 million in 1985.

What could Don Burr have done differently? Like most executives, he probably did not have financial tools that allowed him to run his business as a total system. If he had, he would have seen that a 4.3% improvement in cost control in 1984 could have turned the tide for People Express.

We'll use this circumstance in People Express's story to illustrate how you can target the top-level economic goals of a business so all other goals make sense. If Don Burr had been able to create and execute a balanced plan in 1984, the story of People Express could have been dramatically different. The key to making a balanced plan is an understanding of the meaning of ROI (return on investment) and its marketing and cost control components.

ROI—More Than a Report Card

ROI is often thought of as a report card—an accomplished fact that you have to live with. Report cards can be gratifying if you're doing well, and they can indicate areas of weakness. Otherwise they're useless. To relegate ROI to the same category is a waste. ROI can tell you faster than any other measure the relative emphasis you've been placing on the two largest jobs in running a business: marketing (deciding what's worth doing), and controlling cost (getting things done). Furthermore, charting this year's ROI can help you to determine the optimum way to get to your ROI target for next year.

The formula for ROI (or net assets) is:

$$\frac{net}{sales} \times \frac{sales}{assets} = \frac{net}{assets}$$

Net/sales measures how much profit you can squeeze from gross revenue—your cost control effort. Sales/assets measures your marketing effort—how much sales you can generate, given the total resources of your business.

Note the ROI chart for People Express shown on page 185. The points connected by solid lines on the chart show People Express's actual ROI performance in 1982, 1983, and 1984. In 1985 its ROI went negative and plummeted off the chart.

Net/sales is plotted vertically, on the left side of the chart. Sales/assets is plotted horizontally, on the bottom. The curved lines on the charts show various ROIs; they're calculated by plotting the products of all the combinations of net/sales and sales/assets that result in those ROIs. For instance, a net/sales of 8% times a sales/assets of 1.25 gives an ROI of 10%; so does a net/sales of 5% times a sales/assets of 2; so does net/sales of 4% times a sales/assets of 2.5.

When People Express's performance in cost control and market-

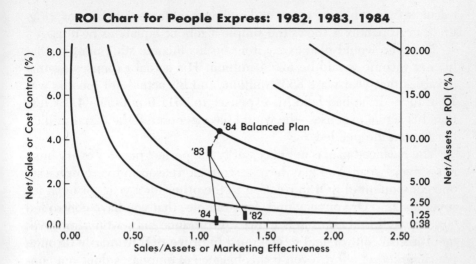

ROI Chart for People Express: 1982, 1983, 1984

ing effectiveness is plotted, a single point shows their net/sales, their sales/assets, and their ROI. For example, in 1984, their net/sales was .34% and sales/assets was 1.1. So their ROI was .38%.

How to Make a Balanced Plan

The dotted line on the chart shows what a balanced plan for People Express for 1984 would have looked like. It would have been the optimum way to achieve an ROI of 5%, with just the right emphasis on marketing, and just the right emphasis on cost control. How could Don Burr have plotted, and then achieved, a balanced plan goal?

First, he would have plotted his 1983 ROI of 3.68% on the chart. Then he would have drawn the shortest possible line to a desirable ROI curve for the next year. We show him aiming for an ROI of 5%. This point represents a net/sales of 4.5% (as opposed to the .34% he actually achieved) and a sales/assets of 1.1 (which he actually did achieve in 1984.)

Next, he would make a sales forecast. Assume his sales forecast for 1984 was $587 million, which is what his actual sales turned out to be. (Remember, Don Burr is very good at marketing and he probably makes accurate sales forecasts.) He could now, using simple algebra, calculate his net income target and ending asset target for the year. (Figure 9 in Appendix A shows the simple algebraic equations he'd use.)

Next, he would plan every item on his income statement so that his net income would be $26.4 million. His actual expenses against payables that year were $535 million, and his actual net income was $2 million. If he had held his expenses to $511.6 million—4.3% less than his actual expenses—he would have generated the $26.4 million net income he needed.

The balanced plan is not necessarily the perfect plan for every business, every year. You may have a strategic reason to overemphasize one component of ROI in relation to the other for a year, or even for several years. Or you may find, for example, that you have controlled costs so well that enormous effort can produce only a tiny improvement in cost control, and so you must improve ROI primarily through your marketing effort, even if this balance of emphases does not constitute a balanced plan on your ROI chart.

But the first cut—plotting what the balanced plan would be, and calculating what it would take to get there—is a pivotal exercise for anyone planning a business.

The point of this illustration is not to criticize Don Burr. His marketing effort was exemplary. His leadership experiment was bold and distinctive. Most executives today are not equipped with comprehensive financial tools and knowledge, and this lack undercuts their other skills, their energy, and their vision.

IBM has used numerous tools over the years to hone financial performance. The balanced plan is one of them. In the early 1950s, I (Lou) had attended an American Management Association meeting where the treasurer of Du Pont made public the formula for ROI (hence its name "the Du Pont formula"). Impressed with the usefulness of the formula, I nonetheless took issue with the assumption implicit in the formula that marketing and cost control deserve equal emphasis. The formula implied that both net/sales and sales/assets were multiplied by a factor of 1. I developed the ROI chart in 1956 to show that, as in Don Burr's case, sometimes a company must place greater emphasis on one component of ROI or the other. Using the chart in the Executive School, I could communicate to executives the concept that they could quantify the relationship between cost control and marketing and keep those two management efforts in balance.

IBM financial executives started using the chart for management purposes. They preferred to compare net income before interest and taxes to invested capital. Figure 10 in Appendix A shows IBM's ROI calculated according to the financial executive's definition of return on investment for ten years. Note how ROI gyrated before 1957, the year in which IBM began to insist that all divisions submit balanced plans.

IBM also plotted every publicly held company in the country, by industry, on the ROI chart. We learned that there is a life pattern of a company on the ROI chart. A young company starts out by making great strides in marketing; then, for a few years, its plans tend to be balanced, as the company matures. As the company settles into its niche, becoming less aggressive in its marketing or less innovative in its product or service, marketing effectiveness drops off. The company tries to stay profitable by squeezing costs. Finally, it loses control of costs and ROI declines, often rapidly.

Since IBM was aware of this pattern, we were able to detect when our ROI was beginning to loop backwards. Twice we deliberately made massive shifts in policy to reverse the pattern and keep our ROI moving up and to the right on the ROI chart. IBM still considers what a balanced plan would be when evaluating financial plans.

How to Set Meaningful Financial Plans

There are two fundamental considerations in setting meaningful financial plans that we have yet to tackle. The first is how to decide which ROI curve to go for.

In the long run, you want your return on investment, or return on capital, to be greater than your cost of capital (or your cost of investment). Like a bank that must lend dollars at a higher rate than it pays for its money, your business ought to produce more with its resources than it pays for its resources. If you find, for instance, that your cost of capital is 10% and the ROI you can generate is only 8%, you might be better off liquidating your business and lending money at 10%.

The second fundamental consideration in setting meaningful financial plans is how to optimize each figure on each line on the Mobley

Matrix to achieve a net income objective, while generating enough cash to be solvent. An example follows.

Herschell Doss, owner of Treeko Electronics, Inc., in Ellicott City, Maryland, uses a Mobley Matrix to scrutinize and plan each piece of his business. He plots ROI to make decisions about highest level financial goals. We'll walk through the executive considerations—applicable to any business—for optimizing each line on the Matrix. We'll use Herschell's financial data for 1986 (Figure 11 in Appendix A) and his ROI chart showing 1984, 1985, 1986 (Figure 12 in Appendix A) to illustrate the management process. We'll explain each continuity equation that is used in the Matrix. A continuity equation specifies a beginning position, the changes to that position, and the resulting ending position. It identifies the factors that cause a status to change over a period of time.

Herschell's industry, wholesale electronics, was in the worst slump in its history from 1983 through 1986, and low-priced foreign competition still shows no sign of letting up. So Herschell is carving a niche in the marketplace that foreign competition doesn't threaten: he adds value to his products by assembling components into sub-assemblies, by testing, and by packaging the sub-assemblies for his customers. As a result, his business grew about 20% in 1986, and has stayed in the black, while most of his competitors are awash in red ink.

To make a plan for 1987, Herschell first looked at his ROI for the prior three years. During 1985, his efforts in marketing and cost control suffered. His ROI dropped from 10% at the end of 1984 to 4% at the end of 1985. In 1986, he held his costs and profit and almost regained his marketing effectiveness of 1984, but ROI barely changed, still hovering around 4%. Interestingly, with all this sales improvement, ROI was barely influenced. Herschell saw that in 1987 he would have to focus on improving profitability. He turned his attention to bottom-line management.

Herschell looked at his cost of capital. He divided his interest expense of $41,000 by his average debt for 1985 and found that the cost of his debt capital was 10%. (His actual cost of debt was somewhat less because of tax deductions for interest.) He decided to target a 10% ROI performance for 1987 in order to at least equal the cost of his capital.

To achieve a balanced plan, it was apparent that practically all of his improvement had to be in cost control for 1987. Using the DuPont formula, Herschell calculated that his sales/assets would have to be 2.86, which was almost identical to his previous year's marketing performance. In order to achieve his 10% ROI, his net/sales would have to be 3.5%.

Herschell made a sales forecast. Nothing in his or any company's financial statements gives this figure. Together with his marketing manager, Herschell made a complete market plan and determined that 1987 sales would be $3 million.

Now, using the same simple math we illustrated with People Express's financial data, Herschell calculated that his net income would have to be $105,000 and his assets for the year would have to average $1,049,000. To achieve such average assets, his ending assets would have to be $1,090,000. To be solvent, his ending cash balance on the top line of his balance sheet could decline by not more than his beginning cash balance of $30,000. He now had the framework within which he could hammer out a detailed set of meaningful financial goals.

Herschell constructed each horizontal line of his Matrix, keeping in mind that his pro forma income statement had to show a net income of $105,000, and his pro forma cash statement had to show a net change in cash of, at worst, −$30,000. However, Herschell doesn't want to play it that tight. He wants a minimum cash balance of $25,000.

For the first line of his planned Matrix, the continuity equation, which adds and subtracts all of the items that affect the beginning balance sheet items and yields the ending balance sheet item, is as shown in the table below.

Beginning Balance Sheet	Balance Sheet Adjustments	Income Statement	Cash Statement	Ending Balance Sheet
Cash			− Change in cash	= Cash
30,000			− 5000	= 25,000

Next, Herschell focused on accounts receivable.

Having determined that sales would lift his beginning receivables of $288,000 by $3,000,000, he decided that collections of $3,005,000 (slightly more than his sales) would give him an acceptable ending receivables of $283,000.

Herschell decided to speed up collections by offering customers an incentive to pay quickly—a 2% discount in 10 days, net 30. A customer who waits the full 30 days to pay is, in effect, paying an annual rate of 36% on the money for the extra 20 days.

Herschell figured that his collection strategy would reduce his receivables turnover from 37.6 days to 34.7 days—a modest and reasonable improvement. He wanted the number of days in his collection period to be large enough so he wouldn't lose customers, and small enough so he wouldn't run out of cash.

Like the turnover of water in a bathtub, turnover of a financial account depends on average throughput and average balance. If a tub contains water, and water can flow in and out of the tub, the turnover of water in the tub depends on the amount of water in the tub as well as the throughput in and out of the tub. For example, economists know that a given amount of money in the economy will produce twice as large a GNP if it circulates twice as fast. Figure 13 in Appendix A describes the "Bathtub Theorem," and details the calculations for turnover strategies.

The continuity equation for Herschell's accounts receivables is shown in the table below.

Beginning Balance Sheet	Balance Sheet Adjustments	Income Statement	Cash Statement	Ending Balance Sheet
Accounts receivable		+ Sales	− Collections	= Accounts receivable
288,000		+ 3,000,000	− 3,005,000	= 283,000

Next, Herschell considered inventory.

For executives of most companies selling a product, inventory is the most baffling account to manage. Volumes are written on inventory control. Most of the issues they cover are important from an accounting standpoint but are not pivotal for strategic decision-making.

You have three fundamental considerations in the overall management of inventory: what goes into inventory (called additions to inventory or cost of inventory), what goes out of inventory (cost-of-goods-sold), and what level of inventory to maintain (the ending inventory position on the balance sheet).

You can add to inventory in only three ways—you can make inventory, you can buy it, or you can "burden" it with manufacturing overhead expenses.

When you make your product, you pay cash to the employees who do the work. This cash outlay is called direct labor, or production, and it appears on the cash statement.

When you buy inventory—whether it is raw materials, subcomponents, or finished goods—you are likely to buy it on credit. This transaction doesn't affect cash (after all, you haven't paid for it yet) and it doesn't affect income (you also haven't sold it yet). You have one of those rare balance sheet adjustments. A credit purchase affects two balance sheet accounts—it increases inventory and it increases accounts payable.

When you "burden" into inventory certain expenses, such as rent, heat, insurance, or depreciation on production equipment, you don't put these expenses on your income statement. Instead, you create balance sheet adjustments that increase inventory and accounts payable. This is called "capitalizing" expenses into inventory, and it is like having your cake and eating it too—for a while. Allocating costs in this manner does not reduce profit until inventory is sold, and it does not reduce cash until purchased goods are paid for. CEOs strapped for cash often don't mind capitalizing expenses into inventory. They can then borrow against the heftier tangible assets.

The cost-of-goods-sold (CGS), which is what is subtracted from inventory because of sales in a given period, cannot be managed directly. By the time CGS appears on your income statement, your key decisions have already been made. CGS is the result of how much you sold (which you generally maximize) and how much you paid for the inventory when you acquired or produced it. If you want to lower CGS in the future, you must make or buy your inventory more cheaply today.

The make/buy decision was crucial for Herschell. By spending cash on direct labor (production) to build sub-assemblies, Herschell adds value to his product. This tactic is defining his healthy niche. The value-added products also generate profit. Herschell planned to double the amount he would spend assembling components. So he projected $420,000 for production.

Herschell wanted to let his inventory level rise in proportion to his sales growth, so he projected an ending inventory of $540,000. Herschell estimated that his value-added approach would modestly improve his CGS/sales strategy, from 70% to 69%. With this he calculated his projected CGS to be $2,070,000. Having established beginning and ending inventory positions, and with CGS calculated, Herschell then completed the continuity equation. He would purchase $1,680,000 of inventory during the year. The continuity equation for inventory is shown in the table below.

Beginning Balance Sheet	Balance Sheet Adjustments	Income Statement	Cash Statement	Ending Balance Sheet
Inventory	+ Credit purch.	− Cost-goods-sold	+ Production	= Inventory
510,000	+ 1,680,000	− 2,070,000	+ 420,000	= 540,000

With this set of numbers, Herschell's inventory turnover would be slightly improved, from 96.5 days to 91.9 days.

Next, Herschell turned to the line for other current assets. Other current assets, as the name implies, is a catch-all—a miscellaneous category for any current asset that is not cash, accounts receivable, or inventory. Current assets, also called operating accounts, are those assets which you expect will become cash within one year.

Bankers and other financial institutions like to see current assets separated from long-term assets, and to see them compared to current liabilities. Current assets minus current liabilities equal working capital. Note that working capital is made up mostly of non-cash values. You can't actually spend working capital, any more than you can spend profit. The only cash in working capital is shown as the cash balance on the top line of the balance sheet. The non-cash accounts that make up working capital are operating transactions that are not yet complete. Examples are accounts receivable, which show sales not yet collected, and accounts payable, which show expenses not yet paid.

The most common other current asset is prepaid expenses. Other current assets can also include short-term intangible assets, such as a loan to an officer of the company. While some other current assets are not amortized—a loan to an officer would not be amortized because it is not a cost of doing business—most other current assets will require amortization.

On the balance sheet, Herschell's beginning other current assets of $14,000 was a loan to an officer. During the year, he planned to prepay $2,000 for an insurance policy, which he would amortize in 1988, and let the loan to the officer stand. His ending other current asset position would be $16,000. The continuity equation for this line is shown in the table below.

Beginning Balance Sheet	Balance Sheet Adjustments	Income Statement	Cash Statement	Ending Balance Sheet
Other current assets		– Amortization	+ Prepayment	– Other current assets
14,000			+ 2,000	= 16,000

The major strategy to consider regarding fixed assets is how much new investment should be made in property, plant, and equipment. Fixed assets are long-term commitments to productivity. You must have operating cash flow (OCF), or get cash through debt or equity, in order to pay for a fixed asset. But having the cash to pay for an asset is only part of your decision. You must be convinced that your new fixed asset will give you a greater profit return than the cost of the money you paid to get it. Sophisticated companies, using analyses like discounted cash flow, try to make sure that an investment will generate enough additional cash flow to cover its cost.

If an asset does not adequately contribute to sales, given its cost of maintenance and depreciation, it should be written off. If it can be sold, so much the better. The sale can create "other income" for the company. A write-off is a balance sheet adjustment. The two balance sheet accounts affected by the write-off are gross fixed assets and accumulated depreciation.

Writing off fixed assets can improve ROI. The ROI for a given net income will go up if assets go down, since the denominator of the net/assets ratio gets smaller in relation to the numerator. This insight is particularly significant in view of the massive liquidation of fixed assets in many American companies over the past decade as we've moved toward an information economy. Companies that liquidate their fixed assets reduce their total assets. This permits them to generate a smaller net income and still show a reasonable ROI.

Herschell has a long-term strategy of gradually increasing his rate of investment in fixed assets; he is purchasing equipment that allows him to do more and more value-added work. In keeping with this strategy, he increased his investment for 1987 to 9% of his total assets of $1,090,000. The dollar figure would be $91,000. His gross fixed assets were to rise to $365,000. Herschell believes that this cash outlay of $91,000 could be financed from operating cash flow (OCF) so that he would not have to borrow or sell stock to stay solvent.

The continuity equation for the year is shown in the table below.

Beginning Balance Sheet	Balance Sheet Adjustments	Income Statement	Cash Statement	Ending Balance Sheet
Gross fixed assets			+ Investment	= Gross fixed assets
274,000			+ 91,000	= 365,000

At the beginning of 1987, Herschell's total gross fixed assets were $274,000, of which $129,000 had been depreciated in previous years as a cost of doing business. Therefore, his net fixed assets at the beginning of 1987 were $145,000. Treeko Electronics' depreciation schedule showed that an additional $43,000 must be charged against income for depreciation. That would increase Herschell's accumulated depreciation by the end of the year to $172,000.

Depreciation schedules must be carefully thought through, because they more or less lock in the depreciation costs for many future years. Depreciation schedules that accelerate depreciation in the early years will hurt profit in those early years but will help it in later years. You might choose this strategy if, for instance, you have a young company and need cash but don't need to show profit to impress investors. If you accelerate depreciation, you'll show less profit in the early years. You'll therefore accrue lower taxes in the early years when you need the additional cash. Straight line depreciation spreads the impact on profit equally over the total life of the asset.

Herschell's continuity equation for accumulated depreciation is shown in the table below.

Beginning Balance Sheet	Balance Sheet Adjustments	Income Statement	Cash Statement	Ending Balance Sheet
Acc. dep.		+ Depreciation		= Acc. dep.
129,000		+ 43,000		= 172,000

Since "other assets" is a catchall category for long-term assets that are not plant property and equipment, a variety of management considerations apply to this line on the Matrix.

Long-term investments, the most common other assets, can be a tantalizing distraction. Be careful how you use your company's resources to engage in business different from your own. If you invest in another company, you assume it will make a higher return than you can by investing your cash in your own business. In making a long-term investment decision, you want to ask yourself if you really want to spread your resources and be an investor or if you would do better concentrating all of your assets in maximizing the returns of your business.

Patents, copyrights, and trademarks—common other assets—have ongoing, long-term value; otherwise, you would not have developed them or bought them. But they do not have permanent value, and so must be amortized.

Capitalizing organization expenses is helpful when your company is getting started. Instead of expensing the costs of startup and organization on your income statement, many of these expenses can be put on the balance sheet as other assets which can be amortized over a number of years. There are several advantages to capitalizing organization expenses if you need to attract outside capital. You reduce the expenses on your income statement and show a higher profit at a time when sales are small and you need to show all the profit you can. When your sales increase, you can cover your amortization costs, continue to show a profit when your sales are good, and recover the cash you laid out in the startup years at a time when you can use the cash for expansion.

Goodwill is another intangible asset. It arises as the result of your acquiring another company. If you pay more for the company than the book value of its tangible assets, you recapitalize the assets, meaning you must make the balance sheet reflect the value you paid for the company. You put value on each of the assets of the company you acquire. If the sum of the values of the new assets doesn't equal what you paid for the company, the difference is capitalized as goodwill. Like other intangible assets, goodwill must be amortized over time.

Industrial companies have typically carried heavy amounts in their fixed asset account for property, plant, and equipment. As more companies become service or information companies, a larger share of their assets become intangible assets. Intellectual property is slowly being defined as a legal concept. We can expect lively debate and considerable change in the near future regarding the theory and practice of valuing intangible assets in financial statements.

For Herschell, other long-term assets at the beginning of 1987 meant one item—an investment in a municipal bond, which won't be amortized. He planned to make no investments in other assets during the year. The continuity equation for other long-term assets is shown in the table below.

Beginning Balance Sheet	Balance Sheet Adjustments	Income Statement	Cash Statement	Ending Balance Sheet
Other long-term assets		− Other amort.	+ Other invest.	= Other long-term assets
21,000		− 0	+ 0	= 21,000

"Taxes due" is usually the first item on the list of liabilities. This is because the government has first claim on your assets. The taxes you accrue for this year whack your net income; the taxes you pay this year for last year's obligation whack your cash.

For planning purposes, Herschell assumed that his total tax obligation would continue to be a little more than half of his net income. He planned to pay the $14,000 from the previous year's tax obligation and accrue $58,000 in 1987.

The continuity equation for taxes is shown in the table below.

Beginning Balance Sheet	Balance Sheet Adjustments	Income Statement	Cash Statement	Ending Balance Sheet
Taxes due		+ Taxes	− Taxes paid	= Taxes due
14,000		+ 58,000	− 14,000	= 58,000

To manage accounts payable, you must ride herd on the transactions that increase payables: expenses, credit purchases to inventory, and manufacturing overhead. You must also control the one transaction that reduces payables: disbursements.

It is useful to keep your variable expenses (also called cost of sales) separate from your fixed expenses. You need to know what you are spending on such items as advertising, commissions, and shipping costs so that you can evaluate the sales you are getting compared to the effort you are expending to get them. To know the relation between your variable expenses and sales for each period, watch the ratio: variable expenses/sales.

You pay your fixed overhead expenses like rent, insurance, and heat whether you make sales or not. These expenses tend to grow with the size of your business. For this reason, watch the ratio: fixed expenses/assets.

We covered credit purchases and manufacturing overhead when we dealt with the inventory line. If you make credit purchases or burden inventory with manufacturing overhead, you'll show these amounts on your balance sheet adjustment statement.

How long you wait to pay your bills has enormous impact on your cash as well as on your vendors' cash. Pay too quickly, and you may have an excessive cash drain before you collect from your customers; pay too late and you may create unhappy vendors. Vendors can be almost as important to your company as employees. Keep on top of the delicate balance by watching your payables turnover, or pay period. The average pay period in days can be calculated from the same type of formula used to calculate the collection period for receivables and inventory turnover.

Don't fall prey to conventional wisdom that says always pay vendors as slowly as possible. If you have plenty of cash and want to improve vendor relations, it's best to speed up disbursements. In addition, you reduce your total assets by spending the cash, thereby boosting your ROI.

Analyzing his fixed and variable expense strategies, Herschell decided that a modest improvement in both his fixed and his variable expenses would give him an expense target of $680,000 for the upcoming year. The combination had to be just right. Since he already had determined in his inventory plan that credit purchases would add $1,680,000 to inventory, his total payables would increase by $2,386,000. Projecting total cash disbursements against payables for 1987 of $2,427,000, Herschell determined that this would not be too great a drain on his cash and, at the same time, he could decrease his payables from $240,000 to $173,000. By paying off more bills than he added, he could shrink his pay period from 34.3 days to 26.8 days. By paying out the additional cash and cutting down his payables, he diminishes his ending assets (as well as ending liabilities and net worth). Paring assets improves his ROI.

The continuity equation for payables is shown in the table below.

Beginning Balance Sheet		Balance Sheet Adjustments		Income Statement		Cash Statement		Ending Balance Sheet
Payables	+	Credit purch.	+	Expenses	−	Disbursements	=	Payables
240,000	+	1,680,000	+	680,000	−	2,427,000	=	173,000

Debt is one of two sources of external cash for your company; the other equity.

The only time you need to borrow is when you do not generate enough cash through operations to invest in your company. This is usually true for a new company and may be true for any company with seasonal downswings in cash flow requiring additional working capital or for a company wanting to make a large investment in plant or equipment. For operating cash a short-term note might suffice; for fixed assets a long-term debt secured by the assets might work. But always the lender must be convinced that your future cash flow from operations can pay the interest and principal when due.

If you have to go outside your company for cash, the best way to decide between the debt route and the equity route is to pick the cheaper. Borrow more money, if that gives you the smallest cost of capital; sell stock, if the cost of that capital is less. By going whichever route is cheaper, you will move toward a balanced capital structure in which a new increment of capital would cost the same whether you get it through debt or equity. This is a happy circumstance because you can then use other criteria to make your decision about which route to go. Perhaps, for example, you want to sell stock and spread ownership around to avoid takeover. Or maybe you'd prefer to take on more debt to leverage your equity. A balanced capital structure allows you to choose either debt or equity comfortably.

To calculate the current incremental cost of debt (what debt will cost if you go for it today), look at the market value of your bonds and the interest rates those bonds are carrying.

$$\text{Cost of debt} = \frac{\text{interest per year}}{\text{market value of bond}}$$

If all of your debt is bank debt, look at your interest rate. Remember that interest is deductible so that the government pays some of your interest.

To calculate the current incremental cost of equity (what equity will cost if you go for it today), take the reciprocal of your price/earnings ratio:

$$\text{Cost of equity} = \frac{\text{net income per year}}{\text{market value of stock}}$$

With the projections Herschell made for the other accounts on his cash statement, he concluded that he would generate enough cash internally so that he would not have to borrow additional money to support his sales growth. He is financing company's expansion both in sales and long-term assets out of operating cash flow.

Herschell's continuity equation for debt is shown in the table below.

Beginning Balance Sheet	Balance Sheet Adjustments	Income Statement	Cash Statement	Ending Balance Sheet
Debt			+ Borrow/ −payback	= Debt
405,000			+ 0	= 405,000

The income and cash accounts that affect other liabilities frequently are used to record transactions that are not related to the usual categories on the income statement and cash statement. For example, "other income" that comes from interest you earn on money market funds or investment in other companies should not be included in your sales account. It is common for accountants to show other income as a negative expense to separate it from sales. Also, interest paid on debt is so important that you may not want to bury it in your payables account. By showing that interest as an "other expense" you isolate it for special attention.

Herschell showed no other liabilities at the beginning of 1987. During the year, he would pay $44,000 of interest on his debt. This obviously would be a cost of doing business, and so it shows as a cost against income. It would also be a cash outlay during 1987, and so would show on the cash statement.

The continuity equation for other liabilities is shown in the table below.

Beginning Balance Sheet	Balance Sheet Adjustments	Income Statement	Cash Statement	Ending Balance Sheet
Other liab.		+ Other exp.	+ Receive/ −payback	= Other liab.
0		+ 44,000	− 44,000	= 0

Herschell owns all the stock in his company. His operating cash flow (OCF) will cover his operating and investing activity, and he plans to sell no stock.

Capital takes many legal forms. Common stock is bought by those seeking a claim to the future stream of earnings of the company. Preferred stock may be sold to stockholders who want more certain cash income with less risk. Other legal categories of capital include paid-in capital, non-voting stock, capital surplus, and treasury stock. They are all capital. The categories simply define various ownership rights of stockholders.

You sell stock if operating cash flow doesn't cover your operations or expansion cash requirements, and if equity is cheaper than debt for you.

Herschell's continuity equation for capital is shown in the table below.

Beginning Balance Sheet	Balance Sheet Adjustments	Income Statement	Cash Statement	Ending Balance Sheet
Capital			+ Paid in/ −out	= Capital
35,000			+ 0	= 35,000

You manage the non-cash component of retained earnings by controlling every item on the income statement to give you the net income you want.

Your cash dividend strategy depends on what kind of stockholders you attract. Many older people depend on cash dividends and hold stock in companies that pay them. If your company has lots of these stockholders, you will feel great pressure to keep dividends coming.

On the other hand, investors who have lots of cash coming in, such as executives with good salaries, want their stake to appreciate—above all, they don't want more cash to pay taxes on. They're quite happy to let you keep the cash in the business, as long as they see the value of their investment going up.

As usual, Herschell planned to pay no cash dividends to himself. Since his profit objective for 1987 was $105,000, his retained earnings at the end of the year would be $419,000.

The continuity equation for Herschell's retained earnings is shown in the table below.

Beginning Balance Sheet	Balance Sheet Adjustments		Income Statement	Cash Statement		Ending Balance Sheet
Ret. earn.		I	Net income	Dividends	=	Ret. earn.
314,000		+	105,000	– 0	=	419,000

When Herschell put the continuity equation for each line on his balance sheet together in one statement, he had the whole story of his business in front of him.

He totaled up his income statement to see that his net income was on target. It was. Had it not been, he would have gone back to see where he could cut costs further. If that were not possible, he would have re-evaluated his ROI target and his marketing plan.

Next, Herschell tallied up his cash statement. His net change in cash would be $7000, giving him a cash balance at the end of the year of $37,000. His cash turnover for the year would be 4.1 days, which means that if he failed to put money in the bank every 4.1 days, he would run out of cash. Herschell felt that 4.1 days was a comfortable term.

If Herschell's plan had not generated enough cash to stay solvent, he would have gone back and re-thought every line on his cash statement, considering whether he could collect more, disburse less, borrow money, or sell stock. Herschell's complete plan is shown on page 203.

The planning technique that Herschell used for 1987 contrasts sharply with the usual methods of financial planning, which simply project balance sheet numbers into the future based on historic trends, or calculate arbitrary percentages of improvement. Extrapolating trends is a sure way to perpetuate mistakes from the past into the future and to ignore necessary changes required to adapt to new circumstances.

Herschell uses a method called "discontinuity planning," in which he looks at what he wants from his total business as well as what must be done to every piece of the business, in order to fulfill his desire for constant operational improvement and for adaptation to a constantly changing environment.

It may look as though this plan required several weeks of financial manipulation and extensive calculations. Actually, Herschell doesn't have to make all of the calculations implied above—his personal computer does it for him. He uses the Mobley Matrix computer program, which can calculate in seconds the seventy-two simultaneous equations it takes to convert any set of strategies Herschell conceives into a set of pro formas.

Herschell enters his strategies into the computer and it tells him what results those strategies will yield. He sees his pro forma income statement, cash statement, balance sheet adjustment statement, and ending balance sheet. If the results of his strategies aren't what he wants, he'll enter different results, and the computer will tell him what strategies he would have to pursue to get the desired results. He works back and forth until he has a plan in which strategies are do-able and results are desirable.

In the process of monitoring progress during the year, Herschell will find that his actual performance will vary somewhat from his plan. He will also dream up "what if" questions that occur to him as a result of new developments. With his computer, he can edit in any possible change and in seconds discover the total impact of that change on all his financial results.

Mobley Matrix for Treeko Electronics, Inc.'s 1987 Plan*

BEGINNING BALANCE SHEET 09/30/86		BALANCE SHEET ADJUSTMENTS		INCOME STATEMENT		CASH STATEMENT		ENDING BALANCE SHEET 09/30/87	
ASSETS								**ASSETS**	
CASH	30		0			CHANGE IN CASH	– 12	CASH	18
RECEIVABLES	288		0	SALES	3000	COLLECTIONS	3005	RECEIVABLES	283
INVENTORY	510	CREDIT PURCH	2100	COST-OF-GOODS SOLD	2070	PRODUCTION	0	INVENTORY	540
OTHER CURRENT	14		0	AMORTIZATION	0	PREPAYMENT	2	OTHER CURRENT	16
GROSS FIXED	274		0			INVESTMENT	91	GROSS FIXED	365
ACCUM								ACCUM	
DEPRECIATION	129		0	DEPRECIATION	43			DEPRECIATION	172
NET FIXED	145							NET FIXED	193
OTHER LONG TERM	21		0	OTHER AMORT	0	OTHER INVESTMENT	19	OTHER LONG TERM	40
TOTAL ASSETS	1008	TOTAL ADJUST	2100					TOTAL ASSETS	1090
LIABILITIES & NETWORTH								**LIABILITIES & NETWORTH**	
TAXES DUE	14		0	TAXES	58	TAXES PAID	14	TAXES DUE	58
PAYABLES	240	CREDIT PURCH	2100	EXPENSES	680	DISBURSEMENTS	2847	PAYABLES	173
DEBT	405		0			BORROW/-PAYBACK	0	DEBT	405
OTHER LIABILITIES	0		0	OTHER EXPENSES	44	RECEIVE/-PAYBACK	– 44	OTHER LIABILITIES	0
CAPITAL	35		0			PAID IN/-OUT	0	CAPITAL	35
RETAIN EARNINGS	314		0	NET INCOME	105	DIVIDENDS	0	RETAIN EARNINGS	419
TOTAL LIAB & NW	1008	TOTAL ADJUST	2100					TOTAL LIAB & NW	1090

This portion of Treeko's financial report shows key performance, turnover, and operations policies for the planned year, as well as the dollar amounts that comprise these ratios.

PERFORMANCE				OPERATIONS			
ANNUAL RATES		**AMOUNTS**		**PERCENTAGES**		**AMOUNTS**	
NET INCOME/AVG ASSETS	10.00%	NET INCOME	105	CGS/SALES	69%	COST-OF-GOODS-SOLD	2070
SALES/AVG ASSETS	2.860	SALES	3000	ADD TO INV/SALES	70%	ADDITIONS TO INVENTORY	2100
NET INCOME/SALES	3.50%	AVERAGE ASSETS	1049	CREDIT PURCH/ADD TO INV	100%	CREDIT PURCHASES	2100
NET INCOME/EQUITY	26.12%	AVERAGE EQUITY	402	MFG OVERHEAD/ADD TO INV	0%	MFG OVERHEAD	0
TURNOVERS (AVG DAYS)		OTHER INCOME	0	PRODUCTION/ADD TO INV	0%	PRODUCTION	0
RECEIVABLES	34.7	INTEREST EXPENSE	44	VARIABLE EXPENSES/SALES	0%	VARIABLE EXPENSES	0
PAYABLES	26.8			**ANNUALIZED RATIOS**			
INVENTORY	91.9	DIVIDENDS	0	FIXED EXP G&A/TOTAL ASSETS	67%	FIXED EXPENSES G&A	680
CASH	2.9						
		SUSTAINABLE	3251	FIXED INVEST/TOTAL ASSETS	9%	FIXED INVESTMENT	91

*Units: Thousands.

Compilation © 1985 Mobley Matrix, Inc. All Rights Reserved.

Herschell uses the Mobley Matrix computer program to prepare thorough financial reports and projections for his banker when he wants a loan. He can project operating cash flow and show his loan officer how and when he'll pay his interest and principal. He also uses the program to analyze companies in which he invests his employee pension fund. (See Appendix B if you'd like to know more about the Mobley Matrix program.)

Herschell's business, like IBM, People Express, MCI, and all other companies, is a subsystem of a larger system, the economic environment. General systems theory holds that subsystems that thrive find their purposes in the larger system of which they are a part. This pattern holds for businesses. The cost of capital directs the highest level profitability goal for a business. The cost of capital—measured by interest rates and stock prices—depends on broader forces such as supply of money and demand for money.

Companies today are operating in a rambunctious, unpredictable economic environment. Executives must ferret out some meaning in the maelstrom.

Chapter 11 Digest

Usual methods of financial planning simply extrapolate trends or calculate arbitrary percentages of improvement—sure ways to perpetuate mistakes from the past into the future and ignore necessary changes required to adapt to new circumstances.

You can fine-tune your financial system so it is balanced and optimally efficient in achieving your purposes; you make a deliberate decision about every piece of the system so that each makes an appropriate contribution to the whole.

Don Burr, CEO of People Express, generated more than 70% average increase in sales for each of his last three full years in business. But his operating expenses mushroomed so that profit and cash flow were inadequate to keep the business aloft for the long haul. Burr needed a balanced plan. The key is understanding the meaning of return on investment (ROI) and its components.

ROI tells you faster than any other measure the relative emphasis you've been placing on the two largest jobs in running a business:

marketing (or deciding things worth doing) and controlling costs (or getting things done). Charting this year's ROI can help you to determine the optimum way to get to your ROI target for next year. (See ROI chart, page 185.)

IBM learned that there is a life pattern of a company on the ROI chart. A young company makes great strides in marketing; it matures and its plans tend to be balanced for a few years; it settles into its niche, becoming less aggressive or innovative and marketing effectiveness drops off; it tries to stay profitable by squeezing costs; finally, it loses control of costs and ROI declines, often rapidly. Aware of this pattern, IBM was able to detect when its ROI was beginning to loop backwards. Twice IBM deliberately made massive shifts in policy to reverse the pattern and keep ROI moving up and to the right on the ROI chart.

When you plan your business, you must optimize each figure in each line on the Mobley Matrix (described in Chapter 10) so as to achieve a net income objective, as well as to generate enough cash to be solvent.

Some key consideration for each balance sheet item, and the income and cash transactions that affect it, are:

Cash: Don't run out.

Accounts receivable: Collect from customers slowly enough to keep them happy and fast enough to keep you solvent.

Inventory: Three things not to get confused—what goes in (called additions to inventory), what goes out (called cost-of-goods-sold), and what level to maintain (ending inventory position). Also, you can add to inventory in only three ways: make it, buy it, or burden it with manufacturing overhead. Especially in the information age, to buy or not to buy, that is the question.

Other current assets: A favorite accounting concept is "working capital," which is current assets minus current liabilities. The only cash in working capital is what's in the cash account at the top of the balance sheet. Don't be fooled—you can't spend working capital.

Fixed assets: Be sure you have enough operating cash flow, or can get enough cash from debt or selling stock, to cover investments in fixed assets and still cover your operating expenses. Sell or write off non-productive fixed assets—the ROI for a given net profit will go up if assets go down.

Other assets: Be careful about investing in other companies—if you do, you're assuming they will make a higher return on the cash than you can.

Taxes due: The taxes you accrue for this year whack your net income; the taxes you pay this year for last year's obligation whack your cash.

Accounts payable: Watch payables turnover—pay too late and make vendors unhappy, pay too soon and run out of cash. Forget conventional wisdom that suggests stringing out your pay period. If you have plenty of cash, pay vendors promptly. You'll keep good relationships, and improve ROI by reducing total assets.

Debt: If your operating cash flow won't cover operations and investments, you have to go outside for cash. Debt is one of two outside sources of cash, the other being equity. Creditors will lend money only if they're convinced that your future cash flow from operations can pay principal and interest.

Equity: If you have to go outside your company for cash, the best way to decide whether to go the debt or equity route is to pick the cheapest. This moves you toward a "balanced capital structure," in which a new increment of capital would cost the same whichever route you choose— then you can choose comfortably based on other criteria.

Retained earnings: Manage every item on the income statement to give you the net income you want. Manage dividends according to the kind of stockholders you want to attract.

The Mobley Matrix computer program lets you plan each piece of the business—you tell it your planned behaviors or strategies, it generates your results, or pro formas, including cash. Or you tell it what results you want, and it tells you what strategies will get you there. You work back and forth until you have a plan in which strategies are do-able and results are desirable. This type of planning optimizes every single piece of a business. (See Appendix B for details.)

◄ CHAPTER 12 ►

The Economic Environment

Worldwide information networks have plunged us into a global economy. An American company is a subset of the larger American economic system, which is now only a subset of a rollicking global economic system. Transnational corporations are busy ordering that largest system, not with grand plans or cosmic schemes—although there are no doubt one or two of those being cooked up in swashbuckling hearts. Rather, incrementally, case by case, in 100,000 negotiations and transactions and decisions and deals every day, transnationals are leapfrogging political ideologies of nation-states and hammering out an integrated world economy.

On the home front: takeover artists, arbitragers, and corporate raiders are ringing in the information age in America. With a keen eye on cash flow, a cool eye on fixed assets, a penchant for risk, and a cavalier pluckiness about debt, financial entrepreneurs are dismantling the artifacts of the industrial age.

The shift from an industrial to an information economy is reshaping the foundations of capitalism. The ownership of private property requires rethinking when the most valuable thing we produce is intangible: information. When my property is a car and I sell it to you, you have the car and I don't. When my property is an idea, and I sell it to you, we both have that idea.

Even for companies that produce and distribute tangible products, the information age is changing the face of ownership of corporate equity. The traditional view that millions of people who own stock in companies are supplying those companies with capital for investment is increasingly inaccurate. Only if you purchase a new issue of stock do you fund corporate expansion—all other stock purchases are simply a transfer of ownership rights. Today, American companies are buying back more stock than they are issuing. Debt and operating cash flow are thundering ahead of equity as a source of cash for plant, property, equipment, and R&D.

Sunset companies are mostly those modeled after machines: ever larger inputs of raw materials, energy, and labor produce ever larger outputs. Sunrise companies, including manufacturing companies, tend to resemble organisms: materials, energy, and size are reduced (called miniaturization) and information is increased.

The most broad and striking forces in our economy—shifts in debt and equity, takeovers and restructuring, companies on the rise and on the decline—make sense if you set them in the larger context of a shift from industrial age to information age. It also helps to step beyond cause-and-effect thinking in order to embrace the economic environment as a complex, interrelated system.

Money: Supply and Demand

The fundamental unit of economics is the transaction. There are always at least two parties to a transaction, and they have needs and wants different from each other. Differences make a transaction possible. Differences make a deal satisfying to both parties and are therefore creative. No difference, no transaction. If both parties get more than they give, new value is created by the transaction.

The most intimate interface between a company and its larger environment is the cost of capital. When the two parties to a transaction are a provider of capital and a user of capital, wealth is created when the user pays the provider for the use of the cash and also makes a return on the cash greater than its cost. The cost of capital settles out of the stormy supply of and demand for cash in the economic environment.

The person venturing into the information age with a new business can troll for cash in those places where cash has piled up as a result of successful industrial age operations. The industrial age has created a lot of wealthy individuals and large companies that have more cash than they know what to do with. Arthur Lipper, publisher of *Venture* magazine and author of the comprehensive book on financing entrepreneurs, Venture's Financing and Investing in Private Companies, says, "There are two kinds of people in the world: those who own money and those who want to use it in the creation of wealth." Individual and institutional investors can't lavish their cash on the large industrial age companies—it is painfully apparent that industrial age companies don't need it.

When a company has a surplus of cash, as so many industrial age companies do, it faces a dilemma: how to invest that cash to improve ROI. If pouring the cash back into the present business won't improve or at least maintain ROI, you have to do something else. If, for example, the market for your product is saturated, and cash spent on expanding operations won't raise revenue because there are no more new customers, and cash spent on R&D won't help because improvement in product or service has reached a point of diminishing returns, then you have to find a way other than your traditional business to make your cash productive.

Right now, lots of industrial age companies are using excess cash to buy back their own stock from stockholders. In 1984, non-farm, non-financial American companies bought back $77.2 billion more of their own stock than they sold. IBM purchased and retired almost $1.5 billion worth of its own stock in 1986, in the start of a projected buyback program that is still underway. GM has announced plans to buy back 20% of its common stock by the end of 1990—estimated cost, upwards of $5 billion. This is a short-term expedient; a company improves ROI by reducing cash and reducing equity—a given return looks juicier when compared to smaller invested capital. It tends to bolster a company's stock price.

Companies can't swallow their tails indefinitely. Sooner or later, the healthy industrial age companies will have to find another way to deal with the mounds of cash they generate from operations. An alternate way to use cash, long-term, is to fashion a joint venture with, or provide capital to, a company that offers a new product, service, technology, or market and thereby creates a desirable return on the cash put to work. In this way, the economic success of one company provides the capital for the growth and expansion of another.

In this way, also, the economic success of one age is providing the capital for the growth and expansion of another. All shifts, whether relatively gentle reformation or boisterous revolution from age to age, must reconcile the old with the new. We don't jettison the old but use it as rich humus out of which the new can sprout.

The throngs of entrepreneurs who desperately need capital can take heart from the fact that a horde of people and institutions out there desperately need a place to put capital so that it can yield a robust return. The booming financial services industry is bringing entrepreneurs and investors together.

The sea of complementary needs to use capital and to invest capital created a huge demand for intermediaries to make the transactions happen. In 1986, almost $6 billion was raised in initial public offerings of stock in financial services companies compared with only $1 billion for technology offerings (industrial machines, computers and electronics) and only $2 billion for new issues by retailers and wholesalers.

The ranks—and coffers—of new financial services companies also swell daily because traditional industrial age money marriage brokers opt out of unusual and risky deals. In any time of rapid change, most deals are risky and the most creative ones often look downright weird, or shady. Some *are* shady. Change agents often skate on the edge of the law, or outside it.

The new financial services companies can structure an enormous variety of transactions with the specific needs of a capital-rich investor married to the specific capabilities of a capital-poor entrepreneur. A financial services company can, for example, issue stock or buy it back, find acquisitions or divest divisions. Meanwhile, many commercial banks and other historic capital brokers slog along trying to structure loans based on industrial age definitions of creditworthiness.

Drexel Burnham Lambert recently ran a full page ad in the Wall Street Journal defending junk bonds. It said that out of 23,000 U.S. corporations with sales exceeding $25 million, only 800 are considered investment grade. Of the fifty states in the United States, only twenty-nine harbor the headquarters of more than five companies with an investment grade rating.

Industrial age creditworthiness was defined by industrial age criteria for a healthy company—dangerous criteria today. In a time of stability, deciding who can create wealth tomorrow by comparing them to who could create wealth yesterday worked pretty well. In a time of change, the future is more important than the past.

Of course, it is always difficult to make predictions, especially about the future. Herein lies the risk—for richer and for poorer. While risk is rampant and to be expected during a shift in age, the relative risk for an investor is lower in financing an information age company than for an industrial age firm. Why?

An investor values a company by anticipating future streams of earnings, by scrutinizing capital structure and, sometimes, by feeling how exciting its product or service is. Young information age companies typically have short, unsteady track records of earnings. Risky. Capital structure is all over the map, often with much of the initial capitalization coming from friendly or even involuntary sources. Arthur Lipper labels the three most common sources of capital for new ventures: cradle equity, from family; pillow equity, from a spouse; and vendor equity, which is all the unpaid bills. Risky. And, of course, exciting products and services sometimes show less than exciting performance in the marketplace. Risky.

However, the striking fortuitous fact about information age companies is that they are growing on operating cash flow. Whereas an industrial age company, because it needed acres of plant, property and equipment, required $5 million in seed capital, $25 million in second round financing, and, if the market was there, $100 million from the public market, the information age company can produce hefty returns with few fixed assets. Software companies, for example, spend R&D money up front, and from then on the big costs are for marketing and for documentation, disks, and discussions with struggling users.

Don Wilson, a leading consultant on new business development in the information age, based in White Plains, New York, plans to help launch a company with an industry-changing management-tool product with $500,000 in "organization capital" followed by $5 million in market development financing. From there, the company is fully expected to grow on its own cash flow from operations. (We spent so much time on cash flow in Chapters 10 and 11 because it is the lifeblood of the emerging information economy.) It's the ability of companies to grow on operating cash flow that makes risk palatable in new information age companies.

In the case of a transaction in which capital flows from someone who needs to invest it to someone who can put it to work, there are at least two things to remember. First, a transaction is healthy when both parties need each other. The entrepreneur should not go to the investor on bended knee. The best transactions for both parties are those in which both are convinced that they need each other and that they must be responsible for negotiations determining what each must give in order that each can gain. Second, if both parties are committed to the success of the venture, the investor can provide help—like financial education—to the entrepreneur.

The relationship between an entrepreneur and an investor is analogous to the relationship between a debtor nation and a lender nation. Just as individuals and institutions can help each other create wealth if they are different, countries can help each other prosper.

American capital is in abundant supply right now. It has not been soaked up by U.S. government debt because Japanese, Western Europeans, and other foreigners have invested heavily in U.S. government securities. Supply of money and demand for money in the U.S. economy are not out of whack in the national economy, because the supply of money in the global economy—the largest system—has covered the needs of the U.S. government and spared individual and corporate cash, which remains for entrepreneurs to gobble up. Here's the story:

Debt and Trade: The Whole Elephant

It is useful to think of cash flow, debt, equity, and investment in the economic environment in the same way we think about them in an individual company. A company will have cash flow from operations. If operating cash flow is not sufficient to cover investing activity (or if it is negative and does not even cover disbursements for operating expenses), then the company will have to go outside for debt or equity capital. The United States does the same thing.

When a Japanese computer company buys transistors from the United States, transistors flow from the United States to Japan and dollars flow from Japan to the United States But when the Japanese company sells the computer to the United States, dollars flow in the other direction.

If too many dollars flow out of the United States in merchant trade, it has a trade "deficit," because Americans are buying more foreign products than foreigners are buying American products. American companies lose customers, unemployment rises, "unfair" competition is blamed, Congress puts tariffs on products sold here, protectionism increases, other countries retaliate, trade wars escalate, and world trade dies. That is the makings of a world depression.

But trade imbalance is not the only piece in the larger worldwide economic system. As you know, three cash flows make up a company's cash financial system. Every company has an operating cash flow resulting from its trading activities; it has investing activity when cash is invested in long-term assets like plant, machinery, and equipment; it has financing activity. If its operating activity does not generate enough cash to cover investment, a company borrows or sells stock (financing). If it invests less cash than it generates it can pay back its debt with the excess cash. Three cash flows go together:

$$\text{Investment cash needs} - \text{Cash flow from operations} = \text{Financing cash needs}$$

When we look only at the U.S. trade balance (which is like operating cash flow) and not at the investing and financing cash flow of the United States, we are feeling only one part of the elephant. A systems approach suggests checking out more of the big creature. For a country, the cash flow relation is similar to that for a company: capital account (net cash that flows in or out as investment capital) minus trade account (net cash from trading activities) equals net cash flow.

In 1972, there was a net inflow of investment capital of $8 billion and a net outflow of trade of $2 billion. This created a cash surplus in the United States of $6 billion.

By 1986, foreigners were investing heavily in American stocks, bonds, and tangible property so that there was a net inflow of $152 billion of investment capital. But trade outflows increased to $126 billion to give the United States a net cash inflow of $26 billion. All this foreign cash helped suppress U.S. interest rates and fed an unprecedented boom in the stock market. Most of this foreign investment came from Western Europe.

For a given country in a given year, investment and operations are not likely to be in balance. In a healthy world economy, however, investment and trade will offset each other over time.

Differences make economics work. Two countries just alike cannot help each other. If countries are different, investors in one country can finance the expansion of operations in another country. If operations are successful, the second country can become the investor in a third country, and so on. But to make this rolling mutuality work, worldwide economic systems must be in place to assure three things:

1. Central banks can finance the imbalance at any given time.

2. Free trade must flourish.

3. Enough companies in each country must have a positive operating cash flow over time.

These are precisely the same criteria for a successful company:

1. It must have a source of capital.

2. It must be able to trade with minimum constraints.

3. It must have a positive operating cash flow over time.

The information age is making it possible for companies to become aware of trading and investment opportunities all over the world. A healthy world economy is a medley of differences cooperating with each other.

Watson Sr., gutsy visionary that he was, announced it from the rooftop of IBM's new World Headquarters, built in 1936 in Manhattan. Painted large on the bricks of the tower were the words, "World Peace through World Trade."

The systems for understanding the economics of a country are less mature than systems for understanding the economics of a company. Raw numbers, like the dollars of national debt, cause great consternation. Can America handle its debt out of its trade—in essence, out of its operating cash flow?

In a company, when you want to give meaning to a number, you compare it to another number, usually the number representing a system of which it is a subsystem. For example, the typical U.S. corporation will generate $1.20 worth of sales each year for every dollar of total investment. We say its sales/assets ratio is 1.20. In the case of the U.S. economy, it is useful to compare raw numbers, like the dollar amount of the U.S. debt, to other numbers which put them in context.

In 1986, the total U.S. debt was $9.3 trillion and the total U.S. GNP was $4.2 trillion. The GNP/debt ratio was .45. In 1950, the GNP/debt ratio was .52 (288.3 billion/558.7 billion). By comparing GNP to debt, we see that even though our raw numbers for debt have increased astronomically, our ability to service our debt, as measured by GNP/debt, has held fairly constant over the past 40 years, hovering around the .50 mark.

The risk of a country's debt is determined by the annual wealth it can create. The United States has been in the same ballpark since the end of World War II. The new wrinkle seems to be that the debt is no longer held only by Americans, but increasingly by foreigners. But global debt is old hat in the world's economic system.

The economic success of one country provides the capital for the growth and expansion of another. Loans to foreign countries are not new, just bigger. The Medici made loans to the English and the Dutch and helped usher in the Renaissance. Antwerp, Amsterdam, and then London became financial capitals of the world. In turn, European wealth provided capital for the building of America. New York became the world's financial capital. There are many signs that Japanese wealth is making Tokyo the next financial capital.

Of course, lending money is always a risk decision, and the interest received on the loan is the reward for the risk investment. If and when the debtor country achieves a measure of economic success, it may either pay back its debt (which rarely happens) or invest its new wealth in the financial instruments of the lending country, thereby returning the capital whence it came.

In the 1950s, the height of the industrial age, money moving to and from foreign countries was just a trickle. The American economy was essentially a closed system. Policy-makers in America saw other economies as similar closed systems to be competed with. Closed systems relate to each other by competing. This fact is the source of our concept of competition in business—we see other companies as closed systems. When countries see each other as closed systems and competitors, it's called sovereignty.

In spite of our assumptions, private companies have been able to produce wealth because they have been able to introduce elements of open-systems behavior—such as dealing with customers and vendors.

The shift to the information age, with its explosion of world trade opportunities and world investment opportunities, has blasted national economic systems wide open. The United States today holds a total of $380 billion of global debts. Much of this represents loans to poorer, developing countries. As usual, there are risks that the money might not really be used to develop the country, leaving little cash to pay principal—or even interest. Today's developing countries waste much of their borrowed money. Governments try to form and run businesses, and they often lack the market discipline to make them efficient. (Also, add corruption and political partisanship.) Most, if not all, foreign loans will not be paid back; in fact, the debts have become equity capital held by banks and governments without the legal frameworks or agreements to treat debt like equity.

In 1987, Citicorp was the first bank to increase its loan loss reserves by $3 billion—a clear signal of bad foreign debts. Stockholders may take a beating, but large banks are not likely to fail. The Federal Deposit Insurance Corporation (FDIC) and other government insurers can protect depositors to some extent—not by paying them off; there is no money to do this. Rather, the government can take the initiative to sell the bank or merge it with other banks in a restructuring that spreads the risks and the losses more broadly.

To deal with existing problem debt, we now need new creative strategies for debt securitization, the creation of international capital markets to spread the risks, and plans for debt-for-equity swaps to legitimize the greater risk of equity ownership. Employee stock ownership plans (ESOPs) and other privatization efforts hold promise for greater productivity in developing nations. Project Economic Justice, for instance, is a mini-Marshall-Plan for economic and social reconstruction in the Caribbean. Conceived by the Center for Economic and Social Justice in Washington, D.C., this plan has the enthusiastic endorsement of both conservatives and liberals in Washington, and more importantly, the support of leaders in the region, including President Arias of Costa Rica. A key proposal of this plan is debt-for-equity swaps. Creditors, such as U.S. banks, would be paid off with shares in state-owned enterprises, which would become profitable concerns, largely owned by the workers, and professionally managed.

We also need to make healthier transactions in the first place. Just as the investor in an entrepreneurial company ought to aim for a healthy transaction in which communication flows between investor and entrepreneur and help can be offered, an investor in another country ought not to hand over the cash and walk away, hoping for a good financial report at the end of the year, or the end of the decade.

It's the transnationals that are extending the microeconomic precision of financial statements into global systems, while fashioning mutually satisfying agreements and closely monitoring progress. Meanwhile the nation-states continue to lumber along with the international economic relations that are the residues of an industrial age.

Even as we applaud the smaller entrepreneurial companies who are becoming the bedrock of the information age economy, we also acknowledge pivotal roles for the large companies. A shining opportunity for corporate giants of our time is to be effective transnational companies. Large companies can apply large-scale systems analysis and decision-making to automation, to uniform needs and wants, to the use of comparative advantage, and to matching the expanding pool of talent growing out of global communication and education.

IBM was a pioneer in this arena of transnationals. Starting as one of the earliest multinationals, its first foreign operations were little more than sales offices for the parent company. As foreign operations grew, they took on more and more responsibility for production, marketing, and finance. These foreign operations became quite autonomous in the 1950s. Finally, IBM became a transnational during the 1960s and 1970s, as the principle of comparative advantage suggested that R&D, manufacturing, and marketing could be integrated in a world wide system. Each foreign operation could then do what it did best.

While foreign divisions relinquished some independence, they gained an opportunity to exploit opportunities throughout IBM's massive global system. And capable, adventurous people in those divisions today greet the possibility of a global career.

A computer-based worldwide information system makes coordination possible in a transnational. IBM continues to stand out as a pathfinder—as one of the few true transnationals. Once more, IBM is timely and distinctive.

Olivetti is a delightful example of a budding information age transnational. Carlo de Benedetti, CEO of Olivetti, faces with verve and vision a dilemma many companies encounter. He says, "All businesses today have to solve an impossible economic equation—how to amortize the higher development costs of new products over their increasingly shorter lives. Globalization is the only answer."

De Benedetti has concluded that marketing must be done globally. Moreover, he sees Olivetti at the center of a world network of entities selling many different products and services. Olivetti's relationships with these entities already run a gamut: from an equity arrangement with Canon in which manufacturing is cooperative and marketing is competitive, to a sales agreement whereby Olivetti competes with DEC in some countries and represents the computer giant in others. Olivetti is roaring into a global market in imaginative ways.

Just as a global economic system invites new ways to do economic transactions, it demands new ways to think about them.

Economic Theory

As the information age dawns, industrial age economic theory no longer explains so well how things work. It tended to give the federal government responsibility for "fine tuning" the American economy: The Federal Reserve Board would make continual adjustments in monetary policy; Congress would make adjustments in fiscal policy. The prevailing economic theory of the industrial age treated the United States as a closed system. An outside poke now and then from the federal government could keep it running smoothly. In a nutshell, macroeconomic theory, born in an industrial age, sanctioned government control over the economy.

The cause-and-effect logic of industrial age economics is giving way to the computerized systems logic of the information age. "Stagflation" of the 1970s said loud and clear "the old macroeconomics is not good enough."

Microeconomics and the school of rational expectations—two free-enterprise-oriented theories—attempt to guide public policy by making computer analyses of all the transactions that take place in free exchange. They take a more open-systems view of the American economy, and try to include in their analyses myriad influences from the larger global economic system, as well as a more detailed perception of transactions within the American economy. These new approaches are upstaging monetary and fiscal theories because they apprehend a little more clearly the complexities of the system.

Deregulation of companies and industries was a natural consequence of the new economics. There is now even a theory of "public choice," which applies economic principles based on price and value to political and court decisions regarding private interests.

Now that all government expenditures are only 20% of total Gross National Product, the new economists believe that the tail should no longer wag the dog.

The evolution of new economic theory cracked the door for a renewed acceptability of private initiative. People of action flung the door wide and rushed through to the lucrative-looking task of restructuring corporate America.

Economics, like other areas of social activity, must live continually with the stress created between the ideal of freedom and the necessity of order. As we become ever more proficient in the design and use of large-scale systems, we will no doubt become more skillful in manipulating the quantifiable variables of the economic social system. But we will continue to be perplexed by those qualitative factors that grow out of the longings of the human heart for freedom, justice, and social order. The voices raised pro and con regarding the restructuring tidal wave in America reflect different perceptions of how economic freedom and justice ought to be ordered.

Takeovers and Restructuring

Gertrude Stein said that America is the oldest country in the world because it came into the twentieth century first. In that sense, American industrial companies are the oldest companies in the world. The second half of this chapter focuses on restructuring and takeovers because these two activities are the attention-grabbing outgrowth of a complex set of important factors in the economic environment. Takeovers and restructuring are not limited to America, and as is the case with all economic activity, they get more global every day. Nonetheless, precisely because America was the superstar of the industrial age, when it comes to a shakedown of older companies, America is "the firstest with the mostest."

For years, corporate success was measured by growth in revenue and profits. The measurement of success is changing. In 1986, the total revenue of the Fortune 500 declined for the first time. Myriad forces contribute to the upheaval in the industrial giants.

An obvious one is the changing nature of the marketplace, which was discussed in depth in the marketing section of this book. Mass markets for industrial age products are relatively few today, and large companies can't afford to gear up for the fast-proliferating specialized niche markets. Just as a bank can't afford to do the paper work to make you a $10 loan, but will be happy to make you a $10,000 loan, a large company can't afford to go for a small market.

The rise of the professional manager after World War II also created a rift that is now coming home to roost—the split between those who own and those who manage. One set of people owns companies, another set manages them. As T. Boone Pickens points out, "The only real stake many managers have in their companies is their jobs." It's awfully tempting to resist change and to hang on for dear life to the work now going on if you think your job may depend on it, and your job is all you have. As we saw in Chapter 3, in a time of change, perpetuating the work going on leads straight to irrelevance. In addition to clinging to the work going on, large corporations tended to cling to the plant property and equipment needed to do that work. It was difficult for managers to imagine selling off all those fixed assets that had been part and parcel of any business they had ever known. Managements had a psychic investment in their assets.

In the 1970s, the institutional investors—pension funds, mutual funds, and insurance companies—began influencing large companies in an unhealthy way. Institutional investors were short-term, bottom-line managers; this quarter's profit had to be larger than last quarter's profit. If these growth expectations did not hold up, the institutional investor simply sold the stock.

Production and service objectives of a company require commitments to the future. Trading objectives do not. Short-term performance makes traders rich and investors poor. Making changes in the business of the business is risky and costs money. You often have to sacrifice short-term results for long-term successes. When companies needed to start making big changes to keep up with a changing era, they dug in their heels.

Peter Drucker cites the example of the video cassette recorder. VCRs were invented in America, but no American company would produce them because market research indicated that they would require a few years of investment before the product would take off.

Many industrial corporations in the 1970s piled up their cash rather than spending it to revitalize themselves. They rolled into the 1980s with loads of cash, tons of dead wood, evaporating markets, declining responsibility to stockholders, aversion to change, and a short-term attitude.

They were ripe for restructuring.

Takeover artists got their attention.

The takeover artists latched onto two advantages that were part of moving into the 1980s: cash and information.

They noticed that there was a formidable amount of cash languishing in the U.S. economy, thanks to individual wealth, corporate wealth, and foreign investment. That cash was just waiting for someone to figure out something new to do with it. The cash had covered nicely the U.S. government debt, with plenty left over to drive up the stock market in the greatest bull market in history.

Takeover artists also managed to take advantage of the ability of computers to make meaning out of data, fast. Computers allowed takeover artists to unscramble the financial data of a potential target to determine the value of the company's resources. Even in the 1970s, analyzing the market value of a corporation's assets would have daunted a cadre of financial specialists. But by the mid-80s, one person, armed with insight and a personal computer, could do it in his or her living room.

While PCs were everywhere in the mid-80s, insight was not. What did the one hundred or so successful takeover artists figure out?

In essence, they grasped the meaning, measure, and might of cash flow. Thus they could see the whole picture of a target company. They could shoot the rapids with both eyes open.

Raiders typically put up some of their own cash and leverage it with large amounts of debt. They show lenders that they can pay back the principal and interest out of the operating cash flows of the company that they plan to make productive. If they plan to liquidate a company, they show that the value of that company's assets, sold off, is greater than the price they pay for the company.

TWA is an interesting takeover in two steps. First, Carl Icahn paid $438 million in 1985 to buy up 73% of TWA's shares of stock. TWA did not get the money; Icahn paid it to other stockholders for their shares. In this first step, Icahn bought the right to control the company so that he could restructure it to his liking.

In July 1987, TWA Chairman Icahn announced a plan to take TWA private by having another of his companies buy 90% of TWA, including Icahn's own shares, in exchange for cash and bonds. The $800 million cash for the deal would come from Drexel Burnham Lambert, Inc., as risky, high-yield junk bonds.

TWA's March 31, 1987 debt was $1.9 billion, with an equity base of $173 million—an eleven-to-one ratio of debt to equity! That's risky. Second quarter 1987 profit of $53 million almost made up the first quarter loss of $55 million. If profits remain flat, TWA will not have enough cash flow to service its enormous debt. If this remains true, TWA's cash of $372 million and cash flow from depreciation of $220 million a year may keep it barely alive for several years. That's a big "if." Icahn obviously believes, and has convinced his lenders, that he can make TWA profitable enough to cover his debt service.

In TWA, as in most other buyouts in which the new owner plans to make the company more productive and not merely liquidate it for the value of its assets, ownership and management are coupled again, as they have not been in forty years. Privatization marries ownership and use.

As the takeover artists careened into a few corporations with the ability to sniff out hidden wealth and value, willingness to break with tradition—people, products, assets, ideas, divisions, companies—and the power to wreak change, the rest of the corporate world took a hard look inside.

What the takeover artists do, when they intend to make a company productive, is restructure it. Restructuring can be any change-making activity from flip-flopping the debt/equity ratio (financial restructuring) to acquiring a new division (operational restructuring). Warily regarding the takeover types, gloomily surveying their own profit performance in recent years, corporations began to restructure themselves.

The *Wall Street Journal* studied the 850 largest companies in North America to learn the nature of their restructuring efforts during the eighteen months between January 1984 and July 1985. The newspaper found that 398 companies had been involved in restructuring—346 voluntarily and only 52 because of takeover transactions. One hundred ninety-seven of these companies did operational restructuring: 315 units, such as divisions, were sold for $73 billion, and 248 units were acquired for $95 billion. One hundred and three of these companies restructured financially; 86 companies bought their own stock back for $52 billion; 56 companies borrowed $16 billion, and 84 engaged in other financial restructuring such as debt-equity swaps or realignments of debt. In this eighteen-month period, all companies bought $117 billion of their own shares, thus reducing their equity.

The declining importance of stockholders to corporations must skew the nature of capitalism itself. Companies are getting cash for new investment from operating cash flow, not from new issues of stock, as was the practice in the first three-fourths of this century. In other words, overall, companies are getting all the cash they need from collections from their customers. Not only can mature companies cover disbursements for operations, but they can also pay for investments in plant, property, equipment, and R&D without selling stock to raise cash.

The vast majority of stocks being traded today on stock exchanges are exactly that—trades of money and ownership rights. These buzzing transactions have no direct monetary effect on the fortunes of the corporations whose shares are being shuffled in the big casino called Wall Street.

In 1984, all U.S. non-farm, non-financial companies generated $334.9 billion from operating cash flow, borrowed $175.7 billion, and bought back $77.2 billion more stock than they sold. Stockholder ownership has been the foundation of capitalism. When corporations no longer need to attract stockholders, the impetus to show profit—and pay taxes on that profit—declines. The impetus to pay dividends also declines.

Alan Greenspan reported in the *Wall Street Journal* in November 1986, that since January of 1984, restructuring activities in all American corporations had reduced equity on corporate balance sheets by $200 billion. Corporate debt had increased $200 billion since early 1984. The big question hanging in the air following this massive operational and financial restructuring is: Will the new structures improve productivity or increase the value of American corporations? Herein lies the risk.

Massive rapid institutional changes always have their downsides. A few greedy people will take advantage of new situations until law or custom catches up to the new game. Many investors will be sucked into the capital markets by rosy predictions of sure success. And Congress is sure to create laws to protect those who are the losers as well as to punish the few who are greedy. In the final analysis, a restructured company must create sufficient operating cash flow to at least service its expanded debt.

The net result of the massive restructuring of corporations is a radical change in capital structure—debt compared to equity. The debt of TWA, for example, swelled 50% between 1984 and 1986, and the airline's equity plunged 67%. TWA must produce a profit of $300 million in three years to survive. Restructured companies often must perform magnificently just to cover interest and principal. If they don't perform, the few stockholders left are likely to lose everything. Debt holders could lose much of their investment and the company itself could be bankrupt.

Many people believe our whole financial system has become too risky. Felix Rohatyn said in 1984, "We are turning the financial markets into a huge casino. Every kind of financial instrument is being created to lure individuals into believing they are investing when they are really speculating. This is speculation on a major scale." And Paul Volker said in 1985, "We spend our days issuing debt and retiring equity—both in record volume—and then we spend our evenings raising each other's eyebrows with gossip about signs of stress in the financial system."

While restructuring has brought risk, it has also delivered opportunity. Henry O. Timmick, himself a beneficiary of restructuring activity, reported in the *Wall Street Journal* in March 1987 that well over 200 of 315 leveraged buyouts in 1986 were "divestitures in which overgrown conglomerates sold parts of their empires to division managers." A new, sometimes reluctant, class of entrepreneurs is hatching as large, lumbering corporations slim down.

It's heartening to hear Timmick speak of his experience on becoming an entrepreneur, "... a production manager asked what company policy was on a particular matter. 'I don't know,' I said. 'It's our company now; we have to create the policy.' From that point on, we set in motion an open-door communications program to get both our managers and employees thinking like spirited owners. This type of aggressive dialogue wasn't necessary under corporate rules where everyone knew his place, but it was an essential ingredient in our new company... our dialogue with employees extended to company finances as well. We opened the books to all managers and they in turn began to appreciate what cash flow was all about. Soon, they were no longer talking about what they had to have, but about what they no longer needed."

In a sense, perhaps, large corporations are acting like Timmick's entrepreneurs—getting rid of what they no longer need. And a healthy transaction shifts what they no longer need to someone who can make it productive.

So where are we headed? What is happening to our industries? The oligarchies of the industrial age are giving way to what looks to be a matrix of companies interacting with human needs and wants.

What then is a company in the information age? If it is not a maker of a specific product or a supplier of a specific service in a defined industry, how do you recognize it? How does it recognize itself over the long haul? If a company is the nexus of a network, like Olivetti, or a collection of capable people working on projects they want to work on, like SAIC, or a knitter of niches, like the U.S. Vehicle Registration Service, or a sprawling transnational like IBM, what gives it an identity?

We believe that in the information age you will be known and will know yourselves by your management systems—the distinctive ways in which you get things done and decide things worth doing.

Chapter 12 Digest

The most broad and striking forces in our economy—shifts in debt and equity, takeovers and restructuring, companies on the rise and on the decline—make sense if you set them in the larger context of a shift from industrial age to information age. It also helps to step beyond cause-and-effect thinking in order to embrace the economic environment as a complex, interrelated system.

Gertrude Stein said that America is the oldest country in the world because it came into the twentieth century first. In that sense, American industrial companies are the oldest companies in the world and the shift to an information age is hitting them hard.

Myriad forces have contributed to the upheaval in the industrial giants: mass markets are drying up, and large companies can't afford to gear up for the fast-proliferating specialized niche markets; the split between those who own and those who manage causes managers to cling to whatever work is already going on, since their job is all they have; powerful institutional investors are looking more at short-term performance than the long-term health of companies.

Many industrial corporations rolled into the eighties with loads of cash, tons of dead wood, evaporating markets, declining responsibility to stockholders, aversion to change and a short-term attitude. They were ripe for restructuring. The takeover artists got their attention.

Takeover artists benefited from two prime weapons of the 1980s: cash and information. They took advantage of the computer's ability to make meaning out of data, fast. Whereas, even in the 1970s the analysis of the market value of a corporation's assets would have daunted a cadre of financial specialists, by the mid-1980s an individual, armed with insight and a personal computer, could do the analysis in his or her living room.

Warily regarding the takeover types, gloomily surveying their own profit performance in recent years, corporations began to restructure themselves. A 1984-1985 *Wall Street Journal* study found that of 398 companies involved in restructuring, 346 had undertaken it voluntarily and only 52 because of takeover transactions.

Restructuring has brought risk: a radical change in capital structure, or debt/equity ratio. Between January 1984 and November 1986, restructuring activities in all American corporations had reduced equity on corporate balance sheets by $200 billion, and increased debt by the same amount. Restructured companies often must perform magnificently just to cover interest and principal. If they don't, the few stockholders that are left are likely to lose everything.

And restructuring has brought opportunity: of some 300 leveraged buyouts in 1986, more than two-thirds were divestitures in which bulky conglomerates sold divisions to their managers. A new, sometimes reluctant, class of entrepreneurs is being hatched as large, lumbering corporations slim down.

The information age is changing the face of ownership of corporate equity. Only if you purchase a new issue of stock do you fund corporate expansion—all other stock purchases are simply a transfer of ownership rights. Debt and operating cash flow are thundering ahead of equity as a source of cash for property, plant, equipment, and R&D. The vast majority of stocks being traded today on stock exchanges are exactly that—trades of money and ownership rights. These buzzing transactions have no direct monetary effect on the fortunes of the corporations whose shares are being shuffled in the big casino called Wall Street. The declining importance of stockholders must skew the nature of capitalism itself.

Many industrial age companies face a dilemma: pouring their cash back into their traditional business won't improve or maintain ROI, because the mass markets for their products are shrinking. So they are using excess cash to buy back their own stock from stockholders. Today, American companies are buying back more stock than they are issuing. Companies can't swallow their tails indefinitely. An alternative to buying back stock is to provide cash, through corporate partnerships such as joint ventures, to companies that offer new products, services, technologies, or markets. The person venturing into the information age with a new business can troll for cash where it has piled up as a result of successful industrial age operations. In this way, the economic success of one company provides the capital for the growth and expansion of another. In this way, also, the economic success of one age is providing capital for the growth and expansion of another.

Since a transaction is healthy when both parties need each other, the entrepreneur ought not go to the investor on bended knee. The relationship between an entrepreneur and an investor is analogous to the relationship between a debtor nation and a lender nation. Just as individuals and institutions can help each other create wealth when they are different, countries can help each other prosper.

It is useful to think of cash flow, debt, equity, and investment in the economic environment in the same way we think about them in an individual company. For example, if a company's operating cash flow is not sufficient to cover investing activity (or if it is negative and does not even cover disbursements for operating expenses), then the company must go outside for debt or equity capital. Countries do the same. For any country in any year, investment and operations are not likely to be in balance. In a healthy world economy, however, investment and trade will offset each other over time.

In the 1950s, the height of the industrial age, money moving between the United States and foreign countries was just a trickle both ways. The American economy was essentially a closed system. Policymakers in the United States saw other economies as closed systems to be competed with. The shift to the information age, with its explosion of world trade and investment opportunities, has blasted closed systems wide open.

The United States today holds a total of $380 billion of global debts. Most, if not all, foreign loans will not be paid back; in fact, they have become equity capital held by banks and governments without the legal frameworks or agreements to treat debt like equity. To deal with problem debt, we need new creative strategies for debt securitization, international capital markets to spread the risks, and plans for debt-for-equity swaps.

It's the transnationals that are extending the microeconomic precision of financial statements into global systems, while fashioning mutually satisfying agreements and closely monitoring progress. Meanwhile the nation-states continue to lumber along with the international economic relations that are the residues of an industrial age.

What then is a company in the information age? If it is not a maker of a specific product or a supplier of a specific service in a defined industry, how do you recognize it? How does it recognize itself over the long haul? We suggest that in the information age it is your management systems that tell you who you are—the distinctive processes by which you get things done and decide the things worth doing.

◄ REFERENCES ►

Bennis, Warren and Burt Nanus: *Leaders: The Strategies for Taking Charge*, Harper and Row, New York, 1985.

Bhide, Amar: "Hustle as Strategy," *Harvard Business Review*, September–October, 1986.

Cleveland, Harlan: *The Knowledge Executive*, E. P. Dutton, New York, 1985.

Deming, W. Edwards: *Out of the Crisis*, MIT Center for Advanced Engineering Study, Cambridge, 1986.

Emery, Frederick: *Systems Thinking*, Penguin Books, Harmondsworth, England, 1969.

Fromm, Erich: *The Art of Loving*, Harper and Row, New York, 1956.

Kharasch, Robert N.: *The Institutional Imperative: How to Understand the United States Government and Other Bulky Objects*, Charterhouse Books, New York, 1973.

Koestler, Arthur: *The Act of Creation*, Macmillan, New York, 1964.

Lipper, Arthur III: *Venture's Financing and Investing in Private Companies*, Probus Publishing, Chicago, 1988.

Lovelock, Christopher: *Services Marketing*, Prentice-Hall, Englewood Cliffs, N.J., 1984.

Mueller, Robert: *Corporate Networking*, Free Press, New York, 1986.

Piore, Michael and Charles Sable: *The Second Industrial Divide: Possibilities for Prosperity*, Basic Books, New York, 1984.

Pirsig, Robert M.: *Zen and the Art of Motorcycle Maintenance*, Bantam Books, New York, 1974.

Thomas, Lewis: *The Lives of a Cell*, Bantam Books, New York, 1974.

Toffler, Alvin: *Future Shock*, Random House, New York, 1970.

◄ APPENDIX A ►

The Double Pyramid of the Executive

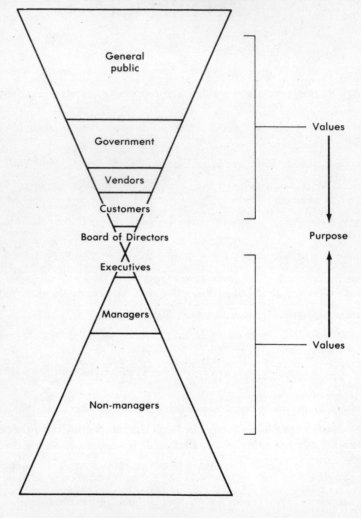

Figure 1. A company has two pyramids. The lower is the familiar one in which all employees have positions. The upper, inverted, pyramid represents all those intersts outside the company that must be served. Purpose integrates the values and interests of people in both pyramids.

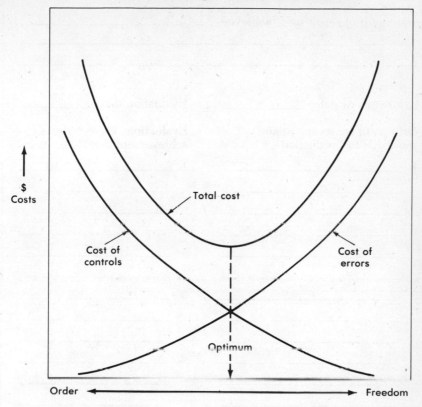

**Total Cost Curve
for Optimizing Freedom and Control**

$
Costs

Total cost

Cost of
controls

Cost of
errors

Optimum

Order ⟵——————————————⟶ Freedom

Figure 2. There's a cost to keeping control. There's also a cost to fixing errors. When you increase control you decrease errors; when you decrease control you increase errors.

You can overdo anything. Diminishing returns set in. The secret of control is that the amount of control you exercise should be "just right"—not too much, not too little. You can optimize freedom and control by measurements or by intuition.

The total cost curve shows that the optimum balance of freedom and control is where the cost of maintaining controls roughly equals the cost of fixing errors; this is the minimum total cost.

The same curve that illustrates total cost appears in economics as the "Laffer curve," which relates revenue to rate of taxation. It appears in psychology as the productivity/stress curve, and it appears in atomic physics in the binding energy/atomic weight curve.

Result Form

Statement of result to be achieved _____

_____

_____

Achievement date: _____   Evaluation date: _____

Criteria of achievement and standards for evaluation	Evaluation: Were criteria of achievement met?

1. _____   1. _____

   _____   _____

   _____   _____

2. _____   2. _____

   _____   _____

   _____   _____

3. _____   3. _____

   _____   _____

   _____   _____

4. _____   4. _____

   _____   _____

   _____   _____

Agreement to result by (at least two people):   Evaluation by:

_____   _____

_____   _____

Next decision or next result required:

_____

_____

Figure 3. A form that can be used to document the achievement of results.

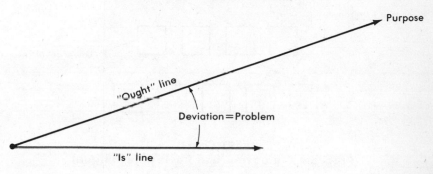

**The Teleocratic Management System Chart
(showing problem solving)**

Purpose

"Ought" line

Deviation=Problem

"Is" line

Figure 4. The complex of purpose, goals or results, and plans constitute the "ought" line. They all are created so everybody can agree to what they ought to do in order to achieve what they want.

But some things don't go the way they ought to. Perception of what "is" is equally important. When the "is" deviates from the "ought," we say we have a "problem."

This vector is one way to illustrate graphically the Teleographic Management System. Another graphic representation of the system is a "hierarchy of purpose chart," which organizes goals and plans in a hierarchy similar to an organization chart. You will find such a chart in Figure 5.

Hierarchy of Purpose Chart

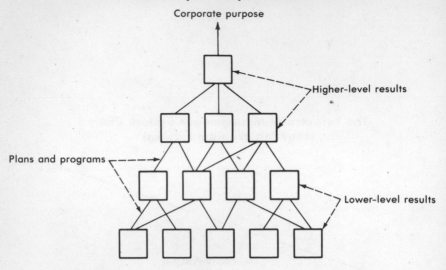

PERT Chart
(Program Evaluation and Review Technique)

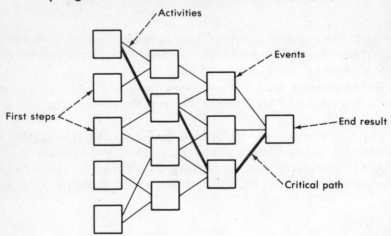

Figure 5. The Hierarchy of Purpose Chart (*top*) interrelates all key results and plans and programs of a corporation or any of its components. The PERT Chart (*bottom*), like the Hierarchy of Purpose Chart, shows all key events (goals or results) and the activities (plans and programs) required to move from event to event. It gives precise control over every part of a task, and the end result continually identifies the critical path (longest time) to the desired end result.

234

Teleocratic Management System Chart
(showing the components of ROI
imposed over the management system)

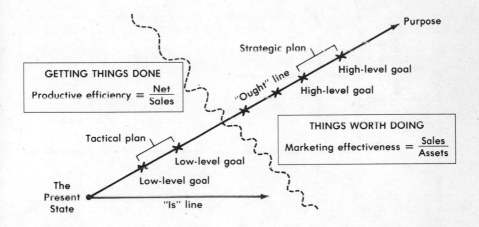

Figure 6. Return on investment (ROI) measures overall company performance. It combines the measure of productive efficiency in getting things done (net/sales) with the measure of marketing effectiveness (sales/assets) to give ROI (net/assets). The Du Pont Formula for ROI is:

$$\frac{net}{sales} \times \frac{sales}{assets} = \frac{net}{assets} \text{ or ROI}$$

The lower left-hand part of the teleocratic management system chart tends to reflect how you are getting things done. As you move up and to the right, toward corporate purpose, the chart tends to reflect the things you've decided are worth doing.

This chart relates key elements of people management to key elements of money management.

World Views and Leadership

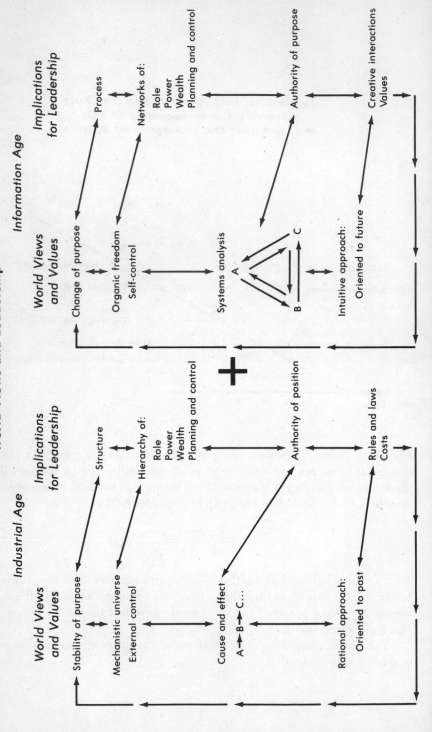

Industrial Age

World Views and Values

Implications for Leadership

Stability of purpose

Structure

Mechanistic universe
External control

Hierarchy of:
Role
Power
Wealth
Planning and control

Cause and effect
A → B → C....

Authority of position

Rational approach:
Oriented to past

Rules and laws
Costs

Information Age

World Views and Values

Implications for Leadership

Change of purpose

Process

Organic freedom
Self-control

Networks of:
Role
Power
Wealth
Planning and control

Systems analysis

A
C
B

Authority of purpose

Intuitive approach:
Oriented to future

Creative interactions
Values

Figure 7. Elements in these charts are selected and suggestive. These schematics are not intended to be complete models; rather, they are designed to suggest certain contrasts between the consequences of two different views. The left half of this schematic identifies, in the first column, a series of major value assumptions which emerged in the 15th century and which profoundly affected the way organizations were ordered

The style of leadership that reflected these values was first autocratic and then bureaucratic. The key elements of a bureaucratic management system are shown in the second column. The right half of this schematic identifies, in the third column, another broader set of values that emerged in the 20th century. These values provide more options for leadership.

The style of leadership that is appropriate to these newer values is called teleocratic leadership. The key elements of a teleocratic management system are shown in the fourth column.

The elements of teleocratic leadership should not replace useful elements of bureaucratic leadership, but rather provide powerful new leadership options. With these enlarged value and style options, the teleocratic leader can better deal with the great variety of complex situations inherent in the information age business environment.

Values Typologies

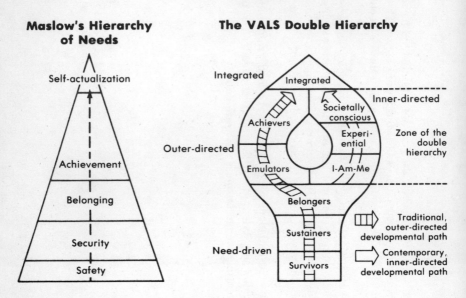

Figure 8. Maslow's hierarchy of needs suggested a growth process for those who kept growing, from safety needs to self-actualization needs. The VALS survey data introduces different terms for the different levels of development. More importantly, it suggests a new parallel path for Belongers to move toward Integrateds, through the inner-directed values as well as through the outer-directed.

To calculate People Express's net income target:

$$\frac{net}{sales} = 4.5\%$$

$$\frac{net}{587} = 4.5\%$$

$$net = \$26.4 \text{ million}$$

To calculate People Express's ending asset target:

$$\frac{sales}{average\ assets} = 1.1$$

$$587 \div \frac{beginning\ assets\ +\ ending\ assets}{2} = 1.1$$

$$587 \div \frac{416\ +\ ending\ assets}{2} = \$1.1 \text{ million}$$

$$ending\ assets = \$651.2 \text{ million}$$

Figure 9. These equations show how Don Burr could have calculated a net income target and ending asset target for 1984.

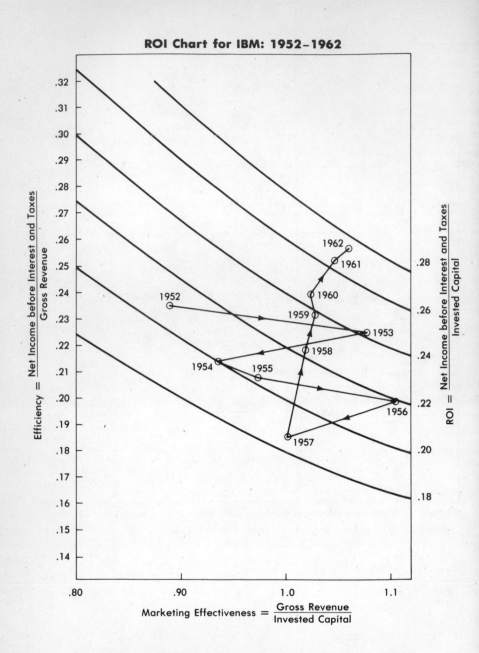

Figure 10. Plot of return on sales vs. capital turnover ratio.

Mobley Matrix for Treeko Electronics, Inc., 1986*

BEGINNING BALANCE SHEET 09/30/85		BALANCE SHEET ADJUSTMENTS		INCOME STATEMENT		CASH STATEMENT		ENDING BALANCE SHEET 09/30/86	
ASSETS								**ASSETS**	
CASH	9		0			CHANGE IN CASH	21	CASH	30
RECEIVABLES	287		0	SALES	2791	COLLECTIONS	2790	RECEIVABLES	288
INVENTORY	526	PURCH	+1800	COST-OF-GOODS-SOLD	1967	PRODUCTION	151	INVENTORY	510
OTHER CURRENT	12		0	AMORTIZATION	0	PREPAYMENT	2	OTHER CURRENT	14
GROSS FIXED	202	W/O	0			INVESTMENT	72	GROSS FIXED	274
ACCUM		W/O	0	DEPRECIATION	32			ACCUM	
DEPRECIATION	97							DEPRECIATION	129
NET FIXED	105							NET FIXED	145
OTHER LONG TERM	2		0	OTHER AMORT	0	OTHER INVESTMENT	19	OTHER LONG TERM	21
TOTAL ASSETS	941	TOTAL ADJUST	1800					TOTAL ASSETS	1008
LIABILITIES & NETWORTH								**LIABILITIES & NETWORTH**	
TAXES DUE	10		0	TAXES	23	TAXES PAID	19	TAXES DUE	14
PAYABLES	258	PURCH	+1800	EXPENSES	686	DISBURSEMENTS	2504	PAYABLES	240
DEBT	366		0			BORROW/-PAYBACK	39	DEBT	405
OTHER LIABILITIES	0		0	OTHER EXPENSES	41	RECEIVE/-PAYBACK	−41	OTHER LIABILITIES	0
CAPITAL	35		0			PAID IN/-OUT	0	CAPITAL	35
RETAIN EARNINGS	272		0	NET INCOME	42	DIVIDENDS	0	RETAIN EARNINGS	314
TOTAL LIAB & NW	941	TOTAL ADJUST	1800					TOTAL LIAB & NW	1008

This portion of Treeko's financial report shows key performance, turnover, and operations policies for the year, as well as the dollar amounts that comprise these ratios.

PERFORMANCE				OPERATIONS			
ANNUAL RATES		**AMOUNTS**		**PERCENTAGES**		**AMOUNTS**	
NET INCOME/AVG ASSETS	4.31%	NET INCOME	42	CGS/SALES	70%	COST-OF-GOODS-SOLD	1967
SALES/AVG ASSETS	2.863	SALES	2791	ADD TO INV/SALES	70%	ADDITIONS TO INVENTORY	1951
NET INCOME/SALES	1.50%	AVERAGE ASSETS	975	CREDIT PURCH/ADD TO INV	92%	CREDIT PURCHASES	1800
NET INCOME/EQUITY	12.80%	AVERAGE EQUITY	328	MFG OVERHEAD/ADD TO INV	0%	MFG OVERHEAD	0
TURNOVERS (AVG DAYS)		OTHER INCOME	0	PRODUCTION/ADD TO INV	8%	PRODUCTION	151
RECEIVABLES	37.6	INTEREST EXPENSE	0	VARIABLE EXPENSES/SALES	10%	VARIABLE EXPENSES	274
PAYABLES	36.4			**ANNUALIZED RATIOS**			
INVENTORY	96.5	DIVIDENDS	0	FIXED EXP G&A/TOTAL ASSETS	44%	FIXED EXPENSES G&A	412
CASH	2.6						
		OPERATING CASH FLOW	114	FIXED INVEST/TOTAL ASSETS	8%	FIXED INVESTMENT	72

Units: Thousands.

Figure 11

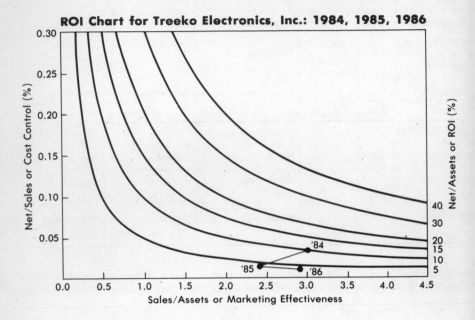

Figure 12

Bathtub Theorem

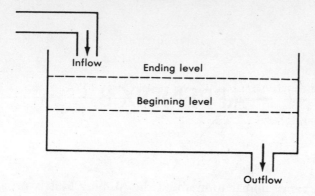

$$\begin{matrix} \text{Turnover} \\ \text{rate} \end{matrix} = \text{average throughput} \div \text{average balance}$$

$$= \frac{\text{inflow} + \text{outflow}}{2} \div \frac{\text{beginning level} + \text{ending level}}{2}$$

For Herschell's receivables plan:

$$\begin{matrix} \text{Turnover} \\ \text{per year} \end{matrix} = \text{average throughput} \div \text{average balance}$$

$$= \frac{\text{inflow} + \text{outflow}}{2} \div \frac{\text{beginning position} + \text{ending position}}{2}$$

$$= \frac{\text{sales} + \text{collections}}{2} \div \frac{\text{beginning receivables} + \text{ending receivables}}{2}$$

$$= \frac{\$3,000,000 + \$3,005,000}{2} \div \frac{\$288,000 + \$283,000}{2}$$

$$= 10.5$$

$$\begin{matrix} \text{Turnover} \\ \text{in days} \end{matrix} = 365 \div 10.5$$

$$= 34.7 \text{ days}$$

Figure 13. Economists know that a given amount of money in the economy will produce twice as large a GNP if it circulates twice as fast. The Bathtub Theorem illustrated here shows why this is so. If a tub contains water, and water flows in and out of the tub, the turnover of water in the tub depends on the average amount of water in the tub as well as the throughput in and out of the tub. The figure illustrates how the theorem looks, the equation, and the application to Herschell's receivables plan.

243

◄ APPENDIX B ►

If you'd like more information about the Mobley Matrix program for managing and planning cash, profit, and assets, or information about other products and services, write to:

McKeown & Co., Inc.
P.O. Box 39155
Washington, D.C. 20016

or call 800-772-1990

◄ INDEX ►